Germany
1993

To the Library of
Harvard Divinity School

In gratitude for the privilege
of studying at your fine
institution from 1963 - 1964.

Sincerely,

Roger David Aus

BARABBAS AND ESTHER
and
Other Studies in the Judaic Illumination
of Earliest Christianity

SOUTH FLORIDA STUDIES IN THE HISTORY OF JUDAISM

Edited by
Jacob Neusner
William Scott Green, James Strange
Darrell J. Fasching, Sara Mandell

Number 54
Barabbas and Esther
and
Other Studies in the Judaic Illumination
of Earliest Christianity

by
Roger David Aus

BARABBAS AND ESTHER
and
Other Studies in the Judaic Illumination
of Earliest Christianity

by
Roger David Aus

Scholars Press
Atlanta, Georgia

BARABBAS AND ESTHER
and
Other Studies in the Judaic Illumination
of Earliest Christianity

©1992
University of South Florida

Publication of this book was made possible by a grant from the Tisch Family Foundation, New York City. The University of South Florida acknowledges with thanks this important support for its scholarly projects.

Library of Congress Cataloging in Publication Data
Aus, Roger, 1940-
    Barabbas and Esther and other studies in the Judaic illumination of earliest Christianity / by Roger David Aus.
        p. cm. — (South Florida studies in the history of Judaism)
    Includes index.
    ISBN 1-55540-753-6 (hard)
        1. Bible. N.T.—Criticism, interpretation, etc. 2. Bible. N.T.—Relation to the Old Testament. 3. Rabbinical literature—Relation to the New Testament. 4. Christianity and other religions—Judaism. 5. Judaism—Relations—Christianity. 6. Church history—Primitive and early church, ca. 30-600.   I. Title. II. Series.
BS2387.A87   1992
225.6—dc20   92-32059
                                                                             CIP

Printed in the United States of America
on acid-free paper

TO UTHA
(PSALM 23:4)

Contents

Preface ix

1. The Release of Barabbas (Mark 15:6-15 par.; John 18:39-40), and Judaic Traditions on the Book of Esther 1
2. The Death of One for All in John 11:45-54 in Light of Judaic Traditions 29
3. Luke 15:11-32 and R. Eliezer ben Hyrcanus's Rise to Fame 65
4. The Magi at the Birth of Cyrus, and the Magi at Jesus' Birth in Matt 2:1-12 95
5. Three Pillars and Three Patriarchs: A Proposal Concerning Gal 2:9 113
6. The Relevance of Isa 66:7 to Revelation 12 and 2 Thessalonians 1 125
7. God's Plan and God's Power: Isaiah 66 and the Restraining Factors of 2 Thess 2:6-7 143
8. Paul's Travel Plans to Spain and the "Full Number of the Gentiles" of Rom 11:25 163
9. The Liturgical Background of the Necessity and Propriety of Giving Thanks According to 2 Thess 1:3 193

Index of Modern Authors 201

Preface

When I took the comprehensive doctoral examinations in New Testament Studies at Yale University at the end of the sixties, I received my poorest marks in the "Jewish Background of the New Testament." My 1971 dissertation, inspired by Nils A. Dahl and very capably guided by Wayne Meeks, was *Comfort in Judgment: The Use of Day of the Lord and Theophany Traditions in Second Thessalonians One.* In this motif study, I was forced to become much better acquainted with the Masoretic Text, the Septuagint, the pseudepigrapha, Qumran, the Samaritans, Philo, Josephus and the rabbis, as well as with several Hellenistic sources. Since then I have dealt primarily with Judaic materials in seeking to illuminate specific New Testament passages, not denying, however, the occasional cross-fertilization with Hellenistic sources.

The more I have worked with Judaic materials, the more I have come to appreciate the great debt early Jewish Christians owed to their mother faith. Their thought patterns, and the way they dealt with specific passages from the Hebrew or Greek bible, betrayed their Jewish heritage. I now find it absolutely necessary, for example, when analyzing the gospels, to understand and appreciate the nature of *haggadah*. Without such an understanding, often the wrong questions are asked of a text. In addition, the hotly debated issue of the historicity of a specific passage, provoked by fundamentalists or some evangelicals, unfortunately at times defers attention from the religious meaning(s) of the text. The question of historicity is frequently completely out of place in regard to the religious truth(s) an early author wished to convey. Specific examples of this are found in the sections "Historicity" in the first two essays of this collection. Others can be observed in my volumes *Water into Wine and the Beheading of John the Baptist.* Early Jewish-Christian Interpretation of Esther 1 in John 2:1-11 and Mark 6:17-29 (BJS 150; Atlanta: Scholars, 1988), and *Weihnachtsgeschichte, Barmherziger Samariter, Verlorener Sohn. Studien zu ihrem jüdischen Hintergrund* (ANTZ 2; Berlin: Institut Kirche und Judentum, 1988).

Since the English translations of the Babylonian Talmud and Midrash Rabbah by Soncino Press in London in the 1930's, more and more Judaic sources have been made available to the English-speaking world, thanks to the work, for example, of Jacob Z. Lauterbach, Judah Goldin, William G. Braude, Israel J. Kapstein, Reuven Hammer and Anthony Saldarini. Yet it has been Jacob Neusner who, together with his students, has translated or retranslated almost every major Judaic writing into English, including the Jerusalem Talmud, now nearing its completion. Every student of the New Testament must be grateful to him for providing easier and more competent access to Judaic sources. The translations he has provided are no substitutes for the original texts, but rather provide the student less competent in rabbinic Hebrew and Aramaic with easier access to them. At that point the real work of interpretation begins.

I am very grateful to Professor Neusner for proposing the idea of this collection of essays, and for accepting them in the series *South Florida Studies in the History of Judaism*. My thanks also go to the Max Richter Foundation of Rhode Island for subsidizing the costs involved in printing this volume. The last seven studies are reproduced by permission of the publishers. Except for orthographical standardization, several bibliographical notations, and minor expansion of some footnotes, no changes have been made in the original contents.

The first two essays appear here for the first time. They deal with an area which has recently engaged my attention more and more, the Judaic background of the trial and crucifixion of Jesus. Essays three and four concern other gospel passages, Jesus' parable of the Prodigal Son, and the visit of the Magi or "wise men" to Jerusalem and Bethlehem.

Essay five begins the section dealing with the Pauline Corpus by treating the relevance of Judaism's three patriarchs, called "pillars," to the pillar apostles of the early Jerusalem church. Essays six to eight show the relevance of Judaic interpretation of Isaiah 66 to Revelation 12, but primarily to Second Thessalonians 1-2 and Rom 11:25. The ninth and final study deals with the Judaic background of liturgical phrases found in 2 Thess 1:3.

Essays 3, 7 and 9 were originally published in the *Journal of Biblical Literature:* 104 (1985) 443-69; 96 (1977) 537-53; and 92 (1973) 432-38, respectively. Essay 4 appeared in *New Perspectives on Ancient Judaism,* 2, ed. J. Neusner et al. (Howard Clark Kee Festschrift; Lanham, Maryland: University Press of America, 1987) 99-114. Essays 5 and 6 are reproduced from the *Zeitschrift für die neutestamentliche Wissenschaft* 70 (1979) 252-61, and 67 (1976) 252-68, respectively.

Finally, essay 8 was originally published in *Novum Testamentum* 21 (1979) 232-62.

As a parish pastor, I have had to use part of my annual vacation to write a first draft of each essay after gathering the material over a longer period of time. I hope that this, my own brand of "recreation," not only will further the state of scholarship in at least a minor way in regard to the relevant texts, but also will encourage contemporary Jews and Christians to better appreciate their common roots.

Roger David Aus
Berlin, Germany
July, 1991

1

The Release of Barabbas (Mark 15:6-15 par.; John 18:39-40), and Judaic Traditions on the Book of Esther

I. Introduction

The natural sequence to Pontius Pilate's interrogation of Jesus as now formulated in Mark 15:2-5 par. is v 15b: "and having scourged Jesus, he delivered him to be crucified."[1] Between these verses the Barabbas (Βαραββᾶς) incident has been inserted, which now occupies a major place in the passion narrative. It has been described as the "Most enigmatical of all the parts of the Gospel Story of Jesus' trial."[2]

Barabbas is portrayed in Mark and Luke as one of the "rebels" (στασιαστής) in prison (in Jerusalem), who had committed murder[3] in the insurrection (στάσις: Mark 15:6-7; Luke 18:19); in Matthew as a "notorious prisoner" (27:16);[4] and in John (18:40) as a "robber" (λῃστής).

Mark 15:6 states that at the feast (of the Passover) he (Pilate) used to release (ἀπολύω) one prisoner whom they (the crowd or people) requested. The imperfect of the verb implies a repetition of this action. This motif reoccurs in v 8, where the crowd begins to make a request (of Pilate), "as he repeatedly did for them" (ποιέω, imperfect). Matthew in 27:15 states that the governor was "accustomed" (εἴωθα) to release one prisoner whom the crowd desired. Several MSS contain Luke 23:17 at this point, stating that Pilate was "obliged" (ἀνάγκην δὲ εἶχεν) to release one man to them at the festival. Finally, John relates that Pilate

---

[1] Cf. R. Bultmann, *The History of the Synoptic Tradition* (New York: Harper & Row, 1963) 272.
[2] See P. Winter, *On the Trial of Jesus* (Berlin: de Gruyter, 1974²) 131, as well as 142: "The Barabbas episode remains an enigma."
[3] Cf. Acts 3:14.
[4] Cf. also v 24, where Pilate notes that a "riot" (θόρυβος) was beginning.

at this point tells the Jews: You have a "custom" (συνήθεια) that I should release one man for you at the Passover (18:39).

The customary "release" of one prisoner to the Jewish people by the Roman procurator at Passover thus appears to be well attested, at least in the gospels. The repetition of the motif underscores its importance for these writers: four times in Mark (15:6, 9, 11, 15), Matthew (27:15, 17, 21, 26), and John (18:39; 19:10 and 12 twice – its only occurrences in John), and five in Luke (23:16, [17], 18, 20, 22, 25).[5] Of the fifty occurrences of the verb in the four gospels, seventeen deal with the question of the release of Barabbas or Jesus.

Pilate is portrayed as at first trying to rescue Jesus, whom he considers to have done no evil (Mark 15:14 par.). He finds in him no crime deserving of death (Luke 15:22; John 18:38; 19:4, 6). Nevertheless, he finally yields to the demand of the assembled Jews. In Mark 15:15 this is due to Pilate's desire to "satisfy" the crowd; in Luke 23:23 and 25 he yields to their urgency and demand. At this point Matthew has one of the most terrible sentences in the "New" Testament, relating that Pilate washes his hands, declaring that he is innocent of Jesus' blood. The Jews should see to the matter themselves. They then answer: "His blood be on us and on our children!" (27:25) This utterance, cited by numerous Christians throughout the centuries as "the gospel truth," has been the justification for much anti-Semitism, even pogroms of Jews. Finally, Pilate, afraid of the crowd in John (19:8) and of not being Caesar's friend (v 12), in the end hands the Galilean prophet over to be crucified (v 16).

Yet the Paschal pardon or amnesty is not mentioned or alluded to anywhere else in Jewish literature, for example in Philo, Josephus or the rabbis. The closest Jewish parallel proposed up to now is b. Pes. 91a, in regard to sacrificing the Paschal lamb for "one who has received a promise to be released from prison" [on the fourteenth of Nisan].[6] This is a citation of m. Pes. 8:6.[7] The earliest comment on it in turn is t. Pes. 7:11, which states regarding a confined leper (מצורע מוסגר): they slaughter [a Paschal offering] for him on the seventh day [of his being shut up].[8] Thus the passage most probably has nothing whatsoever to do with a release from "prison" or a political amnesty.

---

[5]Cf. also Acts 3:13.
[6]Soncino English 485. Cf. C. Chavel, "The Releasing of a Prisoner on the Eve of Passover in Ancient Jerusalem" in *JBL* 60 (1941) 275.
[7]See Ch. Albeck, *Shisha Sidre Mishna* (Jerusalem: Bialik and Dvir, 1959) 2.170. English in H. Danby, *The Mishnah* (London: Oxford University, 1933) 147. The passage continues by mentioning a sick man and an aged person.
[8]M.S. Zuckermandel and S. Liebermann, *Tosephta* (Jerusalem: Wahrmann, 1970) 167. English in J. Neusner, *The Tosefta* (New York: KTAV, 1981) 2.149.

The same is valid for non-Jewish sources. Nowhere in Roman or Greek materials is there a reference or allusion to the custom of a Passover release. This is agreed upon by Jewish scholars,[9] as well as by Christian experts in both Jewish and non-Jewish sources.[10]

The question must therefore be asked whether the entire Barabbas episode was not created by early Jewish Christians as a *haggadah*, or typically Judaic expansion of the sparse information available to them regarding Jesus' trial before Pilate, for apologetic reasons.[11] Although the earliest Christians knew of the Roman governor's reputation of extreme cruelty, of his executing many innocent Jewish citizens,[12] in the gospels they deliberately removed the main responsibility for Jesus' death from him and transferred it to the leaders of the Jews and to the Jewish people in general. I shall comment on this in section VI.4 below.

Cf. the hiphil of סגר as especially applied to leprosy confinement in M. Jastrow, *A Dictionary of the Targumim, the Talmud Babli and Yerushalmi, and the Midrashic Literature* (New York: Pardes, 1950) 956.

[9]Cf. for example S. Lachs, *A Rabbinic Commentary on the New Testament. The Gospels of Matthew, Mark and Luke* (Hoboken: KTAV, 1987) 427, and the authors he cites on p. 148, n. 1. M. Stern in *The Jewish People in the First Century* (Compendia Rerum Iudaicarum ad Novum Testamentum, Section One), ed. S. Safrai, M. Stern et al. (Assen: Van Gorcum, 1974) 338 can only repeat speculation that the Roman practice in Jerusalem was adopted from an already existent Herodian usage.

[10]See P. Billerbeck in Str-B 1.1031. E. Schürer, *The History of the Jewish People in the Age of Jesus Christ,* ed. G. Vermes and F. Millar (Edinburgh: Clark, 1973) 1.370, states bluntly that "Provincial governors had no right to grant a pardon." In his study *Untersuchungen zum römischen Begnadigungsrecht: Abolitio – Indulgentia – Venia* (Commentationes Aenipontanae 18; Innsbruck: Wagner, 1964), W. Waldstein discusses the Passover amnesty on pp. 41-44 in light of Roman sources. He concludes (p. 44): "Also, no good reason speaks against the assumption that under special circumstances a custom could have established itself like that of granting *venia* to a prisoner at Passover." Yet he too can cite no sources for this custom.

[11]The invention of a custom in order to continue a narrative's plot was also practiced by non-Jewish authors. See the examples from Apuleius, Aristophanes and Vergil in J. Bauer, "'Literarische' Namen und 'literarische' Bräuche (zu Joh 2, 10 und 18, 39)" in *BZ* n.s. 26 (1982) 258-64, especially his reference to F. Fröhlke on p. 262.

[12]See especially Luke 13:1; Josephus, *Bell.* 2.176-77 and *Ant.* 18.62; and Philo, *Leg. ad Gai.* 301-302, speaking of "the executions without trial constantly repeated, the ceaseless and supremely grievous cruelty" (English by F.H. Colson in LCL); as well as other sources in Schürer, *The History* 1.383-387. For early Jewish hatred of Pilate, see also 2 Targ Est 3:1, where he is listed in the genealogy of the arch-enemy Haman. English in P. Cassel, *An Explanatory Commentary on Esther,* trans. A. Bernstein (Edinburgh: Clark, 1888) 304, Aramaic in *Aus Literatur und Geschichte. Zweites Targum zum Buche Esther. Im vocalisirten Urtext* (Leipzig and Berlin: Friedrich, 1885) 41.

Elsewhere I have proposed that Jesus' transformation of water into wine in John 2 and the beheading of John the Baptist in Mark 6 par. are such early Jewish Christian *haggadoth,* based on Judaic interpretation of the book of Esther.[13] Here I suggest that the motif of "release," the name "Barabbas," and much more in the Barabbas episode of the gospels also derives from early Jewish Christian haggadic interpretation of Esther.[14]

First I shall describe the relevance of the Judaic interpretation of the book of Esther in general (II). Then I shall sketch how Psalm 22, interpreted of Esther in early Jewish sources, strongly informs the crucifixion narrative (III). Sections II and III make it more probable that other parts of Esther in Judaic interpretation may have influenced the episode with Barabbas directly preceding the crucifixion (IV). The argument is thus cumulative. I shall then discuss the question of the narrative's historicity (V), finally pointing out the great relevance of the results reached in this study to Jewish Christian relationships today (VI).

II. Esther, Salvation, The Passover Festival, and Crucifixion.

A. The Great Popularity of the Scroll of Esther.

The Scroll of Esther in its first Hebrew form may go back to the fourth century B.C.E. The final form definitely emerged by the second century B.C.E.[15] D. Clines maintains that the "Vorlage" presupposed by the so-called "A" text in Greek, different from the LXX, is older than the proto-MT narrative.[16] C. Moore considers four of the six additions to Esther now found in the LXX to have a Semitic "Vorlage"; they stem from either 78 or, more likely, 114 B.C.E.[17] In his retelling of the Esther narrative in his *Antiquities,* Josephus, a native of Jerusalem whose mother tongue was Aramaic, reflects at the end of the first century C.E.

---

[13]Cf. my *Water into Wine and the Beheading of John the Baptist* (BJS 150; Atlanta: Scholars, 1988).

[14]Cf. R. Bultmann's statement in regard to the primitive passion narrative in *The History* 279: "This was developed at various stages, in part by earlier stories that were available ...." The Esther narrative was one of those available stories.

[15]Cf. C. Moore, *Esther* (AB 7B; Garden City, New York: Doubleday, 1979) LVII-LX.

[16]See his *The Esther Scroll: The Story of the Story* (JSOT Suppl. Series 30; Sheffield: JSOT, 1984) 93. Cf. also the diagram on p. 140.

[17]Cf. his *Daniel, Esther and Jeremiah. The Additions* (AB 44; Garden City, New York: Doubleday, 1977) 155 and 161. See also G. Nickelsburg, *Jewish Literature Between the Bible and the Mishnah* (Philadelphia: Fortress, 1981) 172-175.

knowledge of so much haggadic material that it is extremely improbable he himself invented it.[18]

The number of midrashic works dealing with the book of Esther is greater than for any other biblical book. Of the hagiographa or "Writings," it alone possesses a second targum.[19] Why was the writing so immensely popular? First of all, it dealt with evil Haman's proposed destruction, slaying and annihilation of all the Jews, including women and children, in the Persian empire, from India to Ethiopia (Est 3:13).[20] This was much more than Pharaoh's order to throw only the Hebrew newborn boys into the Nile to be drowned (Exod 1:22). This comparison is made in midrashic sources.[21] Here the threat of total annihilation of the Jews is made. It was the darkest hour in Jewish history up to then,[22] followed by deliverance.

In addition, the annual celebration of the festival of Purim included feasting, the sending of choice portions to one another, and gifts to the poor (Est 9:22).[23] The merriment included drinking, as indicated in the statement of Raba, a fourth generation Babylonian Amora,[24] in b. Meg. 7b: "It is the duty of a man to mellow himself (with wine) on Purim until he cannot tell the difference between 'cursed be Haman' and 'blessed be Mordecai.'"[25]

Finally, part of the observance of this annual festival was the obligatory reading of the entire Scroll of Esther in Hebrew by all Aramaic-speaking males. Many people had even memorized it.[26]

---

[18]Cf. 11.184-296 (6.1-13). On his birth in Jerusalem CA. 37-38 C.E., see *Vita* 5, 7. The *Antiquities* were completed in 93-94 C.E. (20.267). On Josephus' use of Aramaic and Hebrew sources in this work, cf. H. St. J. Thackeray in the LCL edition of Josephus' works, IV. xii-xiii.

[19]These commentaries are listed in L.B. Paton, *The Book of Esther* (ICC; Edinburgh: Clark, 1908) 101-103. See also the art. "Esther" by E. Hirsch in *J.E.* (1904) 5.234; Moore, *Esther* LVII; and G. Gerlemann, *Esther* (Neukirchen-Vluyn: Neukirchener, 1973)1.

[20]For this motif, see also 3:6, 9; 4:7, 8; 7:4; 8:5-6; and 9:24.

[21]Cf. for example Midr. Ps. 22/6 on Ps 22:2 in W. Braude, *The Midrash on Psalms* (New Haven: Yale, 1959) 1.302-303.

[22]See Midr. Ps. 22/15 on Ps 22:1 and Isa 9:1 (Braude 1.309).

[23]On the poor as looking forward for this reason all year to the reading of Esther, see t. Meg. 1:4 (Neusner 2.280).

[24]Cf. H. Strack and G. Stemberger, *Einleitung in Talmud und Midrasch* (Munich: Beck, 1982) 99.

[25]Soncino English by M. Simon, 38.

[26]Cf. the sources from the Mishnah, Tosefta and talmudim noted in *Water into Wine* 2, n.5.

B. Salvation/Deliverance/Redemption in Esther.

Except for the Exodus event, Israel's deliverance from slavery in Egypt, no biblical book is more concerned with salvation or redemption than Esther. This is true although in the MT only one reference to deliverance is made. In 4:14 Mordecai tells Esther regarding the total destruction planned for the Jews: "if you keep silent at such a time as this, relief and 'deliverance' (הצלה)[27] will rise for the Jews from another quarter, but you and your father's house will perish."[28]

This situation already changes dramatically in the LXX, especially in the Additions to the Hebrew text. Several examples are the following. In 4:8 Mordecai appeals to Esther to call on the Lord and to speak to King Ahasuerus regarding the Jews, to deliver (ἐρύω/ῥύομαι: LSJ 694, B5)) them from death. In his prayer, inserted at 4:17, Mordecai states that God wants to save (σῴζω) Israel, and he mentions Israel's salvation (σωτηρία), reminding God that He had redeemed (λυτρόω) Israel out of the land of Egypt. In Esther's prayer, situated before 5:1, she asks God three times to deliver (ἐρύω) the Jews, but especially her from her great fear of asking the king to revoke the decree regarding the total annihilation of the Jews. In Artaxerxes' (Ahasuerus') letter, located after 8:13, the king notes that Haman wanted to destroy Mordecai "our savior" (σωτήρ). He encourages the Jews in his realm to keep a festive day, now and later to be a day of salvation (σωτηρία). Finally, in Mordecai's dream inserted at 10:3 he notes that Israel is now saved (σῴζω), the Lord having saved (σῴζω) His people, rescuing (ἐρύω) them from all their calamities.

The "A" Greek text also emphasizes the motif of salvation at 5:5, 9, 13, 16, 19, 25, 29; 6:2; 7:5; 8:14, 26, 30 and 31.[29] Josephus notes that Esther had saved (σῴζω) the Jewish nation (*Ant.* 11.185), whereas Mordecai had saved (σῴζω) the king's life (255, 258, 278), leading to a day of salvation (σωτήριον) for the Jews (282; cf. also 284).

The same motif is strongly emphasized in rabbinic sources. Several examples are the following. In y. Meg. 1:5, 70d R. Ḥelbo, a fourth generation Palestinian Amora,[30] says the month of Adar with the festival of Purim comes just before the month of Nisan with the festival of Passover "so as to link up one redemption (גאולה) [the one of Purim]

---

[27]Cf. BDB 665, deriving from נצל. It only occurs here.
[28]The RSV states in 7:9 that Mordecai's word "saved" the king, but this is a paraphrase.
[29]Cf. the Greek text in Clines, *The Esther Scroll* 216-47.
[30]Cf. Strack and Stemberger, *Einleitung* 98.

The Release of Barabbas

with another redemption [the one of the Exodus from Egypt]."[31] In b. Meg. 11a, R. Yoḥanan, a second generation Palestinian Amora,[32] asks regarding Ps 98:3, "When did all the ends of the earth see the salvation (ישועה) of our Lord? In the days of Mordecai and Esther."[33]

Very important for the release of Barabbas, to be discussed below, is the discussion between R. Ḥiyya bar Abba and R. Simeon ben Ḥalafta, two fifth generation Tannaim,[34] regarding the "hind of the dawn" in Ps 22:1. They note that the redemption (גאולה) of Israel will be gradual, as the light of dawn gradually spreads out, ending in the Jews' having light and gladness (Est 8:16). The modest "beginning" of this redemption came about at Mordecai's encounter with Bigthan and Teresh, two of Ahasuerus' eunuchs who attempted to kill the king (Est 2:21).[35]

Finally, the benediction to be spoken after reading the Scroll of Esther according to R. Yoḥanan ends with the words concerning God: "who has redeemed you and saved you (הגואל והמושיעך) from the hand of your oppressors."[36]

Judaic traditions on the Scroll of Esther are thus unanimous in emphasizing the motif of salvation in this narrative. This in turn led early Jewish Christians to apply other themes from it to the crucifixion of their own "Savior," Jesus.

C. The Passover Festival in Esther

Most likely for theological reasons the Gospel of John has Jesus crucified on the day of Preparation of the Passover (19:14, 31, 42), when the Passover lambs were slaughtered. This implies that Jesus is the Lamb of God (19:33 and Exod 12:46; John 1:29, 36). It would have been the fourteenth of Nisan (Exod 12:6). Yet the Synoptics unanimously imply that he was crucified on the first day of Passover, the fifteenth of Nisan, since the Lord's Supper for them is the Passover meal the evening before (Mark 14:12, 17 [evening, the beginning of the fifteenth], 26 [part of the Hallel psalms, 113-118] par.).[37]

---

[31] English in J. Neusner, *The Talmud of the Land of Israel,* Megillah (Chicago: University of Chicago, 1987) 19.34.
[32] Strack and Stemberger, *Einleitung* 91.
[33] Soncino English 60.
[34] Strack and Stemberger, *Einleitung* 87-88.
[35] Cf. Midr. Ps. 22/13 on Ps 22:1 and Cant 6:10 in Braude 1.308-309. The Hebrew is found in S. Buber, *Midrasch Tehillim* (Vilna: Romm, 1891) 187.
[36] See y. Meg. 4:1, 74d in Neusner 19.146. Cf. also the statement of Raba in b. Meg. 21b (Soncino 130).
[37] On the Lord's Supper as a Passover meal, cf. J. Jeremias, *The Eucharistic Words of Jesus,* available to me in German as *Die Abendmahlsworte Jesu* (Göttingen: Vandenhoeck & Ruprecht, 1967⁴) 35-56.

Passover, especially the fifteenth of Nisan, also plays a major role in Judaic traditions on Esther. Est 3:7 states that the first month of the Jewish year is Nisan. In v 12 Ahasuerus' secretaries are summoned on the thirteenth of that month to write the edict regarding the destruction, slaying and annihilation of all Jews in the Persian empire, including young and old, women and children (v 13). When Mordecai hears of this terrible plan, he has Esther informed of it and asks her to speak to the king on behalf of the Jews (4:14). She responds by requesting him to fast with all the Jews of Susa for three days and nights, as she and her maids will also do. Then she will go to the king, even if she perishes (v 16) because of the strict royal regulations (v 11).

At this point (4:17) Mordecai "goes away" (עבר), which for the rabbis means that "he made the first day of Passover [the fifteenth of Nisan] pass as a fast day."[38] The First Targum to Esther states that "he 'transgressed' against the joy of the feast of Passover,"[39] as עבר is also employed in Est 3:3. Before this, Est. Rab. 8/6 on 4:16 interprets the three days and nights of fasting as the thirteenth to the fifteenth of Nisan, Mordecai objecting that the last day is the first day of Passover (on which fasting is prohibited).[40] Esther then chides him by replying: "Elder of Israel, why is there a Passover?"[41] That is, a festival can only be celebrated if there is a people still alive to do so.

Esther then goes to King Ahasuerus "on the third day" (of her fast: 5:1), that is, on the fifteenth of Nisan.[42] The dramatic tension of the

---

[38] Cf. b. Meg. 15a (Soncino 88) in the name of Rab, a first generation Babylonian Amora who also studied in Palestine (Strack and Stemberger, *Einleitung* 90).

[39] B. Grossfeld, *The First Targum to Esther* (New York: Sepher-Hermon, 1983), Aramaic 21, English 58.

[40] Cf. m. Ta'an. 2:10 on the feast of Dedication and Purim (Danby 197), certainly also applicable to the other festivals.

[41] Soncino 9.107. Cf. Pirq. R. El. 50 in G. Friedlander, *Pirke de Rabbi Eliezer* (New York: Hermon, 1970) 401, and other sources cited in his n. 3, as well as Grossfeld, *The First Targum* 139-40, n. 36. See also Est. Rab. 9/2 on Est 5:1 (Soncino 9.112). I see no evidence for an early fast of Esther on the fourteenth of Nisan, including the reading of Psalm 22 in the Temple and the synagogue. Against D. Simonsen, "Le Psaume XXII et la Passion de Jesus" in *REJ* 22 (1891) 283-85. See also L. Ginzberg, *The Legends of the Jews* (Philadelphia: Jewish Publication Society of America, 1968) 6.472-73, n. 145 on this issue, as well as R. Marcus' note "G" on Josephus, *Ant.* 11.292.

[42] Although the First Targum calls it the third day of Passover, the earliest sources maintain it is the first day. Cf. Grossfeld, *The First Targum* 140, n. 1, as well as Ginzberg, *Legends* 6.471, n. 142. His citation of Seder 'Olam 39 should read 29, where it is stated that "On the sixteenth of Nisan, Haman was hung on the gallows." See the 1981 Yale dissertation of C. Milikowsky, *Seder 'Olam, A Rabbinic Chronography* 542 and 432. On this work as belonging to the middle

The Release of Barabbas 9

entire Scroll of Esther reaches its zenith in this passage (cf. 9:25). If Esther fails to get through to and persuade her husband to rescind his edict, *all* the Jews in the Persian's realm will perish. For this reason it is greatly expanded in Judaic tradition.

The LXX inserts the addition of Esther's Prayer at this point, which probably had a Semitic "Vorlage."[43] She is taken or seized "in the agony of death" (ἐν ἀγῶνι θανάτου: 4:17k). This is repeated in the "A" text, which reflects a different Hebrew "Vorlage" than that of the LXX.[44] In the latter she asks God to deliver (ἐρύω) the Jews and her from her fear (4:17z) of the king,[45] and ceases her prayer on the "third day" of 5:1. Esther's prayer is paraphrased in Josephus, *Ant.* 11.231-234, and in Est. Rab. 8/6 on Est 4:17.[46]

Commenting on the "third day" of Est 5:1, Est. Rab. 9/2 states that Israel is never left in dire distress more than three days. This was true, for example, of Abraham at the '*Aqedah* or binding of Isaac in Gen 22:4; of Jonah in the belly of the fish in Jonah 2:1; and of the dead, who will be resurrected after three days (Hos 6:2). It concludes by stating that "This miracle [נס] also [of Esther and Mordecai, leading to the deliverance of Israel] was performed after three days of their fasting ...."[47]

The motif of the '*Aqedah* is greatly expanded in the Second Targum, for all purposes a midrash, on Est 5:1, where Esther's fervent prayer causes her throat and lips to become dry, and she reminds God of His promise to Abraham to recall his children then in tribulation "for the sake of the sacrifice/binding of their father Isaac," and that He will then redeem [פרק] them.[48]

This "sacrifice" or "binding" of Isaac is described in Gen. Rab. Vayera 56/3 on Gen 22:6, following a parallel in 56/1 to Est. Rab. 9/2, in regard to the "wood of the burnt-offering": "like one who carries his

---

of the second century C.E., cf. the Abstract 2, as well as pp. 12-24. Cf. also Est. Rab. 10/4 on Est 6:10-11 (Soncino English 9.116).
[43] Cf. Clines, *The Esther Scroll* 69, and Moore, *Esther* LXIV, as well as his volume *Daniel, Esther and Jeremiah. The Additions* 155.
[44] Cf. Clines, *The Esther Scroll* 229 and n. 16 above.
[45] For the "A" parallel, see Clines, *The Esther Scroll* 231, including vv 3 and 12 on p. 233.
[46] Soncino English 9.108. The Hebrew is found in *Esther Rabbah* (Jerusalem: Lewin-Epstein, 1960) 26a.
[47] Soncino English 9.112. There is a parallel in Gen. Rab. Vayera 56/1 on Gen. 22:4 (Soncino English 1.491).
[48] Cassel English 324, Aramaic 57.

cross on his shoulders."[49] This takes place on Mt. Moriah, for the rabbis Jerusalem.

The relevance of the 'Aqedah to Jesus' crucifixion is quite clear,[50] and comparison of Jesus' death and resurrection to Jonah in the belly of the fish is found in Matt 12:40. Hos 6:2 most probably is also alluded to in Luke 24:46 and 1 Cor 15:4.

It is no wonder, then, that Esther's desperate situation and prayer found between Est 4:17 and 5:1, spoken "in the agony of death" and on the first day of Passover, the fifteenth of Nisan,[51] is considered by the rabbis to be described in the words of Psalm 22. Jewish Christians logically later applied this same psalm to their redeemer Jesus' darkest hour, on the Cross. Before sketching the application of Psalm 22 to Esther, a short summary of hanging/crucifying in Esther and Judaic traditions on this Scroll is helpful.

D. Hanging/Crucifixion

The verb "to hang" (תלה) occurs twenty-six times in the Hebrew Bible, twenty times of a person's being hanged. Of these, almost half (nine) occur in Esther. Aside from Ahasuerus' order to hang the rebels Bigthan and Teresh in 2:23, the term is used exclusively of Haman's plan to kill Mordecai, which is then reversed. The evil advisor of the king, along with his ten sons, is hanged on the same "gallows" (עץ: "tree," "wood") intended for Mordecai, the Jew from Jerusalem (2:6).

In the LXX of Esther, the Hebrew תלה is translated by κρεμάννυμι, "to hang." Of the two LXX occurrences of "to crucify" (σταυρόω),[52] both are found in Esther, once in 7:9 translating תלה, and once in the addition at 8:12r, the act located (outside) the gates of Susa. The gallows is called ξύλον; σταυρός, "cross," does not occur.

In the "A" Greek text, κρεμάννυμι is also employed with the exception of 7:14 (6:11), which employs ἀνασκολοπίζω, "to impale," and σταυρόω in the addition at 8:28.[53]

Josephus uses κρεμάννυμι in his retelling of the Esther narrative with the exception of ἀνασταυρόω at Ant. 11.208, 246 and 280. For him, the tree (ξύλον) on which Haman plans to hang Mordecai is not fifty

---

[49]Hebrew in J. Theodor and Ch. Albeck, *Midrash Bereshit Rabba* (Jerusalem: Wahrmann, 1965) 2.598; Soncino English 1.493. See also Jastrow 682 on כתף.
[50]For a masterful treatment of this motif, see S. Spiegel, *The Last Temptation*, trans. J. Goldin (New York: Behrman, 1979).
[51]For the fifteenth of Nisan as the date on which Israel was often redeemed in the past, and on which the Messiah is to come for redemption in the future, see Ginzberg, *Legends* 1.224 and 5.221, n. 76, as well as 2.373 and 5.437-38, n. 235.
[52]The verb ἀνασταυρόω is lacking in the LXX.
[53]See Clines, *The Esther Scroll* 236-37, and 242-43.

cubits (ca. 22 meters or 73 feet)⁵⁴ high, as in Est 5:14, but sixty cubits, a typically haggadic expansion (11.246). At 11.261, 266 and 267 it is called a cross, σταυρός.

In the above sources, especially the latter, a tendency to adapt the Esther account to later contemporary times is observable. Impalement on a stake was considered to have first been a Persian mode of execution. Crucifixion, with a cross-beam, was typically Roman.⁵⁵ The latter emphasis is shown in Est. Rab. 10/5 on Est 6:10-11, where Haman tells Mordecai regarding his intention to hang him: yesterday "I was preparing for you ropes and nails, and God prepares for you royal apparel."⁵⁶

Legendary material regarding this gallows/cross grew rapidly, including the association with Deut 21:23 in 2 Targ Est 9:24.⁵⁷ This Pentateuch prohibition of letting the body of a hanged person remain on the tree overnight is reflected in the removal of Jesus' body from the Cross in Mark 15:42-43 par. and John 19:31, and it is quoted by Paul of Jesus' crucifixion in Gal 3:13. In Est. Rab. 9/2 on Est 5:14 all the trees of creation offer themselves as the wood for Haman's tree/cross, the winner being the thorn.⁵⁸ Finally, Pirq. R. El. 50 has Elijah state that the tree on which Haman is to be hanged derives from the Holy of Holies in the Jerusalem Temple.⁵⁹

In light of the above development of legendary materials regarding Haman's gallows/tree/cross, it is understandable that early Jewish Christians could transfer hanging and tree imagery from the redeeming situation of the Scroll of Esther to another, for them redemptive event: the crucifixion and Cross of Jesus.⁶⁰

III. Psalm 22 Applied to Esther and to Jesus' Crucifixion

Every first semester student of the New Testament at a theological seminary is struck by the similarities between elements of Psalm 22,

---

⁵⁴Cf. O.R. Sellers, art. "Weights and Measures," D.4a in *I.D.B.* 4.836-37 on the cubit.
⁵⁵See J. Schneider, art. σταυρός κτλ. in *TDNT* 7.573; M. Hengel, *Crucifixion* (Philadelphia: Fortress, 1977) 22, n. 1; as well as M. Greenburg, art. "Hanging" in *I.D.B.* 2.522.
⁵⁶Soncino English 9.117. On other relevant sources, see Ginzberg, *Legends* 4.431 and 6.475,n. 159.
⁵⁷Cassel English 342-43, Aramaic 72.
⁵⁸Soncino English 9.111-112.
⁵⁹Friedlander 407.
⁶⁰In *Legends* 6.479, n. 184, Ginzberg maintains that there is some connection between the later legends on Haman's gallows and Jesus' Cross, citing 2 Targ Est 7:10. On the latter, see Cassel English 335-36.

applied in Judaic tradition to the desperate situation of Esther before King Ahasuerus in Est 5:1-2,[61] a situation involving the "agony of death" (LXX and the "A" text), and the scene of Jesus' crucifixion. Here I shall point out six of these similarities, thereby making it even more probable that the motif of Pilate's "release" of a prisoner to the Jews at Passover could derive from Judaic interpretation of other Esther traditions.

1. Ps 22:2 (Eng. 1)

The words "My God, my God, why hast Thou forsaken me (עזבתני)?" are interpreted in Midr. Ps. 22/6 in regard to Esther's three-day fast, ending with Est 5:1-2. On the first day (of a fast) one may say "My God," and on the second. Only on the third day, however, may one say "Why hast Thou forsaken me?" "As soon as she (Esther) cried in a loud voice,[62] 'Why hast Thou forsaken me?' (her cry) was heard immediately."[63] Midr. Ps. 22/16 also maintains that Esther spoke these words, asking God why He performs no miracles (נסים) for her in this hopeless situation.[64]

Jewish Christians applied Ps 22:2 not to the redeemer Esther, but to their own redeemer, Jesus, in his most desperate situation, his agony of death on the Cross. Mark 15:34 states that Jesus, like Esther, "cried in a loud voice"[65]: "Eloi, Eloi, lama sabachthani." The Aramaic is then translated into Greek. Matt 27:46's Aramaic is similar to Mark's here, modifying "Eloi" to "Eli." As P. Billerbeck has pointed out, except for the term "why," the Aramaic of the two evangelists is still found in the present form of the targum to Ps 22:2.[66] The term שבקתני, "Thou hast forsaken me," is from שבק, which can also mean "to remit," "to release,"[67] which as I shall point out below is very important for the "release" of Barabbas.

---

[61]Cf. the statement of Grossfeld, *The First Targum* 58: "in Ps. 22 we have the prayer of Esther before she appeared before the king. The midrash to Ps. 22 contains a paraphrase of Ps. 22, givings details of Esther's life alluded to therein." See also L. Jung, the translator of b. Yoma, on Ps 22:1 in 29a (Soncino 136, n.7): "Queen Esther is reported to have sung this psalm as she came before Ahasuerus ...."
[62]This motif may derive from Ps 22:3, "My God, I *cry* by day."
[63]Cf. Braude 1.302, and the Hebrew in Buber 183.
[64]Braude 1.311; Buber 188. See also R. Levi, a third generation Palestinian Amora (Strack and Stemberger, *Einleitung* 94), on Est 5:2 in b. Meg. 15b (Soncino 91).
[65]See also Mark 15:37; Matt 27:50; and Luke 23:46 for Jesus' crying with a loud voice directly before expiring.
[66]Str-B 1.1042. The Aramaic is found in P. de Lagarde, *Hagiographa Chaldaice* (Leipzig: Teubner, 1873; reprint Osnabruck: Zeller, 1967) 11.
[67]Jastrow 1516-17.

2. Ps 22:8 (Eng. 7)

"All who see me mock at me, they make mouths at me, they wag their heads" is interpreted in Midr. Ps. 22/21 as referring to the situation of the Jews in Susa when Esther appears before Ahasuerus. It is about "Haman's sons who laughed Jews to scorn, shot out their lips at them, and shook their heads at them, saying, 'On the morrow these will be slain, or hanged.'"[68]

At Jesus' crucifixion these words also describe his scoffers: "And those who passed by derided him, wagging their heads ..." (Mark 15:29; Matt 27:39).

3. Ps 22:9 (Eng. 8)

"Let Him (the Lord) deliver him, let Him rescue him, for He delights in him" is interpreted in Midr. Ps. 22/22 of Esther's stating regarding God: "His desire to rescue me rose up within Him."[69]

At the scene of Jesus' crucifixion these words are reflected in Matt 27:43, "Let God deliver him now, if He desires him." Directly before this, the chief priests, with the scribes and elders, state: "He trusts in God." This motif of "trusting in God" derives from Ps 22:5-6 (Eng. 4-5).

Matthew was well aware of Psalm 22 as the background for numerous motifs at Jesus' crucifixion. He, or his source, thus added yet one more from the same psalm.

4. Ps 22:16 (Eng. 15)

The basic motif of "My mouth is dried up like a potsherd, and my tongue cleaves to my jaws" is applied in 2 Targ Est 5:1 to Esther's coming before King Ahasuerus: "With tears she prayed fervently, so that her throat and lips became dry."[70]

In John 19:28 Jesus on the Cross says, "I thirst." He is then given vinegar to drink, after which he dies. Jesus' thirst at this point is "to fulfill the scripture" (v 28), certainly referring to Ps 69:22 (Eng. 21): "for my thirst they gave me vinegar to drink." Yet the basic idea of Jesus' thirst on the Cross may originally have been occasioned by Ps 22:16.

5. Ps 22:17 (Eng. 16)

While the MT now reads "like a lion," the original Hebrew certainly is reflected in the LXX, Syriac and Jerome, who have: "'they have

---

[68]Braude 1.317; Buber 192.
[69]Braude 1.318: Buber 192.
[70]Cassel Aramaic 56; English 323.

pierced' my hands and feet." In Midr. Ps. 22/26, R. Judah (bar Ilai) and R. Nehemiah, two third generation Tannaim frequently in debate with one another,[71] interpret this sentence in different ways of Esther, changing the vocalization of the Hebrew.[72]

In the gospels it is assumed that at his crucifixion nails were driven into Jesus' hands and feet, which were then "pierced."[73]

6. Ps 22:19 (Eng. 18)

"They divide my garments among them, and for my raiment they cast lots" is applied in Midr. Ps. 22/27 to Esther. "One person said: 'I shall take her purple cloak and coat.' Another said: 'I shall take her rings and necklaces.' 'And for my raiment they cast lots.' R. Huna[74] said: 'This was the purple cloak, for it is not customary for a commoner to use it.'"[75] Basically the same tradition is found in 22/7, related to Esther's going to the king without permission in Est 4:16.[76]

At Jesus' crucifixion, the Roman soldiers "divided his garments among them, casting lots for them, to decide what each should take" (Mark 15:24; Matt 27:35; Luke 23:34).[77] This scene is enlarged in John, who alone quotes Ps 22:19 in 19:24. He also differentiates between Jesus' garments and his tunic (χιτών in 19:23).[78]

* * * *

The above six similarities between elements of Psalm 22, applied to the Jewish redeemer Esther in a situation of "the agony of death," and to the Jewish Christians' redeemer Jesus in his situation of the agony of death on the Cross, make it quite understandable that another motif just before the crucifixion, that of "release," may also derive from Judaic Esther traditions.[79] To this I now turn.

---

[71] Strack and Stemberger, *Einleitung* 83.
[72] Braude 1.320-21; Buber 194.
[73] The quotation of Zech 12:10 in John 19:37 refers to the piercing of Jesus' side, not his hands or feet.
[74] Probably a second generation Babylonian Amora: Strack and Stemberger, *Einleitung* 93.
[75] My translation of Buber 194. Braude in 1.321 is paraphrastic and misleading ("armor").
[76] Braude 1.304-305; Buber 184.
[77] In Mark 15:17 and 20 and Matt 27:28 and 31 the soldiers had earlier clothed him in a purple cloak in the mocking scene.
[78] P. Billerbeck in Str-B 2.574-80 also describes the usages of Psalm 22 in rabbinic literature, yet with the exception of John 19:24, he does not apply them to the crucifixion of Jesus.
[79] Other motifs from Judaic Esther traditions may also have influenced the scene of Jesus' interrogation and crucifixion. Cf. Mordecai's being mocked by Haman's

IV. The Release of Barabbas

A. A Mini-Trial.

In the biblical book of Esther there is a mini-trial, which is greatly expanded in Judaic tradition, showing its great popularity and the probability that it was also known to many early Jewish Christians.

Est 2:21-23, repeated in part in 6:2, describes how Bigthan and Teresh, two of King Ahasuerus' eunuchs who guarded the threshold (of his bed-chamber), became angry and attempted to kill the king. The matter became known to Mordecai, who sat at the king's gate. He told it to Queen Esther, who then informed the king. "When the affair was investigated and found to be so, the men were both hanged on the gallows" (v 23).

It should be recalled that the "redemption" of Israel in the time of Esther began at precisely this point, as noted in the Tannaitic tradition cited above in section II,B. Comment on Judaic development of Est 2:21-23 helps to understand the "release"motif to be discussed below in section "B."

1. Rebellion.

Popular curiosity asked how Bigthan and Teresh sought to kill King Ahasuerus. The First Targum on Est 2:21, no doubt reflecting a major if not the major view, states that it was "by sword" (סייפיה) in his bed-chamber.[80] This is probably a word play on סף, "threshold," in the same verse.

A similar tradition is found in Gen. Rab. Vayesheb 88/3 on Gen 40:2, where Rab, a first generation Babylonian Amora who studied with Rabbi in Palestine,[81] states regarding the two plotters: "They placed short daggers (קונדא מכיריאה) in their shoes."[82]

These *haggadoth*, especially the latter, recall the Sicarii, named after the *sica*, a curved dagger with which they assassinated their

---

efforts to put a purple robe on him (see for example Josephus, *Ant.* 11.257, and the soldiers' mocking of Jesus in Mark 15:16-20, Matt 27:27-31); and Mordecai, first abased but later elevated to wearing purple and a crown, and to being called "king of the Jews" (Est. Rab. 10/12 on Est 8:15 in Soncino English 9.121; Pirq. R. El. 50 in Friedlander 408-09; and the major motif of Jesus as "king of the Jews" in the crucifixion narrative). Space does not permit development of these motifs here.

[80]See Grossfeld, *The First Targum* 48 and 13.
[81]Strack and Stemberger, *Einleitung* 90.
[82]Soncino English 2.815; Theodor and Albeck 3.1080. See also Jastrow 782 on this phrase.

political opponents, that is, their fellow Jews who were not willing to rebel against Rome in the first century C.E., up to the fall of Jerusalem.[83]

Bigthan and Teresh in Judaic tradition are thus represented as rebels against the king, willing to employ force, even murder, to establish their goals. Early Jewish Christians thus could easily associate the narrative concerning them with the political rebels crucified with Jesus, and with one of them who was released, Barabbas.

2. Mordecai's Knowledge of Bigthan and Teresh's Plot, and the Name Barabbas.

Est 2:22 simply states: "And the matter became known (ויודע) to Mordecai ...." The *haggadah* sought to fill in this gap by suggesting exactly how the plot of the king's eunuchs became known to Mordecai.

a) *The LXX* in the addition at 1:1m-n already interprets the passage to mean: "And Mordecai was resting in the courtyard with Gabatha and Tharra, the two eunuchs of the king who guarded the courtyard. Mordecai overhead their deliberations, and he investigated their plans, and he learned that they were preparing to lay hands on King Artaxerxes, and he reported to the king concerning them." At 2:22 the LXX simply states: "And the matter was made known (ἐδηλώθη) to Mordecai." The question is left open as to who disclosed it to him.

b) *The Greek "A" text* varies from this somewhat. It states at A 11-13 that "Mordecai slept in the king's courtyard beside Astaos and Thedeutes, the two eunuchs of the king. He overhead their words and their plots, how they were planning to lay hands on Ahasuerus the king to put him to death. But Mordecai, being well disposed [to the king], made a report concerning them."[84]

In both the LXX and the "A" text the eunuchs presume that Mordecai, next to them, is sleeping. Yet he hears their plotting and reports it to Esther or the king.

c) In *b. Meg.* 7a a baraitha or Tannaitic tradition not found in the Mishnah has four early rabbis maintain that the book of Esther was composed under the inspiration of the holy spirit. R. Meir, a third generation Tanna,[85] quotes "And the matter became known to Mordecai" from Est 2:22 as his proof for this. M. Simon, the English

---

[83]Cf. "Appendix B: The Fourth Philosophy: Sicarii and Zealots," by C. Hayward in Schürer, *The History* 2.598-606, especially p. 601.
[84]Clines, *The Esther Scroll* 216-219. The Greek "A" text omits a translation of Est 2:22.
[85]Strack and Stemberger, *Einleitung* 82.

translator in the Soncino edition of the Babylonian Talmud, correctly asks: "Who revealed it to him if not the holy spirit?"[86]

This opinion is repeated in 2 Targ Est 2:22.[87]

d) *The First Targum* at 2:22 states that "The matter became known to Mordecai because he was well-versed in speaking seventy languages ...."[88] Rabbinic tradition attributes this to his being a member of the Sanhedrin, whose members knew this many languages. Bigthan and Teresh are here described as plotting in their native Tarsian or Coele-Syrian, which Mordecai could nevertheless understand.[89]

e) *Josephus*. A fifth solution, most important for the release of "Barabbas," is found in this Jewish historian. In *Ant.* 11.205-206 Josephus interrupts his narrative on Est 2:21 to supply information on 5:2, the reason why Esther was deathly afraid of approaching the king, and for her special prayer on this occasion.[90]

This is very important to note, for it shows that Judaic tradition already in the first century C.E. linked Esther's encounter before the furious king with the "mini-trial" narrative of 2:21-23.

Josephus continues his retelling of the Esther story by stating in § 207 that the two chamberlains "plotted against the king, but Barnabazos, the servant of one of these eunuchs, who was a Jew by race, discovered their plot and revealed it to Mordecai ...." This naming of Mordecai's informant is only found here in Judaic sources.

The name Βαρναβαζος is Persian and most probably derives ultimately from an actual plot to assassinate Artaxerxes. Photios' excerpts from the fifth century B.C.E. "Persika" of Ktesias relate, for example, that after Artapanos and the eunuch Spamitres kill Xerxes (in 465 B.C.E.), they set up Artaxerxes as king. Nevertheless, Artapanos also plots against the new king, sharing this information with Megabyzos. The latter, however, reveals (μηνύει) everything, and Artapanos himself is executed along with the eunuch Spamitres.[91]

This entire narrative appears to lie behind the plot of the two eunuchs Bigthan and Teresh to assassinate King Ahasuerus, really Xerxes but called in the LXX Artaxerxes.[92] Judaic tradition also relates

---

[86]Soncino 36, n. 10.
[87]Cassel English 303, Aramaic 40.
[88]Grossfeld, *The First Targum* 48 and 14.
[89]Cf. the relevant texts translated in Grossfeld, *The First Targum* 106-107.
[90]See also n. "d" on § 206 in the Loeb edition by R. Marcus, whose translation I quote on § 207.
[91]Cf. the text in F. König, *Die Persika des Ktesias von Knidos* (Archiv für Orientforschung, 18; Graz, 1972) 12-13 on §§ 29-30.
[92]Cf. Moore, *Esther* XXXV and XL.

that the deed took place in his bed-chamber.⁹³ Megabyzos' role of informing the king corresponds to that of Barnabazos in Josephus.

Megabyzos historically is the same as Bagabuḫša, whose name has various spellings such as Bagabasus.⁹⁴ I suggest that since Aramaic was the *lingua franca* of the Persian Empire,⁹⁵ Jews living there "Aramaized" the name of the informant Bagabasus, it becoming Barnabaz, perhaps now meaning "son of the distributor (of royal largesses)."⁹⁶ As such it was carried to Palestine, where Aramaic was also spoken.

For a Jewish Christian describing the circumstances of Jesus' crucifixion in light of Judaic traditions on the Esther narrative, it would have been only a small step to drop the nun and exchange samek for zayin in Barnabaz: בר אבס, Βαραββας,⁹⁷ similar to the frequently found name בר אבא.⁹⁸

3. The Interrogation/Trial and Crucifixion.

After Bigthan and Teresh's plot to assassinate King Ahasuerus became known to Mordecai, he told it to Queen Esther, who in turn informed the king. "When the affair was investigated and found (to be so), the men were both hanged on the gallows" (Est 2:23).

This incident was also enhanced from an early time in Judaic tradition. While the LXX at Est 2:23 states that the king examined (ἐτάζω) the two eunuchs and hanged (κρεμάννυμι) them, addition A at 1:1o says that he "closely examined" (ἐξετάζω) them, and "when they had confessed, they were led off" (ἀπάγω – to be executed). The second half of this sentence is also found in the "A" Greek text.⁹⁹

To this should be compared the Roman soldiers' "leading away" (ἀπάγω in Matt 27:31 and Luke 23:26, ἐξάγω in Mark 15:20) Jesus to Golgotha in order to crucify him.

---

⁹³See First Targ Est 2:21, noted above in "1. Rebellion," as well as other sources cited in Ginzberg, *Legends* 6.461, n. 88.
⁹⁴König, *Die Persika* 75-76, quoting Justin, 3.1. On the slaying of Xerxes by Artabanus, captain of the royal bodyguard, who wished to transfer the rule to himself, and who was aided by the eunuch Mithradates, the king's chamberlain, who led Artabanus into the king's bed-chamber, cf. Diordorus of Sicily, Library of History 11.69 (Loeb edition by C.H. Oldfather). This work was published at the latest between 36-30 B.C.E. (Loeb 1.xi, n. 2).
⁹⁵Moore, *Esther* XXXVIII, n. 39, as well as the references in *Water into Wine* 6.
⁹⁶See Jastrow 867 on נבו.
⁹⁷On these processes, see S. Krauss, *Griechische und lateinische Lehnwörter im Talmud, Midrasch und Targum* (Berlin, 1898; reprint Hildesheim: Olms, 1964) 1.110 and 3, n. 1.
⁹⁸Cf. for example Str-B 1.1031.
⁹⁹Clines, *The Esther Scroll* 218-219.

The Release of Barabbas

The First Targum notes that at the investigation "the truth" was discovered.[100] The Second Targum states that the matter was found "true" or "reliable."[101] Josephus also notes that the king sought out "the truth."[102]

After the truth of the assassination plot was ascertained, according to Josephus the king "crucified" (ἀνασταυρόω) the guilty eunuchs.[103]

After Jesus' interrogation or mini-trial before Pontius Pilate, who according to the Evangelist John asked "What is truth?" (18:38), this representative of the king or Caesar in Rome also had Jesus crucified.

B. A Release.

Directly before the mini-trial and crucifixion described in section "A" above, Est 2:18 speaks of a "remission" or "release." The proximity of this verse and Judaic interpretation of it to the unit 2:19-23, including in its interpretation the name Barnabazos, makes it probable that it served a Jewish Christian author with the motif of the "release" of Barabbas instead of Jesus at his trial scene.

In a generous mood because of his wedding feast, King Ahasuerus in Est 2:18 "made a הֲנָחָה to the provinces, and he distributed presents with royal liberality." This noun occurs only here in the Hebrew Bible and derives from the root נוח, "to rest." Some lexicographers interpret it as "a giving of rest, i.e., perh. holiday-making."[104]

The RSV has the above meaning in a footnote ("granted a holiday"), but in its main text prefers "granted a remission of taxes." The First Targum interprets the rare Hebrew as a "remission/release of taxes" (שיבוק כרגא).[105] The Second Targum has: "granted remissions/releases to his entire realm" (ושבק שביקין לכולי עלמא).[106] A. Sulzbach translates the latter phrase as "and he granted remissions of punishment/amnesties [Straferlasse] to his entire realm,"[107] an interpretation which is thoroughly justifiable, as will be shown shortly. Here it should be noted that the same Aramaic root, as a noun and a verb, as found in Jesus'

---

[100]Grossfeld, *The First Targum* 48 and 14, and his n. 42 on p. 109.
[101]English in Cassel 303, Aramaic 40.
[102]*Ant.* 11.208, with ἐξευρίσκω.
[103]*Ibid.* Cf. Ginzberg, *Legends* 4.392 and 6.462, n. 91 for their being nailed to a cross.
[104]Cf. for example BDB 629. In rabbinic Hebrew it means "rest, ease, relief" (Jastrow 357).
[105]Grossfeld, *The First Targum* 47 and 13. On שיבוקא, cf. Jastrow 1557.
[106]Aramaic in Cassel 39; his English over interprets. A. Sulzbach in *Targum Scheni zum Buch Esther* (Frankfurt: Kauffmann, 1920) 49 notes that part of the rest of the text here is in disorder.
[107]Sulzbach, *ibid.*

citation of Ps 22:2 on the Cross, שבק, is employed in both targums at this point.

While the "A" Greek text has the plural ἀφέσεις ("he made 'remissions' to all his territories") at this point,[108] the LXX has the singular, as in the Hebrew: "He made a remission/release ἄφεσις to those under his rule." There is no mention of taxes, agreeing with the Second Targum as against the First. The term ἄφεσις means "letting go, release," and already in Plato it means with the genitive φόνου: quittance, release from murder.[109] This possible interpretation makes Est 2:18 very appropriate as the background for the release of an imprisoned murderer such as Barabbas.

While Est 2:18 can also be viewed as a remission of taxes in some rabbinic sources,[110] elsewhere it is interpreted as a release from a) infirmities, or b) prison. The latter is of most relevance for the release of Barabbas.

a) *Infirmities.* In Gen. Rab. Vayera 53/8 on Gen 21:6, a narrative is related in the name of R. Samuel b. R. Isaac, a third generation Palestinian Amora:[111]

> When the matriarch Sarah was remembered [gave birth], many other barren women were remembered with her; many deaf gained their hearing; many blind had their eyes opened; many insane became sane. For "making" is mentioned here [in Gen 21:6], and also elsewhere, viz. "And he made a release to the provinces" (Est 2:18). As the "making" mentioned there means that a release (דורייה) was granted to the world, so the "making" mentioned here means that a "release" [from their infirmities] was granted to the world.[112]

The term דּוֹרָיָיה can mean "freedom, remission of tribute or fine, pardon."[113] Here it has nothing to do with the remission of taxes, but with release from physical infirmities.

b) *Prison.* The healing of the blind, crippled, mute and insane is also related regarding Sarah's giving birth in Gen 21:6 in Pesiq. R. 42/4 on Gen 21:1. After this follows:

> What happened can be compared with what a king did for a friend. When an occasion of gladness befell his friend, the king wished to show to what extent his friend was esteemed by him. So he granted releases/amnesties (דוריות) to all by opening the prisons.

---

[108] Clines, *The Esther Scroll* 222-23.
[109] LSJ 288.
[110] Cf. for example b. Meg. 13a (Soncino 77); Aggadat Esther in S. Buber, *Aggadath Esther* (Vilna, 1925) 23; and Leqaḥ Ṭob in S. Buber, *Aggadic Books on the Scroll of Esther* (Vilna: Romm, 1886) 96.
[111] Strack and Stemberger, *Einleitung* 95.
[112] Theodor and Albeck, 2.562-63. See the parallels cited there.
[113] Jastrow 290.

This is inferred by analogy between the texts Gen 21:8 and Est 2:18, whereby the latter is interpreted as "he opened the prisons."[114]

The same term דוריה in the sense of the release of a political rebel from prison is found in Midr. Ps. 90/7 on Ps 90:1:

> A parable of three men who came to ask a gift (דורון)[115] – some say, to receive a release/amnesty (דוריה) – from the king. The first man came and honored the king, and when the king asked him: "What do you request?" he answered: "Because I incited to rebellion (שמרדתי), I ask that you grant me a release/amnesty (דוריה)." And he granted it to him.[116]

The above texts in their present form are not Tannaitic. Nevertheless, they show that a Jewish Christian wishing to describe Jesus' trial scene in the light of Judaic traditions on the redeemer Esther not only could have borrowed the figure of Barnabazos, the rebel Barabbas, from such traditions on Est 2:21-23. He also could have borrowed the motif of a "release from prison" from the very nearby passage Est 2:18, as others also independently did later. The application of the "Esther psalm," Psalm 22, to Jesus' crucifixion, certainly encouraged him to do so.

Finally, the occurrence of the Aramaic from Ps 22:2, שבק, attributed to Jesus on the Cross ("Why have You 'abandoned' me?") and the same Aramaic verb and noun ("release") found in the two targums on Est 2:18, certainly encouraged the Jewish Christian author of the Barabbas incident, writing in Aramaic, to associate the two. The great dramatic irony in his account could then be that although all his disciples "abandoned" him when he was taken captive in the Garden of Gethsemane, and although the Roman procurator Pilate "released" a political rebel and murderer to the people at the Passover feast, the Heavenly Father in fact did not "abandon" innocent Jesus on the Cross. Instead, He "released" him through death from his terrible suffering there and from the pangs of death by raising him on Easter Sunday (cf. Acts 2:24). In light of the "Suffering Servant of the Lord" texts from the prophet Isaiah, above all Isa 53:4-5 and 12, the earliest Jewish Christians came to believe that this suffering was vicarious, on behalf of all mankind.

---

[114] In M. Friedmann, *Pesikta Rabbati* (Vienna, 1880) 177a. I modify the English of W. Braude, *Pesikta Rabbati* (New Haven: Yale, 1968) 745.
[115] From the Greek δῶρον, gift. Jastrow 289. The close similarity to "release/amnesty" led to much confusion in the texts.
[116] Buber 389; I modify Braude's English somewhat in 2.90.

Excursus on Pilate's Wife

One of the earliest interpretations of the Barabbas narrative is found in Matt 27:15-26. Matthew or the source informing him makes two major additions: Pilate's washing his hands to show that he is innocent of Jesus' blood (v 24), and the dream of Pilate's wife (v 19), also designed to show Jesus' innocence. The latter probably also derives from the Esther narrative, which would indicate that Matthew was already aware of the origin of the Barabbas episode in Judaic interpretation of Esther.[117]

Pilate's wife, called Claudia Procula or Procla in legendary expansion of this material,[118] advises her husband to "have nothing to do with that righteous man [Jesus], for I have suffered much over him today in a dream." This recalls Judaic interpretation of Est 5:14 regarding the advice of Zeresh to her husband Haman, not to do anything evil to Mordecai, frequently called "righteous" in rabbinic sources.[119] She cannot prevail, however, against Haman's friends, who convince him to hang/crucify Mordecai,[120] frequently also called the redeemer of Israel.[121] This incident takes place just before the next verse, Est 6:1, which relates that King Ahasuerus could not sleep during the same night. Judaic interpretation also speaks here of his being "disturbed" and of his dreaming.[122]

If Zeresh's advice stands behind that of Pilate's wife to him, as seems probable, this is yet one more indication of the continuing influence of Judaic Esther traditions on the Barabbas narrative.

V. The Historicity of the Barabbas Narrative

In light of the reconstruction made above, it can be ascertained that early Jewish Christians sought to interpret Jesus' death on the Cross by means of material already familiar to them. They applied motifs and

---

[117] See section III.3 above for Matthew's adding another motif from Psalm 22 to Jesus' crucifixion. He knew his Scripture very well.

[118] Cf. the Gospel of Nicodemus 2 and the Acts of Pilate, as well as the history of exegesis of this verse, in E. Fascher, *Das Weib des Pilatus (Matthäus 27, 19), Die Auferweckung der Heiligen (Matthäus 27, 51-53). Zwei Studien zur Geschichte der Auslegung* (Hallesche Monographien, 20; Halle: Niemeyer, 1951) 5-31.

[119] Cf. for example b. Meg. 10b (Soncino 59) and 13b (Soncino 78). See also the end of the passage cited in n. 120 regarding Mordecai as "righteous."

[120] 2 Panim Aḥerim on Est 5:14 in Buber, *Aggadic Books* 72. On this, see also Ginzberg, *Legends* 6.475, n. 159.

[121] Cf. LXX Est 8:12n; Josephus, *Ant.* 11.278; and 2 Targ Est 3:14 (Cassel Aramaic 50, English 314). By saving the king, Mordecai saved Israel.

[122] Cf. Est. Rab. 10/1 on Est 6:1 (Soncino 9.115) and other sources noted by Ginzberg, *Legends* 4.433-435; and 6.475, notes 163-168.

phrases attributed in Judaic tradition to the redeemer Esther to their own redeemer, Jesus of Nazareth. If this is true, Jesus never uttered for example what is startlingly close to the targum of Ps 22:2 in a loud voice from the Cross, nor did passersby wag their heads at him, nor were lots cast among the attending soldiers for his garments. All these phrases and motifs were *later* applied to him from Judaic Esther traditions, now viewed through Jewish Christian eyes.

The same is true of the Barabbas narrative. Pilate, known in all other sources as cruel, vindictive and without any reverence whatsoever for the life of others, never washed his hands in innocence after acceding to a mob's demand for the release of a murderer, Barabbas. Both the figure of Barabbas himself and the "custom" of a Passover release are Jewish Christian borrowings from, and further development of, Judaic traditions on Est 2:18-23. They cannot be rescued historically, for example, by proposing the later attachment of an historical, originally separate Barabbas event to the condemnation of Jesus.[123]

The earliest passion narrative may have had Jesus bound and led away from an *ad hoc* meeting of the Sanhedrin to Pilate, who after a brief interrogation delivered him to be crucified (Mark 15:1, 15b, 20b par.). The only certain thing that can be stated after this is the inscription of the charge against Jesus on the Cross, reading: "The King of the Jews" (15:26).[124] Pilate was only too willing to crucify someone he considered a political rebel, a possible danger to Rome.

After *all* the disciples "forsook" Jesus and fled when he was taken captive in the Garden of Gethsemane (Mark 14:27, 50 par.), there were no witnesses at Pilate's interrogation of Jesus and at the crucifixion with the possible exception of a number of female followers who viewed the latter from afar at Golgotha (15:40-41 par.). These incidents were later described and elaborated through the believing eyes of those who had experienced a vision of Jesus in Galilee (14:28; 16:7 par.; John 21; cf. 1 Cor 15:5), or by their followers.

The question of historicity should not be addressed to haggadic material such as the Barabbas incident. The Jewish Christian

---

[123]Cf. E. Klostermann, *Das Marcusevangelium* (HNT, 3; Tübingen: Mohr, 1950⁴) 159, and J. Ernst, *Das Evangelium nach Markus* (Regensburg: Pustet, 1981) 458. For ten reasons against the historicity of the Barabbas episode, see also H. Cohn, *The Trial and Death of Jesus* (London: Weidenfeld and Nicolson, 1972) 164-168.

[124]Cf. N. Dahl, *The Crucified Messiah and Other Essays* (Minneapolis: Augsburg, 1974) 23-24, 28. See also the statement of M. Dibelius quoted in W. Grundmann, *Das Evangelium nach Markus* (THNT, 2; Berlin: Evangelische Verlagsanstalt, 1977⁷) 420, and n. 4.

attribution of phrases and motifs from Judaic interpretation of the Esther psalm, Psalm 22, to Jesus at his crucifixion is motivated by the fact that the two figures were both redeemers of Israel. The earliest Jewish Christians, hearers of this episode, would have recognized this attribution and appreciated it as a normal haggadic method. The application of Esther motifs to the passion narrative then continued, resulting in the Barabbas episode.

The creation and further development of the Barabbas episode within the four gospels is similar to the use of Judaic Esther materials to explain the precise manner in which John the Baptist was killed in Mark 6 par.[125] It helps to fill in a great gap in the earliest passion narrative, between Jesus' being delivered to Pilate in Mark 15:1, and the latter's having him scourged, and delivering him to be crucified in v 15b. The procurator's soldiers carry out this order in v 20b. Just before this, they mock Jesus with a purple cloak and a crown in vv 16-20a par. This probably also goes back to the mocking of the redeemer Mordecai in Judaic traditions on Est 6:11, with precisely these two articles.[126]

The Barabbas narrative in Mark 15:6-15a par. allows the author twice to emphasize the contents of the later inscription on the Cross, Jesus as "King of the Jews" (vv 9, 12 and 26; cf. v 2). In addition, he uses the story to portray Jesus as innocent of any crime deserving of death, in contrast to the murderer/rebel Barabbas (vv 7, 14). The character Barabbas is here a dramatic foil to Jesus. Finally, although the author indicates that Pilate wished to "satisfy" the crowd (v 15a), thus himself bearing the final responsibility for Jesus' death, he shifts the main blame for this from the Roman to the envious chief priests, who deliberately stir up the crowd or mob against the Galilean prophet (vv 10-11). The terrible further development of this is Matt 27:25.

The traditions informing the passion narrative of the Gospel of Mark, commonly held to have been written shortly before or after 70 C.E.,[127] in 15:1-15 already make the Jewish people primarily responsible for Jesus' crucifixion. In doing so, they may reflect some scattered Jewish persecution of Christians (Mark 13:9, 11; Acts 3-5; 8:1; 9:1-2; 12:1-3). Yet two other factors were much more influential.

Jewish Christians now claimed to be the "true" Israel, that God had made a "new" covenant or testament with mankind in Jesus of Nazareth. Those Jews who refused to believe in him as the Messiah were no longer truly Israel, they now ostensibly belonged to the "old"

---

[125]See my study cited in n. 13.
[126]Cf. n. 79.
[127]Cf. W. Kümmel, *Einleitung in das Neue Testament* (Heidelberg: Quelle & Meyer, 1964[13]) 55.

covenant. A daughter religion in the state of puberty, Christianity, was rebelling here against its own mother, Judaism. It was seeking to assert its own self-identity, in part by distancing itself from its own roots.

Secondly, already before 70 C.E. it may have been advantageous for Christians, pacifistic "non-rebels," to lean towards Rome, the occupying military power in Palestine and ruler of the world. The indications leading up to the unsuccessful Jewish rebellion of 66-70 C.E. already decades before may have signaled to Christians that it would be advantageous to place as much formal distance between themselves and much of the Zealotic-minded section of the Jewish populace as possible.

VI. The Relevance of This Study for Jewish-Christian Relations Today

If what is stated above in section "V" is basically correct, it has important ramifications for Jewish-Christian relations today.

1) Christian New Testament scholars with very few exceptions are not able to deal adequately with Judaic, especially rabbinic sources, as part of the background of the NT accounts. Many remain dependent on collections of background materials such as those of P. Billerbeck, J. Lightfoot, C. Montefiore and M. Smith.[128] Although more and more Judaic sources are becoming available in English translation, thanks in great part to Jacob Neusner and his students, Christian students of the NT must become more knowledgeable in Hebrew, including rabbinic Hebrew, in order to appreciate and properly evaluate the original sources.

2) After gaining linguistic proficiency, Christian students of the NT must learn to appreciate the internal workings of midrash,[129] especially of *haggadah* as the "creative (re-)writing of history or narrative."[130] Early Jewish Christian *haggadah* sought to apply biblical phrases and motifs to Jesus, for example from the Esther story, reinterpreting them for a new situation such as the Galilean prophet's trial and crucifixion. Where there were gaps in the original, historical account, early Jewish Christians, as they were accustomed to do, filled them in, newly

---

[128]Cf. Str-B; Lightfoot's *A Commentary on the New Testament from the Talmud and Hebraica, Matthew – 1 Corinthians* (Peabody, MASS: Hendrickson, 1979; original 1859, *Horae Hebraicae et Talmudicae*), four volumes; Montefiore's *Rabbinic Literature and Gospel Teachings* (New York: KTAV, 1970); and Smith's *Tannaitic Parallels to the Gospels* (JBL Monograph Series, 6; Philadelphia: SBL, 1968).
[129]An example is G. Porton's *Understanding Rabbinic Midrash,* Text and Commentary (Hoboken: KTAV, 1985). See also Strack and Stemberger, *Einleitung* 222-32.
[130]I. Heinemann, quoted in Strack and Stemberger, *Einleitung* 225.

interpreting and expanding a special motif such as Jesus' being condemned by Pilate as "king of the Jews." The Barabbas narrative also does this pre-eminently and is typical of *haggadah,* filling in a gap regarding the unknown contents of Pilate's interrogation/trial of Jesus before delivering him to be crucified (Mark 15:15b).

3) Jewish scholars working in an area of studies including the NT era should be more willing to apply their special knowledge, as well as linguistic and methodological proficiencies, to NT narratives, for example to specific passages in the gospels. A false reticence regarding "laboring in someone else's vineyard" should be overcome, as well as that involved in presenting seemingly negative results to a Christian audience. If it can be shown, for example, that as Moses, the redeemer of the Israelites from slavery in Egypt, was later glorified in Judaic tradition already at his birth because of this act, application of Moses birth motifs to the birth of the Christian redeemer, Jesus, in order also to glorify him becomes more understandable.[131] Tracing the path this glorification took is not negative or irreverent. It can also lead to a deeper religious understanding of the texts and thus should not be viewed as destroying the "gospel truth" as perceived by Christian fundamentalists. Historical research, including that of Jews dealing with "Christian" texts, is not detrimental to Christians' faith.

4) Most importantly, the above study of the release of Barabbas causes us to rethink completely the question of who was responsible for Jesus' crucifixion. Especially after Jesus' prophetic "cleansing" of the Temple in Jerusalem (Mark 11:15-18 par.), and his accusing the Jewish leaders of exploiting/misusing God's vineyard, Israel (12:1-12 par.), the priestly aristocracy there must not only have become suspicious of the Galilean's great popularity, but also have considered it expedient to get rid of him, the sooner the better. Primarily Sadducees, known for their severity,[132] they allowed no challenge to their own power and prestige, or to their own positions in the "business" of the Temple. Dependent financially on the regular offerings and those made at the annual pilgrimage festivals, and fearful of any disturbance leading to Rome's further intervention in their own affairs, they would have been willing to accept any purported "evidence" in order to accuse Jesus of blasphemy (Mark 14:64), deserving of death.

---

[131]Cf. my essay "Die Weihnachtsgeschichte im Lichte jüdischer Traditionen vom Mose-Kind und Hirten-Messias (Lukas 2, 1-20)" in *Weihnachtsgeschichte, Barmherziger Samariter, Verlorener Sohn.* Studien zu ihrem jüdischen Hintergrund (Berlin: Institut Kirche und Judentum, 1988) 11-58.

[132]Cf. Josephus, *Ant.* 20.199 and the subsequent stoning of Jesus' brother James and others in 200. See also Pss. Sol. 4:1-3 (*OTP* 2.655). For the Sadducees' association with the wealthy, cf. *Ant.* 13.298.

The Release of Barabbas

Because they probably were no longer allowed to execute someone for this reason (John 18:31), they delivered Jesus to Pilate, making a number of accusations against the Nazarite (Mark 15:1, 3). The procurator will have understood their accusation of Jesus' claiming to be the Messiah (משיח; 14:61) in Greek as "king" (βασιλεύς) of the Jews because of the usual contemporary designation מלך המשיח: "the king, the Messiah," "the messianic king."[133] The two terms were intimately connected, which would have been explained to Pilate. As such, it was no problem for him, very cruel and also desirous of retaining his own position, to condemn Jesus to death as a political rebel, an enemy of the only true king, the Roman emperor Tiberius.

Thus a very small group of Jerusalemites bore some responsibility for delivering Jesus to Pilate.[134] Yet only the latter could condemn him to death. He therefore must bear the major burden of crucifying an innocent victim. Above all, the entire scene of the Jerusalem crowd, crying out: "Crucify him! Crucify him"! belongs to the Barabbas episode, a Jewish Christian dramatic development. It never took place historically. The crowd, i.e., a large number of Jews, never shouted: "His blood be on us and on our children!" (Matt 27:25)

If this is the case, nineteen centuries of Christian use of the Barabbas narrative to demonstrate Jewish "deicide," and to make Jews scapegoats for every major national or local disaster because they insisted on "killing our Lord," has been completely unwarranted in spite of the gospels' statements.[135] It was the Roman Pilate who condemned Jesus to death, at the instigation not of *the* Jews, but of a very small number of the self-serving priestly aristocracy in Jerusalem. Indeed, the latter had to take Jesus captive at night in the Garden of Gethsemane because the Galilean prophet was so popular with his fellow Jews (Mark 11:18; 12: 12, 37; 14:2; 15:10).

Making the above exegetical conclusion in regard to the Barabbas narrative known both to contemporary Jews and Christians cannot but help to allow the members of these mother and daughter faiths now to approach each other more openly and fairly. That would be Jesus-like.

---

[133] Str-B 1.6-7.
[134] Cf. the statement of C.G. Montefiore in *The Synoptic Gospels,* ed. L. Silberman (New York: KTAV, 1968) 1.375: "The deepest responsibility is the priests'; and here probably the story is true enough."
[135] See also H. Cohn, *The Trial* 261-75 and 319-31.

2

The Death of One for All in John 11:45-54 in Light of Judaic Traditions*

Introduction

The three synoptic gospels have an extensive trial scene with Jesus before the fully assembled Jewish Sanhedrin or Council in Jerusalem (Mark 14:53 – 15:1 par.). The Evangelist John, in contrast, mentions only a short interrogation of the Galilean prophet before the (former) high priest Annas, who then sends Jesus bound to his son-in-law Caiaphas, the reigning high priest. From there Jesus is led to the praetorium of the Roman procurator Pilate (18:12-28). John omits all the details of this encounter between Jesus and Caiaphas and has here no meeting of the Sanhedrin or Council. By means of a note in v 14, however, the Evangelist refers the reader back to the scene in 11:45-54, where, in contrast, the full council is gathered and the decision is made to put Jesus to death. For the Fourth Evangelist, therefore, the trial narrative in chapter eleven is very important, taking the place of one which would naturally be expected at the end of the gospel.[1]

Yet 11:45-54 is, as E. Bammel contends, "a strange story."[2] For example, the Pharisee Nicodemus, a "ruler of the Jews," a "teacher of

---

* I thank E. Levine of Haifa, D. Catchpole of Exeter, and C. Wolff of Berlin for critically reading this essay and providing me with several bibliographical references. I was privileged to lecture on it on June 7, 1991, in Professor Wolff's John course at the Humboldt University.
[1] A.E. Harvey would even contend that "it is possible to understand the Fourth Gospel as a presentation of the claims of Jesus in the form of an extended trial." See his argumentation for this thesis in *Jesus on Trial. A Study in the Fourth Gospel* (London: SPCK, 1976), quote p. 17.
[2] Cf. his article "EX ILLA ITAQUE DIE CONCILIUM FECERUNT" in *The Trial of Jesus*, Festschrift C.F.D. Moule (London: SCM, 1970) 11-40, quote p. 11. Harvey, *Jesus on Trial* 98, calls it a "puzzling passage." For recent secondary literature on the pericope, see J. Becker, *Das Evangelium nach Johannes. Kapitel 11-21* (ÖTKNT, 4/2; Gütersloh: Mohn; Würzburg: Echter, 1984²) 364-

Israel" (3:1,10), earlier says to the chief priests and his fellow Pharisees, in other words the Sanhedrin,[3] in defense of Jesus: "Does our law judge a man without first giving him a hearing and learning what he does?" (7:51; cf. vv 45 and 50). Why then does he not defend him again in absentia in the trial scene of chapter eleven? In addition, it is striking that throughout the entire gospel Jesus himself acts or speaks, taking the initiative and being the center of attention. Only here is he the silent object of others' deliberations. It is Caiaphas who utters the decisive sentence in 11:50. This fact alone tends to point to material appropriated from elsewhere.[4]

Finally, 11:45-54 contain a number of terms which only occur here. The term συνέδριον, "Sanhedrin," in v 47 does not reoccur in John. "The Romans," οἱ Ῥωμαῖοι in v. 48, is singular in all four gospels. Except for Pilate's own interrogation of Jesus in 18:35, the expression τὸ ἔθνος, "the nation," occurs in John only in the cluster 11:48, 50, 51 and 52. In the four gospels, λογίζομαι is found in a quotation of Isa 53:12 in Mark 15:28 t.r. and Lk 22:37, but elsewhere only in John 11:50 ("consider, ponder"; RSV "understand"). With the exception of 16:7 and the reference back to Caiaphas' statement in 18:14, συμφέρει, "it is expedient," is found in John only in 11:50. The latter is also true for ὁ λαός, "the people," in 18:14 and 11:50.[5] While the term "prophet" occurs fourteen times in the fourth gospel, the verb προφητεύω, "to prophesy," is only found in 11:51. The verb διασκορπίζω, "to scatter," also occurs only in 11:52 in John. Finally, "Ephraim," Ἐφραίμ, is found in the entire NT only in 11:54.[6]

65, as well as E. Haenchen, *Johannesevangelium. Ein Kommentar,* ed. U. Busse (Tübingen: Mohr, 1980) 421.
[3]On the real constituency of the Sanhedrin at the time of Jesus, in contrast to the post-70 C.E. terminology which John has adopted, cf. E. Schürer, *The History of the Jewish People in the Age of Jesus Christ,* ed. G. Vermes, F. Millar and M. Black (Edinburgh: T. & T. Clark, 1979) 2.199-226, and E. Lohse, art. συνέδριον in *TDNT* 7.860-871.
[4]The same can be maintained for the narrative of the beheading of John the Baptist in Mark 6:17-29. Cf. my *Water Into Wine and the Beheading of John the Baptist* (Brown Judaic Studies 150; Atlanta: Scholars, 1988) 70.
[5]The textual history of 8:2 is unclear.
[6]For another analysis, cf. T. Mohr, *Markus- und Johannespassion* (ATLN, 70; Zurich: Theologischer Verlag, 1982) 126. Relying on J. Finegan, R. Bultmann in *Das Evangelium des Johannes* (Meyer; Göttingen: Vandenhoeck & Ruprecht, 1964) 313 maintains that vv 45-54 are a Johannine construction, employing no source. The philological analysis above excludes this view. See also F. Hahn, "Der Prozess Jesu nach dem Johannesevangelium. Eine redaktionsgeschichtliche Untersuchung," in *Evangelisch-Katholischer Kommentar zum Neuen Testament,* Vorarbeiten 2 (Zurich: Benziger;

The above philological analysis points to 11:45-54 as a unit with a very high amount of vocabulary peculiar to it. Again, while the Evangelist most probably moulded and shaped the pericope somewhat (see below), the many *hapax legomena* cited above make it probable that the core was appropriated by him from an outside tradition.

It is the purpose of this essay to describe the Judaic background of that basic tradition.[7] After an analysis of early Jewish, primarily rabbinic accounts of the deaths of the two Judean kings Jehoiakim and Jehoiachin (I), I shall point out part of the scriptural background of these narratives in 2 Samuel 20:1-22, the story of Sheba ben Bichri's political revolt against King David. The latter biblical account by itself also provides the background for several other features in John 11:45-54. Relevant motifs and terms from the text's further development in early Jewish writings will then be noted (II). Next, I will suggest why a high priest was made the main figure in the Johannine trial scene of chapter eleven. I will analyze both his ability to prophesy (III), as well as his intimate connection to the scapegoat, which takes upon itself all the sins of the whole people (IV). Finally, I shall discuss the language and extent of the original narrative (V), as well as the question of its historicity (VI).

I. Early Jewish Accounts of the Deaths of Kings Jehoiakim and Jehoiachin

A number of motifs and verbal similarities to John 11:45-54 derive from early Jewish traditions concerning the Babylonian king Nebuchadnezzar and his subjugation of the Judean king Jehoiakim and his son Jehoiachin (2 Kings 24 and 2 Chronicles 36) at the beginning of

---

Neukirchen: Neukirchener, 1970) 25-27 for the Evangelist's reliance on a (written) "Vorlage."

[7]While several early pagan writers note the general principle of the death of "one for many," a direct connection between them and the Jewish-Christian author of John 11:45-54 is very improbable. It is more appropriate first to analyze Judaic sources before looking elsewhere. This, however, does not deny the possibility of cross-fertilization between "Hellenistic" and Palestinian sources. See J. Wettstein's *Novum Testamentum Graecum,* Tomus I (Amsterdam: Dommerian, 1752; reprint Graz 1962) 919 for quotations from Xiphilinus, Suetonius and Tacitus, as well as A. Wikenhauser, *Das Evangelium nach Johannes* (RNT, 4; Regensburg: Pustet, 1961^3) 223 for Dio Cassius. Origen in XXVIII.19 on John 11:50 (in *Das Evangelium nach Johannes,* ed. and trans. R. Gögler, Einsiedeln/Zurich/Cologne: Einsiedeln, 1959, pp. 352-53) speaks of Greek narratives involving self-sacrifice "which we should not despise," yet they simply do not match the redemptive sacrifice of Jesus for the whole world. H. Windisch in *Der zweite Korintherbrief* (Göttingen: Vandenhoeck & Ruprecht, 1924^9) 182 on 2 Cor 5:14 also calls attention to passages in Vergil, Plato and Epictetus.

the sixth century B.C.E.[8] Although several of these rabbinic sources were already noted by J. Wettstein in 1752,[9] and since then have been cited by several commentators,[10] no extensive analysis of them has been made up to now, and much of relevance to the Sanhedrin trial scene in John eleven has been overlooked. A sketch of these accounts is therefore helpful at the outset (sections A and B), followed by an analysis of their relevance to John 11:45-54 in section C.

A. Jehoikim

Gen. Rab. 94/9 Vayyigash on Gen 46:26-27[11] relates an early rabbinic (Tannaitic) tradition that when Nebuchadnezzar comes to (Jerusalem to) conquer Jehoiakim, he first stays in Daphne of Antioch. The Great Sanhedrin (סנהדרי גדולה) goes there to greet him and asks: "Has the time arrived for this house [= the Temple] to be destroyed?" (הגיע לו זמנו של בית הזה ליחרב).[12] The Babylonian king says no, but since Jehoiakim has rebelled against (מרד ב)[13] him, he will only depart if they surrender Jehoiakim to him. The members of the Sanhedrin inform their Judean king that Nebuchadnezzar demands him. He defends himself by asking if it is right to do so, sacrificing[14] one life for another. He even quotes Deut 23:16 about not "delivering" a servant to his master. They reply that his grandmother/ancestress[15] did so to Sheba the son of Bichri, and they then quote 2 Sam 20:21, "Behold, his head

---

[8]For the historical situation, cf. J. Bright, *A History of Israel* (Philadelphia: Westminster, 1959) 302-06, as well as G. Hentschel, *2 Könige* (Echter Bibel, 11; Würzburg: Echter, 1985) 116-119.

[9]Cf. his *Novum Testamentum Graecum,* Tomus I, 919. I shall refer to the specific accounts in the course of this essay. To these should be added y. Sheq. 6:2(3), 50a, occasioned by the mention of Jeconiah's Gate in Jerusalem (see below).

[10]Cf., for example, A. Merx, *Das Evangelium des Johannes* (Berlin: Reimer, 1911) 298-99, and Str-B 2.545-46.

[11]Cf. the Hebrew and Aramaic in J. Theodor and Ch. Albeck, *Midrash Bereshit Rabba* (Jerusalem: Wahrmann, 1965) 3.1185. A vocalized text is given in *Midrash Rabbah* (Hebrew), ed. M. Mirqin (Tel-Aviv: Yavneh, 1980) 4.159-160. An English translation is offered by H. Freedman in the Soncino edition of Midrash Rabbah (2.879), and by J. Neusner in *Genesis Rabbah. The Judaic Commentary to the Book of Genesis* (Brown Judaic Studies 106; Atlanta: Scholars, 1985) 3.323.

[12]The verb חרב is frequently employed of the destruction of the Temple. See the passages cited in Jastrow, *A Dictionary* 498.

[13]Cf. 2 Kings 24:1.

[14]On דחי, cf. Jastrow 291, and m. Ohol. 7:6.

[15]The text has זקינך, "your grandfather/ancestor," but it should be corrected to the reading of MS ח: זקינתך, because it refers to the wise woman of 2 Sam 20:16. On the term, cf. Jastrow 409.

shall be thrown to you over the wall." Because Jehoiakim will not listen to the members of the Sanhedrin, they seize him and lower him over the city wall (to Nebuchadnezzar to be killed).

The prophet Jeremiah had predicted that Jehoiakim would be buried "with the burial of an ass, dragged and cast forth beyond the gates of Jerusalem" (Jer 22:19; cf. 36:30). For this reason the above midrash, now continued in Lev. Rab. Metzora 19/6 on Lev 15:25,[16] asks how Jehoiakim died through the hands of Nebuchadnezzar. In dialogue with R. Nehemiah, R. Judah (bar Ilai), a third generation Tanna,[17] says that the Babylonian king took him and carried him around through all the cities of Judah, then "sat publicly over him in judgment" and put him to death. Afterwards he tore open an ass and placed Jehoiakim's corpse in it, as Jer 22:19 states.

The phrase וישב לו בפראדימוס, the best text here, is translated by D. Sperber as "and he sat for the examination publically (sic)."[18] This "public trial" of the rebel king is presumed to take place outside the Jerusalem city wall, from which Jehoiakim was lowered.

Finally, a narrative now found in both b. Sanh. 82a and 104a[19] relates that Jehoiakim's "skull" (גולגלתא), thrown down by the townspeople at the gates of Jerusalem, was found there much later by an early rabbi's grandfather.[20] Jer 22:19, as above, is quoted in the story. I shall comment on this "skull" and the site of Jesus' crucifixion, Golgotha, below.

* * * *

The above Jehoiakim midrash most probably was composed on the basis of events which took place in the second half of the first century B.C.E., and thus relatively close to the time of the writing of the Gospel

---

[16]Cf. M. Margulies, *Midrash Wayyikra Rabbah.* A Critical Edition based on Manuscripts and Genizah Fragments with Variants and Notes, 5 vols. (Jerusalem: Ministry of Education and Culture of Israel, American Academy for Jewish Research, 1953-60) 431-35. An English translation is offered by J. Israelstam in Soncino 4.245-47, a German by A. Wünsche in *Bibliotheca Rabbinica* (Leipzig: Schulze, 1883-84; reprint Hildesheim: Olms, 1967) 5.127-28. The notes by J. Fürst on p. 277 are valuable corrections.
[17]Cf. H.L. Strack and G. Stemberger, *Einleitung in Talmud und Midrasch* (Munich: Beck, 1982[7]) 83.
[18]Cf. his *A Dictionary of Greek and Latin Legal Terms in Rabbinic Literature* (Bar-Ilan: Bar-Ilan University Press, 1984) 151-52. See the text and variants in Margulies, 433-34.
[19]Cf. Soncino English 544 and 706-07.
[20]R. Perida was a Tanna active ca. 200 C.E. See *Str-B* 5/6.216.

of John, which most scholars place at the end of the first century C.E.[21] The following background material is of relevance to the Jehoiakim midrash and thus indirectly to John 11:45-54.

The last king of the Jewish Hasmonean dynasty was Antigonus, whom the Roman general Pompey led captive back to the capital of the empire in 63 B.C.E. From there he escaped, however, and bribed the Parthians to set him up as king.[22] Antigonus then reigned from 40-37 B.C.E.[23] Anthony, whom 100 Jewish officials (most probably also including members of the Jerusalem Sanhedrin) approached at his headquarters in Daphne near Antioch to prevent the Idumean Herod from becoming king,[24] hated Antigonus because he had received his royal title from the Parthians and not the Romans. He thus considered Antigonus a promoter of "sedition."[25]

The Hasmonean took refuge in Jerusalem, which Herod besieged in 39 B.C.E., first offering amnesty to those who would surrender.[26] In 37 B.C.E. Herod besieged the city anew, this time aided by the Roman general Sossius. When the situation became desperate for him, Antigonus threw himself at the feet of Sossius, who first put him in irons and under strict guard, then took him to Anthony (in Daphne of Antioch) in chains.[27] The manner of Antigonus' death is related in various sources.

Josephus, quoting the older historian Strabo of Cappadocia,[28] states that Anthony beheaded Antigonus, being the first Roman to do this to a king.[29] By means of a large bribe, Herod had persuaded him to commit this act.[30] Plutarch, who died ca. 120 C.E.,[31] repeats this statement in Anthony 36. In his "Roman History" (49.22.6), Dio Cassius, writing about 200-220 C.E.,[32] adds that Anthony "bound [Antigonus] to a cross

---

[21] Cf., for example, R. Brown, *The Gospel According to John, I-XII* (AB 29; Garden City, New York: Doubleday, 1966) LXXXV-VI for 90-100 C.E. as most probable for the final written form of John.
[22] Josephus, *Ant.*, 14.379.
[23] For the sources, cf. Schürer, *The History* 1.281-86, as well as the art. "Antigonus," 9), by U. Wilcken in PW 1.2419-20.
[24] *Ant.*, 14.324-26. Perhaps the number 100 suggested the "Great" Sanhedrin of the Jehoiakim midrash. See also *Bell.* 1.243-44.
[25] *Ant.*, 14.382,384; *Bell.*, 1.283.
[26] *Ant.*, 14.402; *Bell.*, 1.295.
[27] *Ant.*, 14.481,488; *Bell.*, 1.353,357.
[28] In the LCL edition of *The Geography of Strabo*, H.L. Jones notes that he was born in 64 or 63 B.C.E. (I.xiv).
[29] *Ant.*, 15.9. See also *Bell.*, 1.357: he "fell beneath the (executioner's) axe" – πέλεκυς.
[30] *Ant.*, 14.490.
[31] Cf. the LCL edition of Plutarch's Lives by B. Perrin, I.xii.
[32] Cf. the LCL edition by E. Cary, I.xi.

and flogged [him]–a punishment no other king had suffered at the hands of the Romans, – and afterwards slew him."

This ignominious death of the last Hasmonean, "king of the Jews," with flogging and a cross, ending in beheading, appears to have exerted great influence on the Jehoiakim midrash sketched above. In addition, it offers relevant points of comparison to the death of Jesus, also thought by the Roman Pontius Pilate to be a political insurgent, "king of the Jews." Pilate also had the Galilean prophet scourged and crucified.

B. Jehoiachin

Leviticus Rabbah continues the Jehoiakim midrash sketched above by now relating the events involved with Jehoiachin, called here Jeconiah.[33] After Nebuchadnezzar kills his father, he appoints the son in his place and returns home to Babylon. There the inhabitants of the city ask him, "What have you done?" (מה עשיתה). When he replies that he put the rebel Jehoiakim to death and set up his son in his place, they remind him with a proverb that the son will certainly turn out to be like the father.[34]

Nebuchadnezzar immediately returns to Daphne of Antioch,[35] and approximately the same scene as before repeats itself. The Great Sanhedrin comes down from Jerusalem to meet him and asks if the time has come for the Temple to be destroyed. He again replies no, he only wants Jeconiah, and then he will withdraw. The members of the Sanhedrin inform Jeconiah of Nebuchadnezzar's wish. The midrash then asks: "What did Nebuchadnezzar do to him?" (מה עשה לו ג). It replies that he imprisoned and then exiled him. Yet the Great Sanhedrin goes into exile with Jeconiah, to whom Jer 22:28 is applied:

---

[33] Jer 22:24,28 and 37:1 call him Coniah, and 1 Chr 3:16 Jeconiah. The rabbinic narrative is found in Margulies, *Midrash Wayyikra Rabbah* 435-40, an English translation in Soncino 4.247-49, and German in Wünsche, *Bibliotheca Rabbinica* 5.128-29.

[34] On Nebuchadnezzar's fear of Jehoiachin's revolting, see also Josephus, *Ant.*, 10.99. The proverb is very old. See the official chronology of early Judaism, Seder 'Olam 25, dealing with Jehoiachin. The text is found in C. Milikowsky, *Seder 'Olam: A Rabbinic Chronography* (1981 Yale dissertation), Hebrew 399, English 527.

[35] For the same motif, cf. also Lam. Rab. Proem 30 (Soncino 7.56). Here Nebuchadnezzar, the captain of his guard Nebuzaradan, and the destruction of Jerusalem in three and one half years seem to reflect Vespasian, Titus and their destruction of the same city from 66-70 C.E. See 4:12 § 15 (Soncino 7.225-26), and 1:5 § 31 (Soncino 7.101). In 2:10 § 14 (Soncino 7.177) the same motif of Nebuchadnezzar's coming to Daphne, with the Great Sanhedrin's meeting him there, is applied to Jeconiah's successor, Zedekiah.

Coniah is a despised, broken pot. He will be childless, having no offspring to succeed him "in sitting on the throne of David" (v 30).

When (because of this exile) the Heavenly Court then absolves God of His vow regarding Jeconiah's childlessness (cf. 1 Chr 3:17-18),[36] the Great Sanhedrin asks whether in its days the royal house of David should cease, for which Ps 89:37 is cited, a verse treated messianically in rabbinic sources.[37] They ask, "What shall we do?" (מה נעשה). "Let us win the favor of the queen's hairdresser/governess" (גדלת)[38] who will positively influence the queen. She in turn will do the same with King Nebuchadnezzar. This takes place, and Jeconiah is allowed to have sexual relations with his wife. Since she has her menstrual period, however, he abstains. After his wife waits, then purifies and immerses herself, God rewards the king by pardoning all Jeconiah's sins, and offspring is assured. The Davidic line will thus continue. Because of this precept of menstruation, the entire midrash is related to Lev 15:25.

Josephus, a Jerusalem Jew writing at the end of the first century C.E.[39] and thus approximately at the same time the Fourth Gospel was composed,[40] notes in *Ant.* 10.100 that Jehoiachin was by nature kind and just (χρηστὸς ὢν καὶ δίκαιος), not considering it right to allow the city of Jerusalem to become endangered on his account. He therefore delivers (παραδίδωσι) his mother and other relatives to the Babylonian commanders, voluntarily leaving the city. In the parallel account in 10.230, Josephus stresses that Jehoiachin with his wives and children and all his other relatives "handed himself over completely voluntarily (παραδόντι... ὅλης ἑκουσίως αὐτὸν)[41] for the sake of his native city, that it might not be taken and razed...."

It is also Josephus who demonstrates what a positive example Jeconiah still was to first-century C.E. Palestinian Jews. In *Bell.* 6.2.1 the Jewish historian relates how the Roman general Titus, about to capture Jerusalem in 70 C.E., offers the rebel commander John of Gischala the opportunity to leave the city and to fight the Romans outside, thus saving the Temple from destruction. When John refuses, Josephus himself addresses him in Aramaic with the following words (103-106):

---

[36]Cf. b. Sanh. 37b-38a (Soncino English 237-38); Cant. Rab. 8:6 § 2 (Soncino 9.307); and the end of Lev. Rab. 19/6 in Margulies 450 (Soncino 4.249 quotes Jer 3:22 instead).
[37]Cf., for example, Gen. Rab. Vayechi 97 on Gen 49:8 (Soncino 2.901).
[38]Jastrow 213.
[39]Cf. *Vita* 7, and *Ant.*, 20.267 (93/94 C.E.).
[40]Cf. n. 21.
[41]Cf. LSJ 514 on ἑκουσιάζομαι as offering oneself freely.

Yet, to be sure, John, it is no disgrace to repent (μετανοῆσαι) of misdeeds, even at the last; and if you desire to save your country, you have a noble example (καλὸν ὑπόδειγμα) set before you in Jeconiah, king of the Jews (βασιλεὺς Ἰουδαίων). He, when of old his conduct had brought the Babylonian's army upon him, of his own free will (ἑκὼν) left the city before it was taken, and with his family endured voluntary (ἐθελούσιον) captivity, rather than deliver up (παραδοῦναι) these holy places to the enemy and see the house of God in flames. Therefore is he celebrated in sacred story by all Jews, and memory, in a stream that runs down the ages ever fresh, passes him on to posterity immortal. A noble example, John....[42]

This is part of a long speech composed later upon Josephus' desk. Yet the main thought is certainly historical, that Titus asked Josephus to persuade the rebel leader to sacrifice himself for the sake of the whole city, particularly the Temple. To do so, Josephus had ample cause to cite Jeconiah, the "king of the Jews," as a positive example known to "all Jews."

A major support for the thesis that Jehoiachin/Jeconiah was still very well known in the first century C.E. is found in m. Sheq. 6:3 and Mid. 2:6, which state that the western-most of the northern gates of the Temple Court was called the "Gate of Jeconiah" because through it the king "went forth when he went into exile," a reference to 2 Kings 24:12.[43] Of the thirteen gates,[44] only one was named in honor of a king, Jehoiachin/Jeconiah. If this gate belonged to the rebuilt post-exilic Temple, this shows that knowledge of it was retained at least until the composition of the Mishnah ca. 200 C.E.[45] If it belonged to Herod the Great's Temple, which appears to have been completed ca. 10 B.C.E.,[45a] every Palestinian Jew, as well as guests from the diaspora, would have been aware of it from the annual pilgrimage festivals up to 70 C.E. Josephus' statement that Jehoiachin was known to "all Jews" thus gains greatly in plausibility.

---

[42]The English translation is that of H. St. J. Thackeray in the LCL edition. Wettstein (*Novum Testamentum Graecum,* I.919) had already called attention to this passage.

[43]English in Danby 158 and 593. See also t. Sheq. 2:18 (Neusner 2.177) for R. Simeon (ben Yoḥai), a third generation Tanna (Strack and Stemberger, *Einleitung* 82), as quoting 2 Chr 36:10 dealing with Jehoiachin in comment on m. Sheq. 6:1-3.

[44]The texts note a total of thirteen gates, while at m. Midd. 1:4 seven are named (Danby 590).

[45]Cf. Danby xiii.

[45a]Cf. the description of Josephus, and the sources cited in Schürer, *The History* 1.292. In his article "Jehoiachin" in *J.E.* (1904) 7.84, L. Ginzberg attributes the Jeconiah Gate to the Second (Herodian) Temple.

The above emphasis in Josephus on Jehoiachin's/Jeconiah's positive character, like the end of Lev. Rab. 19/6, completely contradicts the biblical account in 2 Kings 24:9 and 2 Chr 36:9. In his appeal to John of Gischala to "repent" and act like Jeconiah/Jehoiachin, Josephus betrays knowledge of the Judean king as a model of repentance in early Jewish tradition. After thirty-seven years of imprisonment in exile,[46] Jehoiachin "repented" of his earlier behavior and became a role model in regard to this theme, as attested by numerous rabbinic sources.[47]

Finally, it should also be noted that not only was Zerubbabel, who helped to rebuild the Temple after the exile,[48] one of Jehoiachin's grandsons (1 Chr 3:19; Zechariah 4).[49] The Messiah himself is to be one of his descendants. Tanḥuma Toledot 14 on Gen 27:33[50] says, for example, that the Messiah is to proceed from Zerubbabel, an ancestor of Anani (1 Chr 3:17-24). The latter is interpreted as the Messiah, he who comes with the "clouds" of Dan 7:13. The same tradition is found in Tanḥuma B Toledot 20.[51] It is also reflected in the Targum of 1 Chr 3:24 on "Anani," interpreted as "the King Messiah who is destined to be revealed."[52] Matt 1:11-13 also includes Jehoiachin/Jechoniah and Zerubbabel in the genealogy of Jesus the Messiah (see also Luke 3:27).

---

[46]Cf. Jer 52:31; Seder 'Olam 28 (Milikowsky 420 and 536); 'Abot R. Nat. B 17 (Hebrew in Schechter 37, English in Saldarini 117), where Jehoiachin's innocence in regard to rebellion is maintained; and 2 Targ. Est 1:1 (English in Cassell 265), spoken by Daniel to Evilmerodach.

[47]Cf. Lev. Rab. Tzav 10/5 on Lev 8:2 (Soncino 4.128); Cant. Rab. 8:6 § 2 (Soncino 9.306-307); Pesiq. R. 47/1 on Lev 16:1 (English in Braude 797-98); Pesiq. Rab Kah. 24/11 on Hos 14:2 (English in Braude and Kapstein 376-78); Baruch 1-2. The latter can be dated to the second century B.C.E. See G. Nickelsburg, *Jewish Literature Between the Bible and the Mishnah* (Philadelphia: Fortress, 1981) 113. See also n. 36.

[48]Cf. Ezra 2:2; 3:2,8; 4:2,3; 5:2 and Neh 7:7; 12:1.

[49]See also the rabbinic sources in L. Ginzberg, *The Legends of the Jews* (Philadelphia: Jewish Publication Society of America, 1913; reprint 1968) 6.381, n. 135.

[50]Cf. the Hebrew with a German translation in F. Singermann, *Midrash Tanḥuma* (Berlin: Lamm, 1927) 178-79.

[51]Cf. S. Buber, *Midrasch Tanchuma* (Vilna: Romm, 1885) 1.139-40. A German translation is given by H. Bietenhard, *Midrasch Tanḥuma B* (Judaica et Christiana, 5; Bern: Lang, 1980) 1.149-50.

[52]Cf. an English translation in S.H. Levey, *The Messiah: An Aramaic Interpretation. The Messianic Exegesis of the Targum* (Cincinnati: Hebrew Union College – Jewish Institute of Religion, 1974) 140. He also refers to Dan 7:13, and to b. Sanh. 98a (Soncino English 663-64). Ginzberg, *The Legends* 4.287 and n. 136 in 6.381, also refers to 'Aggadat Bereshit 44 (ed. S. Buber, Cracow: Fischer, 1903), p. 89 in this regard as well as to b. Sanh. 96b (Soncino 654).

The Death of One for All 39

C. Analysis

There are numerous motif and verbal similarities between the Judaic traditions on Jehoiakim and Jehoiachin, and John 11:45-54, seen in the larger context of Jesus' trial. The following six stand out.

1. The Sanhedrin

In the continuous Tannaitic midrash on both Jehoiakim and Jehoiachin, the "Great Sanhedrin" of Jerusalem plays a major role in regard to the Babylonian enemy, who is capable of destroying the Temple (and the city). The only place the "Sanhedrin" occurs in John is in 11:47, also in a context of avoiding the destruction of the Temple (and the "nation") by the occupying power, the Romans.

2. The Destruction of the Temple

In the Jehoiakim/Jehoiachin midrash, the Sanhedrin is primarily concerned with the possibility of the Babylonian Nebuchadnezzar's "destroying" (חרב) "this house,"[53] the Temple. To avoid this, the members are even willing to surrender Jehoiakim to him, whom he then kills.

In John eleven, the "chief priests and Pharisees" in the Sanhedrin are afraid that if they allow Jesus to continue performing signs/miracles such as the raising of Lazarus from the dead, all the people will believe in him, "and the Romans will come and destroy (αἴρω)[54] our holy place and our nation" (v 48). Caiaphas adds that it is expedient "that one man should die for the people, and that the whole nation should not perish/be destroyed (ἀπόλλυμι),[55] v 50.

The RSV correctly adds "holy" to "our place" in v 48 because the Jerusalem Temple is definitely meant. One relevant passage in the MT with "place," מקום, is Jer 17:12: "the place of our sanctuary." Here "of our sanctuary," however, specifies the "place." A. Schlatter also cites here Jer 7:14, where "the house" and "the place" are parallel, meaning the Jerusalem Temple.[56] Yet ὁ τόπος standing alone to mean the Temple is basically a Jewish Greek expression, as shown for example in 2 Macc 5:19, "But the Lord did not choose the nation for the sake of the [holy] place, but the [holy] place for the sake of the nation."[57] Place (Temple) and nation also occur in John 11:48.

---

[53] On ב(ה)ית as the Temple, see Jastrow 168,2).
[54] Cf. BAG 24: conquer, take over; remove; blot out.
[55] Cf. BAG 94: mid., be destroyed, ruined; perish; die.
[56] Cf. his *Der Evangelist Johannes* (Stuttgart: Calwer, 1948) 257. His other examples are unconvincing.
[57] Cf. also 3:18; 5:17; 13:23; 3 Macc 1:9,23,29, as well as H. Köster, art. τόπος in *TDNT* 8.187-208, especially 198-199 and 204. One rabbinical usage of the

It should be noted that already in the sixteenth century John Calvin related the Sanhedrin's fear that the Romans would come and destroy the Jerusalem Temple to the Babylonian captivity,[58] as it took place under Jehoiakim and Jehoiachin. In the nineteenth century E. Hengstenberg also compared the phrase "and the Romans will come (and destroy both our holy place and our nation)" in John 11:48 to Jer 36:29, "the king of Babylon will certainly come (and destroy this land)."[59] Unfortunately, neither Calvin nor Hengstenberg was aware of rabbinic traditions on the two Judean kings. This Jeremiah passage certainly influenced both the Jehoiakim/Jehoiachin midrash, and the author of John 11:45-54 in his phrasing of v 48.

Already at the outset of his gospel, "John" in 2:19 betrays knowledge of a dominical saying regarding the destruction of the Temple (ναός), yet he interprets it there of Jesus' body. In Mark 13:2 par. Jesus is reported to have predicted the destruction of the Temple, but not necessarily by himself. The latter view, however, is ascribed to him by false witnesses at Jesus' hearing before the Sanhedrin in Mark 14:58 and Matt 26:61. (It is missing here in Luke, but is applied by him to Stephen in Acts 6:14 ["this place"].) The high priest demands that Jesus respond to this accusation of wanting to destroy the Temple.

The combination of Jesus, the destruction of the Temple, and the high priest at a meeting of the Sanhedrin, now found in the Synoptics, appears to have been known to the author of John 11:45-54. Writing after the destruction of the Temple in 70 C.E., he creatively moulded this information into a new form, employing elements of the early Jehoiakim/Jehoiachin midrash to do so.

3. Rebellion/Insurrection and Judgment

Because Jehoiakim "rebelled against" Nebuchadnezzar in 2 Kings 24:1,[60] the Babylonian king in the midrash sketched above "sat over him publicly in judgment" and put him to death just outside Jerusalem. The

---

"place" of Isa 5:8 as the destroyed Temple is found in Lam. Rab., Proem 22 (Soncino 7.27), a saying by Resh Laqish, a fourth generation Palestinian Amora (Strack and Stemberger, *Einleitung* 91).

[58]Cf. Johannes Calvins Auslegung der Heiligen Schrift in deutscher Übersetzung, 10. Band. *Das Evangelium des Johannes* (trans. A. Fürer; Moers: Erziehungsverein Neukirchen, 1905) 322.

[59]Cf. his *Das Evangelium des heiligen Johannes* (Berlin: Schlawitz, 1862) 2.275. Jer 36:30 states that Jehoiakim will have none to sit on the throne of David, and the king's dead body will be cast out. This connects it to 22:19, cited in the midrash above.

[60]Cf. 2 Chr 36:13.

Jewish legal chamber, the Sanhedrin, presided over by the high priest,[61] had seized the king and lowered him over the city wall to the waiting Nebuchadnezzar.

Elsewhere in the Gospel of John Jesus is also considered an insurrectionist, a rebel against the authority of the (foreign, Roman) government, especially in regard to the title "king." In 6:15, for example, Jesus must withdraw to a mountain by himself in order to keep the people from making him "king" by force. The trial before the Roman procurator Pilate in Jerusalem in 18:33 – 19:16 also centers on the question of kingship. Only when the crowd maintains that "every one who makes himself a king sets himself against Caesar," does Pilate sit in public judgment over Jesus and hand him over to be crucified (19:12-16). Finally, the title on his cross read: "Jesus of Nazareth, the King of the Jews" (19:19). It indicated that Jesus was crucified as a rebel, an insurrectionist.

Here Pilate, the foreigner, sits in public judgment over, and condemns to death, the (ostensible) royal insurrectionist. While the Sanhedrin plays no role at this point in John, its negative activity has already been extensively described in 11:45-54. Here, as in the Jehoiakim midrash, it actively condemns Jesus to death: "from that day on they took counsel how to put him to death" (v 53).

The same is true for the traditions informing the oldest Synoptic passion narrative, that of Mark. Jesus as "King of the Jews" is emphasized in the trial scene at 15:2,9,12 and 18, and the term also appears as the inscription on Jesus' cross in v 26. In addition, Jesus is closely associated with the rebels involved in insurrection (15:7).

In both the Johannine and the Synoptic passion narratives Jesus is thus portrayed as a messianic pretender, an insurrectionist who promotes rebellion against the world power Rome by maintaining that he himself (and not Caesar) is "king." The author of John 11:45-54 was well aware of this basic theme. He therefore portrayed the Jewish authorities in Jerusalem as not only resisting such a man, but also as seeking to put him to death. If his rebellious stance were to continue, the Romans would come and destroy both the Temple and the nation (John 11:48).

---

[61]The Sanhedrin of the midrash is, of course, that which existed until the destruction of the Temple in 70 C.E. Of the high priest of this time J. Jeremias states: "as president of the Sanhedrin and principal agent of the people at a time when there was no king, he represented the Jewish people in all dealings with Rome." See his *Jerusalem in the Time of Jesus* (London: SCM, 1969) 159.

4. One Life for Others

When Nebuchadnezzar demands his life, and the members of the Sanhedrin inform him of this, Jehoiakim defends himself in the midrash sketched above by asking if it is right to do so, sacrificing or setting aside one life for another or others. This basic thought, of one voluntarily (Jehoiachin) or involuntarily (Jehoiakim) sacrificing his life so that others, a majority, may stay alive, derives ultimately from the biblical and rabbinic narrative of the rebel/insurrectionist Sheba, the son of Bichri, who seeks shelter in the city of Abel. Yet its inhabitants, led by a wise woman, cut off the man's head and throw it over the city wall to the waiting army commander (2 Samuel 20). This episode is specifically quoted in the Jehoiakim midrash, where the wise woman is called Jehoiakim's own ancestor, and I shall analyze it below. Here it suffices to state that the same motif of losing one's own life so that others may remain alive is clearly mirrored in John 11:50-51, Jesus' dying for the people so that the whole nation will not perish.

5. "What Shall We Do?"

In the Jehoiakim/Jehoiachin midrash sketched above there are six similar phrases, the most important being the last:

1. "What did Nebuchadnezzar do to him (Jehoiakim)?"
2. The Babylonians ask Nebuchadnezzar, "What have you accomplished/done?"
3. "What did he (Jeconiah) do?"
4. "What did the young men of Israel do?"
5. "What did Nebuchadnezzar do?"
6. The Great Sanhedrin sat and asked regarding the continuance of the Davidic line, "What shall we do?"

It is the latter sentence which appears to be taken over literally by the author of John 11:45-54 in v 47, where "the chief priests and the Pharisees gathered the council, and said, 'What shall we do?'" This means that the rabbinic passages cited by A. Schlatter, including one with the same phrasing, are irrelevant,[62] as are those from Hellenistic writers.[63] Much more probably, there is literal dependence on the Tannaitic Jehoiakim/Jehoiachin midrash here.

---

[62] Cf. his *Der Evangelist Johannes* 256-57. M.-J. Lagrange, *Évangile selon Saint Jean* (ÉBib; Paris: Gabalda, 1936⁵) 313, maintains that the union of τί ποιοῦμεν and ὅτι betrays a Semitic turn.

[63] Cf. the passages cited by W. Bauer in *Das Johannesevangelium* (HNT,6; Tübingen: Mohr, 1933³) 155-56.

6. Scattering

The Great Sanhedrin in the Coniah/Jehoiachin section of the midrash sketched above is alarmed because of Jeremiah's prophecy in 22:30 regarding the Judean king: "none of his offspring shall succeed in sitting on the throne of David and ruling again in Judah." It therefore asks, "What shall we do?" and, aided by the king's repentance, decides on a scheme to ensure Davidic progeny.

Directly after Jer 22:30 the prophet reproaches the Judean kings, especially those just addressed: Jehoahaz (Shallum), Jehoiakim and Jehoiachin. They had enriched themselves at the cost of others, shed innocent blood, practiced oppression and violence, been rebellious and wicked. Jeremiah writes:

> Woe to the shepherds who destroy and "scatter" (פוץ; LXX διασκορπίζω) the sheep of my pasture! says the Lord. Therefore thus says the Lord, concerning the shepherds who care for my people: You have "scattered" (פוץ; LXX διασκορπίζω) my flock, and have driven them away, and you have not attended to them. Behold, I will attend to you for your evil doings, says the Lord. Then I will gather (קבץ; LXX εἰσδέχομαι) the remnant of my flock ..." (23:1-3).

The Lord's promise of a Davidic king, interpreted in rabbinic sources as the Messiah,[64] then follows.

In the first century C.E. the biblical chapter and verse system we employ today did not exist. Jer 23:1-3 was thus associated almost automatically with what directly preceded it, the censure of Coniah/Jehoiachin.

I suggest that because the author of John 11:45-54 had the Jehoiachin midrash in mind, he appropriated the motif of "scattering" and "gathering" from Jer 23:1-3 and developed it into the statement of v 52: Caiaphas prophesies that Jesus should die "not for the nation only, but to gather (συνάγω) into one the children of God who are scattered abroad (διασκορπίζω)." This, as noted above, is the only occurrence of the latter verb in John. Bilingual (see section V below), the author translated פוץ with διασκορπίζω, as in the LXX, but chose the Greek

---

[64]Cf., for example, the targum in an English translation by R. Hayward, *The Targum of Jeremiah* (Edinburgh: T. & T. Clark, 1987) 111, especially his references in notes 3-4. The targum also substitutes "people" (עם) for "sheep" and "flock" in Jer 23:1-3, "scattering" for "shepherding" in 22:22, and "the house (of the sanctuary)" for Lebanon and Bashan in 22:20 and 23. See Hayward 109-111, and S. Sperber, *The Bible in Aramaic*, III. The Latter Prophets According to Targum Jonathan (Leiden: Brill, 1962) 187-88.

συνάγω over the LXX's εἰσδέχομαι for קבץ, probably under the influence of the same verb in 11:47.[65]

Appendix: Golgotha

As noted above, a rabbinic tradition concerning a Tanna relates that Jehoiakim's "skull" (גולגלתא) was thrown down from the gates of Jerusalem and later found before the city by a rabbi, who recognized it as that of the sinful Judean king.

John 19:17 states that the site of Jesus' crucifixion was "the place of a skull, called in Hebrew [Aramaic] Golgotha (Γολγοθα)."[66] Jesus "went out" to it, so it lay outside the walls of Jerusalem.[67] In addition, according to John 19:41 there was a garden with a tomb in the place where Jesus was crucified. V 42 states that Jesus was buried in this tomb because it was close at hand (cf. 19:20). Only the area north of the city wall was known at this time as a garden area.[68]

For the above reasons I suggest that the site of Jesus' crucifixion, Golgotha, was somewhat outside the (second) northern wall of Jerusalem. In dependence on the westernmost northern gate of the Temple Court, Jeconiah's Gate (so named because it was the site from which the famous Judean king left the city for Babylonian exile), popular belief[69] may have attributed the same direction to the site at which his father Jehoiakim was let down over the (earlier) city wall to be killed by Nebuchadnezzar. Rabbinic tradition relates that his "skull," גולגלתא, was later found there. This site could have been simply called in the vernacular[70] גולגלתא, "the place of (Jehoiakim's) skull," especially if it was

---

[65]John employs συνάγω only five times elsewhere in his gospel. The verb frequently translates קבץ in the LXX, as the concordance shows. On the occurrence of פץ in 2 Sam 20:22, see below.
[66]On the dropping out of the second lambda, cf. G. Dalman, *Grammatik des jüdisch-palästinischen Aramäisch* (Leipzig: Hinrichs, 1905²) 166, n. 1: this is Greek influence.
[67]Cf. also Mark 15:20 ("they led him out") and Matt 27:32. It is significant that b. Sanh. 43a (Soncino 281) records Jesus' execution on the eve of Passover in regard to m. Sanh. 6:1, with the "place of stoning," here illustrative of all forms of execution, as outside the city.
[68]Cf. the convincing arguments set forth by J. Jeremias in *Golgotha* (Leipzig: Pfeiffer, 1926) 3, as well as in his *Jerusalem in the Time of Jesus* 43.
[69]Much knowledge of the Temple erected at the return of the Jews from their Babylonian exile, including its further development, will have remained in Palestine even after Herod the Great erected a larger new edifice shortly before the birth of Jesus. To do so, he tore down the former building. Cf. Josephus, *Ant.*, 15.385-391.
[70]Cf. the hill opposite to and north of the Antonia fortress in Jerusalem, called "in the local dialect" Βεζεθα (Josephus, *Bell.*, 5.151; also 2.328). It probably derives from בֵּי זֵיתָא, "place of olive(s)," "Olivetown." See Jastrow 160 on בֵּיתָא. It

The Death of One for All

later used for Jewish decapitations,[71] and, when the Jews no longer possessed this right of capital punishment,[71a] for Roman executions. Jerome, who died in nearby Bethlehem in 420 C.E. and was often dependent on Jewish traditions, comments for example on "Golgotha" in Matt 27:33 by saying that in contrast to other views, the term means "the place of the decapitated."[72]

Unfortunately, this proposal must remain within the realm of "informed guessing."

* * * *

The six motifs and terms analyzed above, all deriving from the Tannaitic Jehoiakim/Jehoiachin midrash, show striking similarities, and in part even exact verbal agreement, with motifs and terms in John 11:45-54. While each of the six could be questioned individually, cumulatively they speak very strongly for the suggestion that the author of the gospel account was acquainted with this midrash in some early form. Other factors, deriving from a major biblical source of the midrash and the latter's development in another direction, will now be analyzed for their relevance to John 11:45-54.

II. 2 Sam 20:1-22, and Its Judaic Development

The Jehoiakim/Jehoiachin midrash surveyed above maintains that the wise woman of the city Abel is the "ancestress" of King Jehoiakim, and 2 Sam 20:21 is explicitly quoted. This biblical chapter, especially in early Jewish interpretation, also lies behind certain motifs and terms in John 11:45-54. I shall first analyze the relevance of the Hebrew text to the Jehoiakim/Jehoiachin midrash and to John 11:45-54, and then its Judaic development, with its own relevance.

---

should also be noted that according to Josephus, a native of the city, the second wall of Jerusalem began from the gate in the first wall, which "they called" Γενναθ (*Bell.*, 5.146). This very probably derives from the singular construct form, גִּנַּת, of the Aramaic גִּנְתָא, "garden." See Jastrow 240. It was thus called in the vernacular "Garden Gate," and led to the north.

[71] One of the four Jewish methods of execution. See m. Sanh. 7:1, and especially 7:3 (Danby 391). For examples of the victims, see m. Sanh. 9:1 (Danby 395) as well as b. Sanh. 52b (Soncino 355), and for Roman sources of beheading, n.2 on p. 354.

[71a] A baraitha states that this took place forty years before the destruction of the Temple, i.e., ca. 30 C.E. Cf. y. Sanh. 1:1, 18a (English in Neusner 31.12), and 7:2, 24b (Neusner 31.201), as well as b. Shab. 15a (Soncino 63).

[72] Cf. Saint Jérôme, *Commentaire sur Saint Matthieu*, ed. E. Bonnard (SC 259; Paris: Cerf, 1979) II 288-291, as well as Jerome's commentary on Eph 5:14 in Migne, P.L. 26.559.

A. The Hebrew Text

1. Rebellion

Sheba, the son of Bichri, a Benjaminite and thus from northern Israel, decides to lead a political revolt against King David in Jerusalem. He is characterized as a worthless fellow/base/a good-for-nothing (בליעל איש, v 1), who "lifted up his hand against King David" (v 21). All the men of Israel, that is the north, thereupon withdraw from David and follow him (v 2).

In the Jehoiakim midrash analyzed above, the king also openly rebels against Nebuchadnezzar and is therefore put to death by him. Also, from fear of Jehoiachin's rebelling against him, the Babylonian king exiles him to his own native city.

In John 11:45-54 the members of the Jerusalem Sanhedrin note that if they let Jesus continue to perform signs/miracles like that of the raising of Lazarus from the dead, "every one will believe in him," and the Romans will come and destroy both Temple and nation (v 48). For this reason they decide to have him put to death. Elsewhere, as pointed out above, the early traditions informing the passion narratives of John and the Synoptics portray Jesus as a threat to the rule of Rome, for he is thought to be a "king," a "rebel/insurrectionist."

2. Ephraim

2 Sam 20:21 notes that Sheba ben Bichri comes from the hill country of "Ephraim."

The only occurrence of Ephraim in the NT is in John 11:54, where after the Sanhedrin's decision to put him to death, Jesus goes to "the country near the wilderness, to a town called Ephraim."

This site is usually identified by commentators[73] with Aphairema in 1 Macc 11:34, which is quoted in Josephus, *Ant.* 13.127.[74] It lay some four miles or seven kilometers northeast of Bethel[75] and is most probably the present et-Taiyibeh. Yet the site is not near the "wilderness," as maintained in John 11:54. This geographical note remains puzzling and cannot simply be explained, as R. Schnackenburg does, by maintaining the Evangelist himself knew of a tradition that Jesus had stayed there once, or more often.[76]

---

[73]Cf., for example, J.N. Sanders and B.A. Mastin, *The Gospel According to St. John* (Black's, 4; London: Black, 1968)281.
[74]See also *Bell.*, 4.551 for Vespasian's capturing it, together with Bethel, in 68 C.E.
[75]The two towns are most probably also meant in 2 Chr 13:19.
[76]Cf. his *Das Johannesevangelium* 2.453.

The "D" text at this point has after "the country/area" Σαμφουριν. I suggest that this is due to a translation into Greek of the Hebrew or Aramaic, "its name (being) Ephraim," with שם or שמא.[77] Far from being a gloss, which would make no sense in the light of the following "city called Ephraim," it would then betray the influence of 2 Sam 20:21, "a man from the hill country (הר) of Ephraim, Sheba ben Bichri his name," שמו. With the omission of the proper name, the Semitic became "the hill country/district, its name Ephraim."

This suggestion may appear somewhat speculative, as it indeed is. Yet I have learned to be very suspect of John's special geographical details. As I have pointed out elsewhere, while for example there was at least one Palestinian town called Cana in Jesus' time, the Evangelist's account of his turning water into wine there in 2:1-11 is basically a Jewish-Christian development of Judaic traditions on Esther one, and is not historical.[78] There is thus good reason for the Synoptics' not mentioning Cana, as they also omit Ephraim. The author of John 11:45-54 appears to have appropriated the latter place name from 2 Sam 20:21, a text he knew stood behind the Tannaitic Jehoiakim/Jehoiachin midrash sketched above, from which he extensively borrowed.

Finally, the place name "Ephraim" does not derive from the idea of a dying "Messiah ben Joseph/Ephraim."[79] P. Billerbeck in Str.-B. 2.292-294 convincingly shows that the relevant rabbinic sources for the latter only appear after the Bar Kochba rebellion of 132-35 C.E., at least a third of a century after the final composition of the Fourth Gospel.

3. A Decision to Kill the Rebel

Although Sheba ben Bichri had as yet done no violence, his leading the revolt of the northern tribes provoked David very much, resulting in the king's now seeing his own authority endangered. He thus tells Abishai in 2 Sam 20:6 that Sheba will do them more harm than the revolt of his own son Absalom (chapters 15-19). Abishai should thus take David's servants and pursue Sheba "lest he get himself fortified cities and snatch away our eyes," i.e., do David and Judea irreparable harm. King David's instructions to "pursue" Sheba (emphasized by repetition in vv 6,7,10 and 13) are correctly understood by Abishai's brother Joab, who demands that the man be handed over to him by the

---

[77]Cf. already J.H. Bernard and A.H. McNeile, *A Critical and Exegetical Commentary on the Gospel of John* (Edinburgh: T. & T. Clark, 1928; reprint 1958) 2.408, taking up a suggestion of Harris. This is also advocated by C.K. Barrett in *The Gospel According to St. John* (London: SPCK, 1962) 340.
[78]Cf. the study mentioned in n. 4.
[79]See, for example, M. Barker, "Caiaphas' Words in Jn 11.50 refer to Messiah ben Joseph" in *The Trial of Jesus,* Festschrift C.F.D. Moule 1970, pp. 41-46.

inhabitants of Abel Beth-maacah, to which he had fled (v 21), and which Joab had besieged. The military commander certainly intends to kill him, as the "wise woman" of the city interprets him. She thus has Sheba killed.

In the Jehoiakim midrash, King Nebuchadnezzar also has the Judean king killed because he has rebelled against him.

In John 11:53 the Sanhedrin of Jerusalem also decides to put Jesus, from the northern province of Galilee, to death because of fear that his activities would do them, the Temple and the nation great harm by provoking the Romans, who would consider Jesus a rebel against their power.

4. Destruction

When Joab besieges Abel of Beth-maacah, casting a mound against it and battering the wall to break it down, a "wise woman" from the city asks him why he seeks to "destroy" (להמית, literally to cause to die, kill), to "swallow up" (בלע)[80] the city (v 19). Joab replies that this is far from his intention; he does not want to "swallow up" the city or "destroy" (שחת)[81] it (v 20). He only wants the fugitive Sheba.

This motif of destruction is not only mirrored in the Jehoiakim/Jehoiachin midrash, where the Sanhedrin asks Nebuchadnezzar whether the time has arrived for the Temple to be "destroyed." It is also reflected in John 11:48, where the members of the Jerusalem Sanhedrin express their fear that because of Jesus the Romans will come and "destroy" (αἴρω) the Temple and the Jewish nation.

5. One Life for Others

In 2 Sam 20:21 Joab tells the wise woman of Abel Beth-maacah that he does not intend to destroy the whole city. However, because Sheba has rebelled against King David: "Give him up alone (לבדו), and I will withdraw from the city." Thereupon, following the counsel of the wise woman, the inhabitants cut off the head of Sheba and throw it out to Joab before the city wall. He then returns to Jerusalem.

The life of one person, innocent of any violent action against King David, is thus sacrificed for the good of the whole city, the whole people.

This motif from the Samuel narrative is employed in the Jehoiakim midrash, where Nebuchadnezzar demands of the Jerusalem Sanhedrin only the rebel king: "Give him up to me, and I will go away," almost a literal borrowing from 2 Sam 20:21. Then, in a debate on whether it is

---

[80]BDB 118: swallow down, up, engulf; devastate; destroy.
[81]BDB 1007-08: hiph. spoil, ruin, damage, destroy.

right to sacrifice one life in order to preserve others, specific mention is made of Jehoiakim's ancestress, the wise woman of Abel, who killed Sheba in such a context.

The same motif is emphasized in John 11:50, where the high priest Caiaphas, head of the Sanhedrin, states: "it is expedient for you that one man (εἷς ἄνθρωπος) should die for the people, and that the whole nation should not perish."

6. All the People

Before the inhabitants of Abel Beth-maacah cut off Sheba's head and throw it out to Joab, the female leader goes to "all the people" (כל-העם) in her wisdom (2 Sam 20:22). This phrase also occurs in vv 12 and 15, and "all" is found in vv 2,7,12 and 13.

This emphasis on "all" the people is also found in John 11:45-54. In v 48 the Sanhedrin fears, because of Jesus' signs/miracles, that "all" (πάντες) will believe in him. Caiaphas scolds them for their lack of knowledge. They do not understand that it is expedient for them "that one man should die for [all] the people (ὁ λαός), and that the whole nation (ὅλον τὸ ἔθνος) should not perish" (v 50).

In the LXX, λαός almost always translates עם, and ἔθνος frequently stands for the same Hebrew noun. The two Greek terms can hardly be distinguished in John, as noted by several of the commentators.[82] The fact that λαός only occurs in 11:50, repeated in 18:14, and ἔθνος only in 11:48,50,51 and 52, with the exception of the trial scene before Pilate in 18:35, may point to a special scriptural background for the Sanhedrin scene. I suggest that it is 2 Samuel 20.

7. Scattering

After Sheba alone was killed for the sake of the whole city of Abel Beth-maacah, Joab blew the trumpet, and his men "dispersed" (פוץ) from the city, each to his tents/home (2 Sam 20:22).

The same Hebrew verb for "scattering/dispersing" is employed in Jer 23:1-2 of Jeconiah. Since the author of John 11:45-54 was well aware of the Jehoiakim/Jehoiachin midrash, which quotes the adjacent 22:30, as argued above, this terminology most probably influenced his choice of διασκορπίζω in 11:52, the only occurrence of the verb in John. The fact

---

[82]Cf., for example, H. Strathmann, art. λαός in *TDNT* 4.32-39 and 50-57, especially 52: "In Jn. this usage betrays a certain concern to ignore the distinction which Jews would sense between λαός and ἔθνος." See also Schnackenburg, *Das Johannesevangelium* 2.450, especially n. 4.

that the verb פוץ also occurs in 2 Sam 20:22[83] probably encouraged his choice of this term.

* * * *

The above seven motifs and terms are reflected in the Tannaitic Jehoiakim/Jehoiachin midrash and/or in John 11:45-54. Again, while an individual motif or term may be questioned, cumulatively they provide strong evidence for 2 Samuel 20 as lying not only behind the midrash sketched above, but also the gospel trial narrative with the Sanhedrin.

The post-biblical development of 2 Samuel 20 provides even more evidence of its relevance to John 11:45-54.

B. Judaic Development

1. The Septuagint, the Targum and Josephus

a) *The Septuagint*

2 Kingdoms 20:22 has πᾶς ὁ λαός, which also occurs in vv 12 and 15. If the author of John 11:45-54, with λαός in v 50, himself translated his Semitic narrative into Greek, as a Jewish Christian he most probably knew of LXX usage of λαός in 2 Kingdoms 20. If someone else before him translated it, the same could be true.

Otherwise the LXX of 2 Kingdoms 20 shows little connection with John 11:45-54.

b) *The Targum*

It emphasizes the motif of "gathering" (כנש) by inserting it in vv 4,5 and 14. It also inserts "the people" into "the inheritance of the Lord" in v 19. Finally, like a midrash, it refers to Deut 20:10 by saying in v 18: "Remember now what is written in the book of the law to inquire in this city ... if they are at peace."[84]

While the targum's emphasis on "gathering" may in part have influenced the "gathering" of John 11:52 (cf. the discussion of Jer 23:3 above), it seems otherwise to have exerted no influence on the text.

c) *Josephus*

The Jewish historian retells the narrative of 2 Samuel 20 at the end of the first century C.E. in his *Ant.* 7.278-92. This passage betrays so many elements typical of early Jewish haggadah that it is clear Josephus

---

[83]The LXX employs here διασπείρω (LSJ 412).

[84]Cf. the text in Sperber, *The Bible in Aramaic* 2.198-99. An English translation with notes is offered by D. Harrington and A. Saldarini, *Targum Jonathan of the Former Prophets* (Edinburgh: T. & T. Clark, 1987) 196-98. Although some materials in it date from a later period, several experts believe it basically stems from the end of the first and the beginning of the second century C.E. (p. 13).

The Death of One for All 51

did not invent them all himself, but was dependent on contemporary Jewish interpretation of the passage. Relevant motifs and terms are the following.

α) Sheba is an "evil man" (ἀνήρ τις πονηρός).⁸⁵ Josephus adds that he rejoiced in στάσις, "sedition" (278),⁸⁶ going so far as to declare war on King David (279). He is an "enemy" (282 and 292), an evil person whom no one knows, i.e., a stranger (291). This description emphasizes Sheba's character as a political rebel whom no one would miss if he were killed.

The same type of imagery is employed of the evil, rebel King Jehoiakim in the midrash sketched above, which quotes 2 Samuel 20. It in turn stands behind John 11:45-54, where the Romans are assumed to fear rebellion/insurrection on the part of Jesus.

β) David orders Amasa to "collect (συναγαγόντ'; 280) as large an army as possible" in order to make war on Sheba. The same verb, συνάγω, occurs in John 11:47. The major influence here, however, was the "gathering" in Jer 23:3, next to a statement quoted in the Jehoiachin midrash sketched above (22:30).

γ) David tells Joab "it is not expedient" (οὐκ εἶναι σύμφορον) to grant Sheba "a breathing-space lest he prepare a greater force and cause them more harm and trouble than Absalom had done" (281).⁸⁷ He and Abishai should thus pursue the enemy and try to engage him, (with the intent of killing Sheba). Stated positively, "it is expedient" to dispose of Sheba before greater trouble begins.

The Greek σύμφορος means "suitable, useful, profitable, expedient," and συμφορῶς ἔχειν "to be expedient."⁸⁸ It derives from συμφέρω, and it has the same meanings as συμφέρον.⁸⁹ Josephus' usage of it in this context points to the presence of this motif in early Jewish interpretation of the usefulness or expedience of killing Sheba, still reflected in the midrashim (see below).

This motif stands in the background of Caiaphas' remark in John 11:50, "You do not understand that it is 'expedient' (συμφέρει) for you that one man should die for the people, and that the whole nation should not perish."

---

⁸⁵Cf. the targum's גבר רשיע. For other similarities to the targum, see the "undermining the walls" of par. 288, with n. "d" by R. Marcus, as well as the beginning of the wise woman's speech in 289, with n. "e," which should be supplemented with a reference to Deut 20:10.
⁸⁶LSJ 1634. Because of the same phenomenon, Herod Antipas had John the Baptist killed at the wilderness prison of Machaerus. See *Ant.,* 18.118.
⁸⁷Translation by R. Marcus in the LCL edition.
⁸⁸LSJ 1688.
⁸⁹LSJ 1687.

δ) When the wise woman of Abel speaks to Joab, she says God chose kings and commanders in order to "remove" (ἐξαιρῶσι) the Hebrews' enemies and to give them peace from them (289). Yet Joab seeks to "destroy" and to do evil to the city, although it has done no wrong. Joab then prays to God and asserts that he does not intend to kill any of the people or "destroy" (ἐξελεῖν) such a great city. He wants them rather to hand over the rebel Sheba, and he will leave the city (290).

These two Greek verbs are the present conjunctive and second aorist infinitive of ἐξαιρέω, which can mean "to remove" people from their country, as well as "to get rid of, make away with, destroy."[90] The verb has the same root as ἀροῦσιν in John 11:48, the future of ἀείρω-αἴρω, which can also mean: "to remove, make away with, destroy."[91] The Sanhedrin is also afraid that the Romans will come and "destroy"' the Temple and their nation. This motif of destruction, however, entered John 11:45-54 via the Jehoiakim/Jehoiachin midrash, which in turn is in part based on 2 Samuel 20.

Of the above four points of possible contact between Josephus' retelling of the Sheba ben Bichri narrative and John 11:45-54, the term "to be expedient" is of the greatest relevance.

2. The Midrashim

As indicated by Josephus' retelling of the 2 Samuel 20 narrative, which incorporates many haggadic elements, there was very early Judaic interpretation of the Sheba ben Bichri incident. In addition to many later, Amoraic elements, the relevant midrashim also include much that is Tannaitic. The large number of variants in these accounts also show how popular the story was. I shall now illustrate four themes from these midrashim which are of relevance to John 11:45-54.

a) *Sheba's Character and Rebellion*

"Sheba ben Bichri" is followed by "his name" in 2 Sam 20:21, which to the rabbis indicated that he was an evil person (רשע).[92] Tanḥuma B Vayyera 11 on Gen 18:25 has Joab call him "a polluted person, an idolator," who is "guilty" (חייב).[93] To allow the residents of Abel Beth-

---

[90] LSJ 581. It is often confused with ἐξαίρω, which also can mean: to make away with, get rid of (582).
[91] LSJ 27, with reference to Matt 24:39 and the trial scene in John 19:15.
[92] Cf. Num. Rab. Naso 10/5 on Num 6:2 (Soncino 5.361); Ruth Rab. 4/3 on Ruth 2:1 (Soncino 8.51); and Midr. Samuel 1/6 on 1 Sam 1:1. For the latter, see S. Buber, *Midrash Shemuel* (Cracow: Fischer, 1893) 44. A German translation is offered by A. Wünsche, *Aus Israels Lehrhallen* (Leipzig: Pfeiffer, 1910) 5.11.
[93] Cf. Buber, 1.92; German in Bietenhard, 1.96.

maacah a better conscience in handing over Sheba to Joab, Gen. Rab. 94/9 Vayyigash on Gen 46:26-27, after a speech by the wise woman of the city which is reminiscent of Josephus' version, calls him a "stranger" (אכסנאי).[94] Eccles. Rab. 9:18 § 2 also states this, adding: "Even if he were the best man in the city, we would surrender him."[95] Midrash Samuel 32/3 on 2 Sam 24:24-25 has the inhabitants ask: "Should we perhaps give him [Joab] a good man from the city?" The wise woman then also points to Sheba as a "foreigner."[96] He thus can be sacrificed with impunity.

Finally, the Tosefta, incorporating Tannaitic traditions not found in the Mishnah, has the wise woman state in regard to Sheba: "Any one who rebels against the kingship of the House of David is [in any case] liable for execution (חייב מיתה)."[97]

The above midrashic material on Sheba ben Bichri as a worthless, rebellious figure deserving of death influenced the portrayal of Jehoiakim in the Jehoiakim/Jehoiachin midrash sketched above. This in turn lies behind John 11:45-54, where Jesus' life can also be sacrificed with impunity because the Romans will consider him a rebel against their own authority.

b) *Destruction*

In Gen. Rab. 94/9 the wise woman accuses Joab of being a "destroyer" (קוצר) of Israel by besieging the city of Abel.[98] In Tanḥuma B Vayyera 11 on Gen 18:25 the same assertion is made with the verb אבד.[99] These are variants of the verbs employed in the biblical account. This motif of destruction lies behind that found in the Jehoiakim/Jehoiachin midrash, where the Sanhedrin queries Nebuchadnezzar regarding the time of the destruction of the Temple. The latter, in turn, is reflected in John 11:48.

c) *One for All*

The midrashim developed Joab's words to the wise woman of Abel and the other inhabitants of the city in 2 Sam 20:21, "Give him up *alone,* and I will withdraw from the city," in various ways, all focusing however on whether it is right to sacrifice one life for the sake of others.

---

[94] Theodor/Albeck 3.1183; English in Soncino 2.877.
[95] Cf. *Midrash Rabbah ʻal Ḥamishah Ḥummeshe Torah we Ḥamesh Megillot* (Vilna: Romm, 1884-87) 5.119a. English in Soncino 8.258.
[96] Cf. Buber 141, and the German in Wünsche, *Aus Israels Lehrhallen* 5.168.
[97] Zuckermandel/Liebermann 39; English in Neusner 1.182. Cf. Gen. Rab. 94/9 Vayyagash on Gen 46:26-27 (Soncino 2.878), where Sheba will be "decapitated by divine decree."
[98] Theodor/Albeck 3.1182; Soncino 2.877.
[99] Buber 1.92; Bietenhard 1.96.

The Jehoiakim/Jehoiachin midrash analyzed above shows one direction of the development of this motif. Another is found in Gen. Rab. 94/9, where the wise woman pretends before her fellow citizens to bargain with Joab concerning the number of victims he demands. She reduces the number from 1000 to 500 to 100 to 10, and finally to one: Sheba alone is sacrificed. In her opening statement she maintains that Joab requests 1000 men. Then she asks the citizens: "And is it not better [to sacrifice] 1000 men than that your city be destroyed?" (ולא טב אלף גוברין מלרחרבה מדינתכון).[100] This is repeated in only slightly different phrasing in Midrash Samuel 32/3 on 2 Sam 24:24-25.[101]

This bargaining is borrowed from Abraham's intercession for the inhabitants of Sodom in Genesis 18, where the patriarch reduces the number of righteous men required by God from fifty to ten. The catchword "far be it from thee" in 18:25 linked the narrative to 2 Sam 20:20, and the Sheba midrash in Tanḥuma B Vayyera 11 is related to this verse in Genesis.

It is significant that in the same section of Genesis Rabbah cited above, an incident is related of a revolutionary who is sought by the (Roman) government. He flees to R. Joshua b. Levi, who persuades him to surrender with the words: "It is better that that man [you] be killed than that the [whole] community be punished on his [your] account"[102] (מוטב דלקטול ההוא גברא ולא ליענש ציבורא על ידיה).

The expression "Better is ... than destruction" in these accounts is derived from the Hebrew of Eccl 9:18, "Wisdom is *better than* weapons of war, but one sinner *destroys* much good." The "wise" woman of Abel in Eccl. Rab. 9:18 § 2 is interpreted as possessing this wisdom.[103]

D. Daube has extensively analyzed other rabbinic sources on the theme of sacrificing one person for the sake of others.[104] They thus need not be discussed here. While he also considers Lev. Rab. 19/6 to

---

[100] Theodor/Albeck 3.1184; Soncino 2.878 (this translation); Neusner 3.322.
[101] "Is it not better for you...." Buber 141, and Wünsche, *Aus Israels Lehrhallen* 5.167. The question is repeated here also in regard to 500 men.
[102] Theodor/Albeck 3.1185; Soncino 2.879; Neusner 3.323.
[103] Soncino 8.256-58. In § 1 (8.256) the above expression is employed by Jacob in regard to his brother Esau: "It is better that he should attack me and not my children." Here one person is also willing to sacrifice himself for the sake of others.
[104] Cf., for example, m. Ohol. 7:6. English in Danby 660: "the claim of one life cannot override the claim of another life." See also m. Ter. 8:11-12 (Danby 62) and t. Ter. 7:20 (Neusner 1.182). The latter refers explicitly to Sheba ben Bichri and is quoted in Gen. Rab. 94/9 with the Sheba midrash on 2 Samuel 20 (Soncino 2.878). It is also quoted and commented on in y. Ter. 8:10, 46c. English in A. Avery-Peck, *The Talmud of the Land of Israel, 6. Terumot* (Chicago: University of Chicago Press, 1988) 417-19.

reflect historical conditions at the close of Antigonus' life, and the midrash to be very early, his view that the precedent of Sheba was "only invoked after Bar-Kochba's defeat" in 135 C.E., cannot be held.[105] Caiaphas' statement in John 11:50, at the latest from the end of the first century, contradicts this, for it clearly reflects Judaic traditions which developed out of 2 Samuel 20. They maintain that it is better for an individual to be sacrificed than that a city/community be destroyed. They stand behind the Jehoiakim midrash, which quotes 2 Samuel 20. It in turn influenced John 11:45-54.

d) *The Wise Woman*

The female inhabitant of Abel-maacah, who has her fellow citizens kill Sheba ben Bichri in order to save the whole city, is called a "wise woman" in 2 Sam 20:16. After Joab explains to her that he will stop his siege and withdraw if the Abelites give up Sheba alone, she tells the Judean general: "Behold, his head shall be thrown to you over the wall" (21). Then she goes to the people "in her wisdom," and they decapitate Sheba, tossing his head out to Joab (v 22).

Because of the woman's "wisdom," the Sheba midrash, as noted above, is also related to Eccl. Rab. 9:18 ("*Wisdom* is better than weapons of war, but one sinner destroys much good"),[106] a text which ultimately provided the imagery of "something is better than/it is expedient that" in John 11:50, where being "destroyed," "perishing" also occurs. It is also attached to rabbinic comment on Prov 31:26 ("She opens her mouth with *wisdom*...").[107] It is this characteristic of wisdom which leads the rabbis to assert that she "delivered/rescued" (הצילה) the inhabitants of Abel from death.[108] Her sacrifice of an individual for the good of the community is thus viewed positively.

The Sages were puzzled about the promise the wise woman made to Joab regarding Sheba's head even before she consulted her fellow Abelites. They therefore ask: "How did she know this?" (מנא ידעה).[109]

---

[105]Cf. his *Collaboration with Tyranny in Rabbinic Law* (London: Oxford University Press, 1966), especially 67,51,101 and the quotation from p. 99. He nowhere refers to John eleven.
[106]Cf. n. 103. See also Eccl. Zuta 9:18 in S. Buber, *Midrasch Suta* (Berlin: Mekize Nirdamim, 1894) 150-51.
[107]See S. Buber, *Midrasch Mischle* (Vilna: Romm, 1893) 112. German in Wünsche, *Bibliotheca Rabbinica*, 4(33).76.
[108]Cf. Targ. Pal. Gen 46:17 (Rieder 1.72-73; Etheridge 321), and Midr. Prov 31:36 (Buber, *Midrasch Mischle* 112; Wünsche, *Bibliotheca Rabbinica* 4[33].76).
[109]Gen. Rab. 94/9 in Theodor/Albeck 3.1183; Soncino 2.878.

Their answer is that she reasoned: "he who is insolent toward the royal house of David will be decapitated by divine decree."[110]

The wise woman is thus presented in the Sheba midrash as having special knowledge of the immediate future, not just persuasive abilities, as noted by Josephus in *Ant.* 7. 292. This element of special knowledge of the future in regard to the sacrifice of one for the good of all in part informs Caiaphas' prophecy in John 11:50-51. There it is expedient/better for one man to die for the people so that the whole nation should not perish.

The wise woman of Abel in 2 Samuel 20, quoted in the early Jehoiakim midrash, is often identified in the early Jewish sources cited above as being Serah the daughter of Asher.[111] She is also considered one of the seven mortals who entered Paradise during their own lifetime.[112] Her great popularity in Judaic legend may also have contributed to the Jewish-Christian author of John 11:45-54's being acquainted with details concerning her, including her major role in the handing over of one man to be killed for the good of all others in the city.

III. The High Priest as Prophet

John 11:50-51 says that the high priest Caiaphas "prophesied" that Jesus should die for the people, thus the whole nation would not perish.

This priest's actual name was Joseph and his surname Caiaphas.[113] He officiated as high priest from ca. 18 to 36 C.E., unusually long in light of the one year or less enjoyed by his three predecessors.[114] His was one of the great families in Jerusalem which supplied a large number of

---

[110]The translation is that of H. Freedman in Soncino, as in n. 109. On this, see also n. 97. Cf. also Midr. Samuel 32/3 (in Wünsche, *Aus Israels Lehrhallen* 5.167, where "Und woher kannte sie ihn?" should be revised to "Und woher wusste sie es?"). In Eccl. Rab. 9:18 § 2 (Soncino 8.257) it is the wise woman who asks Joab: "How do you know?" This misses the point of the rabbis' question.

[111]Cf. Gen. Rab. 94/9 (Soncino 2.877); Tanḥuma B Vayyera 11 on Gen 18:25 (Bietenhard 1.95); Eccl. Rab. 9:18 § 2 (Soncino 8.256); Midr. Samuel 32/3 (Wünsche, *Aus Israels Lehrhallen* 5.166); and Midr. Prov 31:26 (Wünsche, *Bibliotheca Rabbinica* 33.76).

[112]Cf. Kallah Rabbathi 3:26, 53a in Soncino, *The Minor Tractates of the Talmud* 460-61; Pesiq. Rab Kah. 11/13 on Exod 13:17 (Braude and Kapstein 212-13); Targ. Pal. Gen 46:17 (Rieder 1.72-73; Etheridge 321); and Targ. Pal. Num 26:46 (Rieder 2.235; Etheridge 438-39).

[113]Josephus, *Ant.*, 18.35 and 95. On Caiaphas, see Schürer, *The History* 2.230; Str-B 1.985; and Ginzberg, *The Legends* 6.85.

[114]*Ant.*, 18.34.

The Death of One for All

high priests,[115] and his father-in-law was the better known Annas (John 18:13,24).[116] His name probably derives from the word "ape" (קוֹף), Aramaic קֵיפָא,[117] and not from the purported Arabic for "seer, foreteller."[118]

Many scholars consider Caiaphas' words an unconscious prophecy regarding the destruction of Jerusalem by the Romans in 70 C.E. Regarding the phenomenon of unconscious prophecy, they point to several rabbinic examples given by P. Billerbeck.[119] 'Avot R. Nat. B 43 even has a list of ten different persons in the Hebrew Bible who uttered unconscious prophecy.[120] Other names could be added.[121] While these sources point to the phenomenon of unconscious prophecy as well-known in Palestine, not one of them has to do with a high priest's prophesying.

It is primarily Josephus, writing approximately at the time of the Gospel of John, who points out examples of the phenomenon of a high priest's prophesying. He calls each of the head priests of former times the "high priest" and describes their prophesying, primarily in the context of battles.[122]

The Jewish historian also notes that John Hyrcanus, who reigned from 135-105 B.C.E., not only was the supreme commander of the Jewish nation. He also was the high priest, and had the gift of prophecy so that he was never ignorant of the future.[123] On the basis of an

---

[115]Cf. m. Par. 3:5 (Danby 700); t. Yeb. 1:10 (Neusner 3:3), repeated in b. Yeb. 15b (Soncino 84) and y. Yeb. 1:6, 3a (Neusner, 21.53). According to the Berlin "Tagesspiegel" of April 21,1991, Israeli archaeologists found the grave site of many members of the "Caiapha" family in the Talpiot section of Jerusalem in 1990. It includes beautifully decorated stone ossuaries with inscriptions, eleven of which contain the name Caiapha.

[116]The fact that Jesus is first taken to Annas, then to Caiaphas, in John, and the mention of Annas as high priest before Caiaphas in Luke 3:2 and Acts 4:5, probably indicate his still strong position within the Sanhedrin. Josephus in *Ant.*, 20.199 says his son, also called Annas, was rash in his temper, following the Sadducees, who are heartless when sitting in judgment. According to this source, the son had Jesus' brother James stoned to death with others (200).

[117]Jastrow 1337. On the Aramaic, see t. Yeb. 1:10 in Zuckermandel/Liebermann 241, line 25. Two MSS have קיפאי.

[118]See Lagarde's special studies cited in T. Zahn, *Das Evangelium des Johannes* (Erlangen and Leipzig: Deichert, 1921⁶) 493, n. 97.

[119]Str-B 2.546.

[120]Cf. Schechter 118, and the English in Saldarini 255-56.

[121]Cf. the sources referred to in the index of Ginzberg, *Legends* 6.387.

[122]*Ant.*, 3.216; 5.159, 345 (the high priest Eli announces to Hannah that God will give her children), 358; 6.115, 122, 254-55, 359; 7.72,76. See also Mark 2:26 for Jesus' calling Abiathar a high priest (cf. 2 Sam 15:35).

[123]*Bell.*, 1.68-69; *Ant.*, 13.282-83. See also the baraitha on him in b. Sota 33a (Soncino 162-63), found also in t. Sota 13:5 (Neusner 3.202).

experience in the Holy of Holies in the Temple, it is related that the high priest Simeon the Righteous also foretold that he himself would die.[124]

Even in the middle of the second century C.E., belief in the prophetic power of the high priest still prevailed on a popular level. This is shown in Justin Martyr's "Dialogue with Trypho the Jew" 52, where the Christian dialogue partner maintains that up to the time of Jesus "there never failed to be a prophet among you [Jews], who was lord, and leader, and ruler of your nation."[125] This describes the high priest very well, whom Josephus labels "the captain of their [the Jews'] salvation" (*Bell.* 4.318), "entrusted with the leadership of the nation" (*Ant.* 20.251, referring to the period after Herod and Archelaus).

The characterization of the high priest Caiaphas as a prophet in John 11:50-51 thus corresponds to popular belief in first-century C.E. Palestinian Judaism. It is completely wrong to seek its origin elsewhere, for example in Hellenism.[126]

The destruction of the Temple (and Jerusalem) in 70 C.E. by the Romans was adumbrated according to Josephus by numerous portents, including the very massive brass eastern gate of the Temple inner court opening by itself during the night in 66 C.E. (*Bell.* 6.293-296). In b. Yoma 39b[127] a baraitha states that the doors of the Temple opened by themselves beginning with forty years before their destruction, thus in 30 C.E. The same predating by forty years is found in the high priest Caiaphas' "unconscious" prophecy of the 70 C.E. destruction of the Temple and Jerusalem already ca. 30 C.E. (John 11:50). Again, the Jewish-Christian author of 11:45-54 betrays his Jewish roots here.

---

[124]Cf. b. Yoma 39b (Soncino 185). See also b. Sota 33a (Soncino 162-63) on a divine announcement to Simeon the Righteous, although the mention of Gaius Caligula shows the text is in disorder. The same tradition is found in t. Sota 13:6 (Neusner 3.202). Note also the revelation given to the high priest Jaddus regarding the coming of Alexander of Macedonia in *Ant.*, 11.326-28.

[125]Cf. *The Ante-Nicene Fathers,* ed. A. Roberts and J. Donaldson (Grand Rapids: Eerdmans, 1979) 1.221. I owe this reference to E. Bammel, "ΑΡΧΙΕΡΕΥΣ ΠΡΟΦΗΤΕΥΩΝ" in *TLZ* 6 (1954) 356, n. 53. His n. 42 has nothing to do with high priests. See also F.E. Greenspan, "Why Prophecy Ceased" in *JBL* 108 (1989) 37-49, especially 45.

[126]Against R. Bultmann, *Das Evangelium des Johannes* 313, who appeals to Hellenism as reflected in Philo, *Spec. Leg.*, 4.192: "the true priest is necessarily a prophet." This, however, has nothing to do with a *high* priest. See C. H. Dodd, "The Prophecy of Caiaphas, John xi 47-53" in *Neotestamentica et Patristica*. Festschrift Oscar Cullmann (NovTSup 6; Leiden: Brill, 1962) 139. Bultmann is followed here by J. Gnilka, *Johannesevangelium* (NEB 4; Würzburg: Echter, 1983) 95.

[127]Soncino English 186.

IV. The High Priest and the Scapegoat

The author of John 11:45-54 does not have Nicodemus, another Pharisee or a Sadducee from the Sanhedrin in Jerusalem state that it is expedient "that one man should die for the people, that the whole nation should not perish" (v 50). Instead, he purposely puts these words into the mouth of the reigning high priest, Caiaphas. There was very good reason for him to do so.

Only Caiaphas was allowed to perform the most sacred rite of Judaism, that of offering substitutionary sacrifices for the sins of the whole people, on the annual Day of Atonement (Yom Kippur) in Jerusalem.[128] This he did *in toto* approximately eighteen times, including the year in which Jesus was put to death. After killing the goat of sin offering for the people and bringing its blood into the Holy of Holies in the Temple, thereby atoning for the holy place, the tent of meeting and the altar, the high priest laid both his hands on another live male goat, confessing over it *all* the iniquities, *all* the transgressions and *all* the sins of the people of Israel. This male goat, which was to bear *all* of Israel's iniquities, was then sent by him into the wilderness (Leviticus 16, especially vv 20-22).

The Mishnah in Yoma 6 describes the ritual of the scapegoat as it most probably was enacted in Caiaphas' time. The account is definitely pre-70 C.E., i.e., from before the cessation of sacrifices in that year. The text of the high priest's prayer of confession, spoken when he laid his two hands upon the unblemished animal, is first given. It mirrors Leviticus 16, emphasizing atonement for *all* of Israel's iniquities, transgressions and sins.

Then the scapegoat was "delivered/handed over" (מסר)[129] to an individual priest to be "led away" (hiph. of הלך). The former term is the same as that employed for Sheba's being "handed over" to Joab to be killed, and it also stands behind παραδίδωμι in John 18:30, 35-36 and 19:11,16 for Jesus being "handed over" to Pilate and "the Jews" in order to be killed.[130]

---

[128] To my knowledge the only commentator to note this is Zahn, *Das Evangelium des Johannes* 496.

[129] Jastrow 810: "to hand over; to deliver, transmit." "Esp. a) to surrender a person to the authorities...."

[130] Cf. 6:64,71; 12:4; 13:2,11,21; 18:2,5; and 21:20, as well as the art. δίδωμι κτλ. by F. Büchsel in *TDNT* 2.169. On "leading [Jesus] away," see ἀποφέρω in Mk 15:1, with "delivering," as well as ἀπάγω in Mark 14:44,53, but especially 15:16, after "delivering" in the previous verse. A more extensive study of the term is found in W. Popkes, *Christus traditus. Eine Untersuchung zum Begriff der Dahingabe im Neuen Testament* (ATANT 49; Zurich and Stuttgart: Zwingli, 1967).

A causeway[131] was made for the scapegoat so that the Alexandrians could no longer pull out its hair while shouting, "Bear [our sins] and be gone!" From Jerusalem to the precipice (צוק)[132] in the (Judean) wilderness ninety *ris* or twelve Roman miles away,[133] there were ten booths. After the last booth, while people "stood at a distance" watching,[134] the priest pushed the goat from behind (or backwards) so that it rolled down the hill and was killed, breaking into pieces. This was then reported to the high priest in Jerusalem.[135]

The high priest's responsibility for the killing of an innocent, unblemished male goat, which died as a substitute for all the sins of all the people of Israel, so that God would not punish them, is reflected in John 11:50. There the high priest Caiaphas recommends that one person, Jesus, also die for the whole people/nation.

Jesus is thus described here in imagery of the Day of Atonement, involving the high priest and a scapegoat, which was forced to sacrifice its life in order to atone for the sins of all. This was imagery which was easily discernible to the Jewish-Christian hearer of the episode, and later to the reader of the gospel. It excludes, however, the thesis frequently maintained that Jesus is portrayed as the Lamb of God from Isaiah 53 in John 11:45-54.[136]

V. The Language and Extent of the Original Narrative

The large number of peculiar terms found in John 11:45-54, as pointed out in the Introduction, makes it very probable that the gospel

---

[131]Archaeological remains of the "scapegoat's gangway," a bridge leading from the southern section of the eastern wall of the Temple precinct to the wilderness, have been found. Cf. the art. "Temple" in *E.J.* (1971) 15.964.

[132]Jastrow 1270. On this, cf. also Sifra Leviticus 177 on Lev 16:7-10, Aḥare Mot, Pereq 2 (Neusner 3.16).

[133]Cf. Jastrow 1475 on ריס.

[134]Cf. John 19:25-26 with "near," but especially the earlier tradition of "afar" in Mark 15:40; Matt 27:55; and Luke 23:49.

[135]Cf. Danby 169-70, with notes, and Albeck, *The Six Orders of the Mishnah* 2.240-42. See also t. Yoma 3:13-15 (Neusner 2.203-04), with the necessity of killing the scapegoat in the ravine in case it did not die at the first attempt. In b. Yoma 66b (Soncino 310) on this passage, R. Eliezer, a second generation Tanna (Strack and Stemberger, *Einleitung* 77), is immediately afterwards asked about *peloni*, "a certain person." R. Herford considers this to be Jesus. See his *Christianity in Talmud and Midrash* (London: Williams & Norgate, 1903; reprint New York: Ktav, 1975) 45-47.

[136]Cf., for example, Origen in *Origenes. Das Evangelium nach Johannes* 28, 18-19 (pp. 352-53), and W.F. Howard, "The Gospel According to St. John" in *I.B.* (1952) 8.651-52.

writer "John" appropriated this pericope as a unit from elsewhere.[137] The background of the episode is clearly 2 Samuel 20, and its interpretation in early Jewish sources. Since there is no clear dependency on the Septuagint of that narrative in the pericope, and since almost all the relevant motifs and terms discussed above are found in the Hebrew midrashim and Josephus, whose mother tongue was Aramaic, it is probable that the language of the original narrative was Semitic. The language of the people, Aramaic, is likely, yet Hebrew cannot be excluded. The author of the Fourth Gospel appears to have been bilingual,[138] and he himself could have translated the episode into Greek. Another possibility is that it had already been translated in a bilingual Jewish-Christian community such as Syria, from where John appropriated it.

* * * *

The following appear to be additions to the pericope made by the Evangelist himself.

11:45-46 connect the Lazarus episode with the fateful meeting of the Sanhedrin in vv 47-53. They very probably stem from the Evangelist's hand.

In 11:47b, "for this man performs many signs" betrays a favorite Johannine term, σημεῖον, found seventeen times in the Fourth Gospel for "miracle," yet much less frequently in the Synoptics. It thus probably derives from the Evangelist's pen.

Another addition made by him may be the motif of the children of God as now being scattered abroad; they are to be gathered into "one" (11:52). Not only diaspora Jews are meant here, but also Gentiles. John mentions the dispersion of the Jews in 7:35, and in 10:16 Jesus as the

---

[137] Mohr, *Markus- und Johannespassion* 128, believes it derives from the Jewish-Christian "Urgemeinde." C.H. Dodd in "The prophecy of Caiaphas" 140 speaks of "an early Palestinian Jewish Christianity still within the body of the Jewish nation...." See also p. 143. W. Grundmann, "The decision of the Supreme Court to put Jesus to death (John 11:47-57) in its context: tradition and redaction in the Gospel of John" in *Jesus and the Politics of His Day*, ed. E. Bammel and C.F.D. Moule (Cambridge: Cambridge University, 1984) 301-02, considers John 11:47-57 to belong to a signs source connected to a passion and Easter narrative. B. Lindars in *The Gospel of John* (NCB 4; London: Oliphants, 1972) 403-07, speaks hesitantly of materials from "Jewish apologetic for the death of Jesus," perhaps developed through debate with the church.

[138] Cf. E. Freed, *Old Testament Quotations in the Gospel of John* (NovTSup 11; Leiden: Brill, 1965) 130: "the evidence for the use of the Heb. text along with the Gk. is strong, as well as, in several clear cases, the traditions of the Targums." See also G. Reim, *Studien zum alttestamentlichen Hintergrund des Johannesevangeliums* (SNTSMS 22; Cambridge: Cambridge University, 1974) 231-32, agreeing with A. Schlatter.

good shepherd states that he must bring into the fold other sheep. Then there will be "one" flock. As in 11:52, this will be accomplished by Jesus' laying down his life (10:15).

The gathering into "one" in 11:52 (cf. also 17:21) thus appears to be Johannine. Yet the motifs of the "scattered" and "gathering" were probably already in his source, as pointed out above in section I.C.6.

In addition, the term "openly" in 11:54 is probably from the Evangelist. In the Synoptics, it only occurs in Mark 8:32, yet it appears a total of nine times in John.

Finally, Jesus' "withdrawal" to Ephraim in 11:54 seems to recall 10:39-40, which would indicate the Evangelist's own formulation. The place name derives, however, from 2 Samuel 20, the biblical background of the Sheba ben Bichri midrashim and that of Jehoiakim/Jehoiachin. It therefore was probably in the Evangelist's source.

Except for these additions, the unit John 11:45-54 seems to have been available to the Fourth Evangelist basically as it is now.

VI. The Historicity of the Narrative

As stated at the outset, in his gospel the Fourth Evangelist omits most of the Synoptics' extensive trial scene with Jesus before the fully assembled Jewish Sanhedrin or Council with the high priest (Caiaphas) in Jerusalem (Mark 14:53-15:1 par.). Instead, he reports a questioning of Jesus by Annas, the father-in-law of Caiaphas, in 18:13, 19-23. Only after this is the Galilean prophet sent bound to Caiaphas, and from there, without a report of any happenings, to Pilate's praetorium (vv 24 and 28). Within this section, in 18:14 the Fourth Evangelist refers back to the episode of 11:45-54, which is a deliberation of the Sanhedrin already at this point, ending in the decision to put Jesus to death.

Which of the gospel traditions is historical, if either? Modern research on the Synoptic trial scene recognizes that it may consist, at least in part, of a number of accusations already made over a number of days, or during earlier periods.[139] Yet the meeting of the Sanhedrin in John 11:45-54 is definitely unhistorical, like the transformation of water into wine at Cana in 2:1-11.[140]

---

[139]Cf., for example, Brown, *The Gospel According to John, I-XII*, 441-42, and Harvey, *Jesus on Trial* 127-28.

[140]Cf. *Water Into Wine* 1-37. S. Ben-Chorin in *Bruder Jesus.* Der Nazarener in jüdischer Sicht (Munich: List, 1972) 194 sees in John 11:50 the real motivation for Jesus' trial, considering the episode historical. In his book *The Priority of John*, ed. J. Coakley (London: SCM, 1987) 223-29, John A. T. Robinson considers the Fourth Evangelist to be historically superior to the Synoptic accounts in regard to John 11:45-53. W. Grimm, "Die Preisgabe eines Menschen zur Rettung des Volkes" in *Josephus-Studien.* Festschrift O. Michel (ed. O.

The Death of One for All

The Jewish-Christian author of the original narrative searched for an adequate means to portray Jesus as giving his one life on the Cross as a sacrifice for all, for an adequate expression of "at-one-ment." The episode of Sheba ben Bichri in 2 Samuel 20, so popular in early Jewish interpretation of the Hebrew Bible that it influenced numerous early midrashim, including those on the kings Jehoiakim and Jehoiachin, occurred to him as eminently appropriate to describe Jesus as dying for the whole nation, for all the children of God. He therefore borrowed extensively from it many motifs and verbal expressions which still can be recognized in 11:45-54. He retold and recast the biblical narrative and Judaic traditions on it in such a masterful way that for centuries Christian readers of the Gospel of John have gained deep insight into the mystery of Jesus' sacrifice of his life on the Cross for all mankind, for both Jews and Gentiles.

The question of historicity should not be asked of such a narrative. It was designed by the very creative author to present a theological truth in a way which was standard practice in first-century Jewish Palestine, and which appealed to the Jewish and Jewish-Christian listener (and later reader) as something already partially familiar to him or her.

As the biblical account found in 2 Samuel 20 was applied by early Jewish interpreters to the "public trial" in Jerusalem of the rebel King Jehoiakim, involving the Sanhedrin; and as the probable historical background of this episode was the placing on a cross, scourging and beheading of the rebel "king of the Jews" Antigonus ca. 37 B.C.E.; and as the biblical narrative was also creatively retold in early Jewish sources concerning King Jehoiachin, who voluntarily left Jerusalem so that the city and people would not be destroyed, and from whom the Messiah was expected, and who was a "noble example" to "all Jews" in the first century C.E.; so the Jewish-Christian author of John 11:45-54 recast the same biblical narrative and its early Jewish interpretation to fit his own hero, Jesus, for him the true "king of the Jews," who voluntarily gave his life in Jerusalem in order to rescue/redeem all.

Betz, K. Haacker and M. Hengel; Göttingen: Vandenhoeck & Ruprecht, 1974) 133, speaks of John 11:47-50 as an "historical fact," which John must have heard about indirectly or directly. See also p. 135. Grimm does not analyze rabbinic development of the Sheba ben Bichri narrative, although he mentions it and Jonah 1:12ff. (140).

3

Luke 15:11-32 and
R. Eliezer ben Hyrcanus's Rise to Fame

Jesus was an original storyteller. His parables even today convey an impressive freshness, an immediateness, an urgent summons to his hearers to rethink an issue now or to act differently from before.[1] Yet it would be naïve to believe that he was not influenced by his age, that he did not also rework motifs and even story material that was well known to his listeners. J. Jeremias pointed out rabbinic parallels to the Laborers in the Vineyard/the Generous Employer, in Matt 20:1-15;[2] the Great Supper in Matt 22:1-10 and Luke 14:15-24, connected with the Rich Man and Poor Lazarus in Luke 16:19-31;[3] and the Guest Without a Wedding Garment in Matt 22:11-13.[4] In regard to the last, it is R. Eliezer ben Hyrcanus and R. Yoḥanan ben Zakkai who comment in *b. Šabb.* 153a on Eccl 9:8, partly in parabolic form, showing that the motifs of clean clothes, repentance, and vigilance were already "school material" in the first century C.E.[5] These two men also play two of the

---

[1] For a small but convenient collection of rabbinic parables for purposes of comparison, see P. Fiebig, *Rabbinische Gleichnisse* (Leipzig: Hinrichs, 1929).
[2] *The Parables of Jesus* (New York: Scribner's, 1963) 138. Against Jeremias, I suspect that both Jesus and R. Ze'ira made use of a "floating" tradition.
[3] *The Parables,* 178 and 183, where Jeremias relies on H. Gressmann as well as on the 1953 Göttingen dissertation of his student W. Salm, "Beiträge zur Gleichnisforschung," 144-46. According to Jeremias, this was "well-known story material" (p. 178).
[4] *The Parables,* 188; see also p. 200 on the Treasure in the Field (Matt 13:44) and the Pearl (Matt 13:45-46), and p. 170 on the Fig Tree (Luke 13:6-9). D. Flusser calls attention to rabbinic parallels to Matt 7:24-27 and Luke 6:47-49 (*Die rabbinischen Gleichnisse und der Gleichniserzähler Jesus,* 1. Teil, *Das Wesen der Gleichnisse* [Judaica et Christiana, 4; Bern: Lang, 1981] 98; see also pp. 143-44).
[5] See an English translation by H. Freedman in *The Babylonian Talmud, Shabbath* (London: Soncino, 1938) 781. Rabban Yoḥanan ben Zakkai, a first-generation Tanna, according to many sources was a pupil of Hillel and was active first in Jerusalem, then after 70 C.E. at Yabneh. One of his main students was

four main roles in a rabbinic story that provides close structural, motif, and verbal parallels to Jesus' parable of the Prodigal Son and the Forgiving Father in Luke 15:11-32. The latter, Jesus' longest story,[6] is called by A.M. Hunter the "paragon of all parables."[7] It is thought by one scholar to have been "the most influential on the mind of the church and of Western man as a whole."[8]

The narrative of R. Eliezer ben Hyrcanus's becoming a scholar, his "rise to fame," is found in *Tanḥuma B, Lech Lecha* 10 on Gen 14:1;[9] *'Abot de Rabbi Nathan* A, 6;[10] *'Abot de Rabbi Nathan* B, 13; [11]*Pirqe Rabbi Eliezer* 1-2;[12] and *Genesis Rabbah, Lech Lecha,* 42/1 on Gen 14:1.[13] Although many different strands of tradition are now found in

---

Eliezer ben Hyrcanus, a second-generation Tanna. See H. Strack and G. Stemberger, *Einleitung in Talmud und Midrasch* (Munich: Beck, 1982[7]) 77.

[6]It has fifty-one lines in the Nestle Greek NT, compared with the next longest parable, that of the Last Judgment in Matt 25:31-46, which has thirty-seven lines.

[7]*Interpreting the Parables* (Philadelphia: Westminster, 1960) 60, 108, as well as Robert Bridges' remark quoted on p. 61. Flusser calls it "ein Meisterwerk der erzählenden Volksprosa" (*Die rabbinischen Gleichnisse* 1. 296).

[8]D. Via, Jr., *The Parables: Their Literary and Existential Dimension* (Philadelphia: Fortress, 1967) 163.

[9]S. Buber, *Midrasch Tanchuma* (Vilna: Romm, 1885) 1. 67-69. This edition is based primarily on MS Oxford Opp. 20, although important variants are given in the notes. The passage is not noted by Str-B, although in a different context three parallel traditions are noted (2. 414).

[10]S. Schechter, *Aboth de Rabbi Nathan* (Vienna, 1887; New York: Feldheim, 1967) 30-31. An English translation is offered by J. Goldin, *The Fathers According to Rabbi Nathan* (Yale Judaica Series, 10; New Haven: Yale University Press, 1955) 43-44.

[11]See Schechter, *Aboth*, 30-33; English translation in A. Saldarini, *The Fathers According to Rabbi Nathan, Version B* (Studies in Judaism in Late Antiquity, 11; Leiden: Brill, 1975) 98-104.

[12]*Pirqe Rabbi Eliezer* (Hebrew) (Jerusalem: Eshkol, 1973) 3-8; English in G. Friedlander, *Pirḳê de Rabbi Eliezer* (London, 1916; reprint, New York: Hermon, 1970) 1-8, especially 1 n. 1. Friedlander based his translation primarily on the MS of A. Epstein of Vienna (p. xiv).

[13]J. Theodor and C. Albeck, *Midrash Bereshit Rabba* (2d ed.; Jerusalem: Wahrmann, 1965) 1. 397-99; English translation by H. Freedman in *Midrash Rabbah, Genesis I* (London: Soncino, 1939) 1. 340. This version is reproduced with minor changes in *Yalquṭ Shem'oni, Genesis Lech Lecha* 72 on 14:1. See *Yalquṭ Shem'oni, Bereshit* (Jerusalem: Kook, 1973) 274. I am very grateful to Dr. N. Oswald of Berlin for aid in analyzing several of the Hebrew sources, as well as for discussing the *Tanḥuma B* narrative with me.

these accounts, they are all related to one another and have basically the same subject matter: Eliezer's leaving his paternal home; his studying Torah with Yoḥanan ben Zakkai in Jerusalem, at first under very adverse conditions; the brothers' jealousy of Eliezer, related to an inheritance motif; and his father's finally recognizing the son's greatness as a rabbinic scholar and becoming reconciled to him. It was for this reason, for example, that the narrative was placed at the beginning of *Pirqe Rabbi Eliezer;* it formed a biographical introduction to this work, which is mostly pseudepigraphical.[14] All five traditions have been translated into English and analyzed as literature by Z. Kagan.[15] J. Neusner has also translated the *Tahuma B* passage, cited the other traditions, and commented on them in his major study of R. Eliezer.[16]

The *Tanḥuma B* tradition contains a large number of loan words[17] and differs in major respects from the others.[18] It also provides most, although not all, of the parallels from the Eliezer narrative to Jesus' parable of the Prodigal Son and the Forgiving Father. A recent German translation by H. Bietenhard has the advantage that it is not an eclectic text, like Buber's, but almost exclusively reproduces Codex Vaticanus Ebr. 34, Buber's "Rome" text.[19] Since the *Tanḥuma B* tradition is now readily available in three independent translations into English and German, no new translation is offered here. Nevertheless, a brief summary of and comment on the narrative are necessary in order for the reader to perceive the parallels to Jesus' parable in their "Eliezer" context. Variants from the other traditions are cited when relevant. In addition, Genesis 14 is suggested as part of the background of the present Eliezer narratives (section I). Following this I shall elucidate Jesus' parable in light of the Eliezer parallels (section II). Then a short discussion of the chronological relationship of the five Eliezer traditions to each other is given, and the proposal is made that Jesus' parable and

---

[14]Friedlander, *Pirke,* 1 n. 1.
[15]"Divergent Tendencies and Their Literary Moulding in the Aggadah," in *Studies in Aggadah and Folk-Literature* (ed. J. Heinemann and D. Noy; Scripta Hierosolymitana 22; Jerusalem: Magnes, 1971) 151-170. In his 1980 Yale dissertation, "Scripture and Fiction," D. Damrosch also analyzed the narrative techniques involved in the Genesis Rabbah Eliezer tradition (pp. 91-97). I thank N. Dahl, now of Oslo, for calling my attention to the latter work.
[16]*Eliezer Ben Hyrcanus: The Tradition and the Man* (Leiden: Brill, 1973) especially 1. 437-46.
[17]There are six Greek and two Latin loan words employed in the narrative; see the footnotes of the Bietenhard translation mentioned in n. 19. Later midrashim substituted Hebrew for such expressions.
[18]Kagan calls it a "unique variant" ("Divergent Tendencies," 158).
[19]Bietenhard, *Midrasch Tanchuma B,* Band 1 (Judaica et Christiana, 5; Bern: Lang, 1980) 72-74.

the Eliezer stories are most probably both dependent on a common oral tradition, a folk tale (section III). Finally, Jesus' specific changes and emphases, as far as ascertainable, are elaborated (section IV).

I.

A. Tanḥuma B Lech Lecha 10, with Consideration of the Other Eliezer Traditions

Tanḥuma B Lech Lecha 10 begins by stating that Rabbi Eliezer was the son of (a) פילוט.[20] S. Buber thought this term derived from פָּלָטִין, "palace,"[21] which in the context is very improbable. It could possibly be a corruption of the Greek πολίτης, implying that Eliezer's father was, like the Jew Saul/Apostle Paul, a Roman citizen. By metathesis, a not uncommon phenomenon in loan words,[22] פוליט could have become פילוט. Bietenhard suggests that it derives, also by corruption, from πολιτευόμενος, used as a loan word in Hebrew to mean "councilman."[23] Yet the term is most probably a corruption of פָּלִיט, "fugitive," in Gen 14:13, for at the conclusion of *Tanḥuma B Lech Lecha* 10 it is stated that R. Eliezer in Jerusalem was expounding on Genesis 14, and the parallel narrative in *Gen. Rab.* 42/1 says specifically that it was on the neighboring verse, Gen 14:15.[24] This derivation from Gen 14:13 is all the more probable since there was extensive rabbinic consideration of the "fugitive" here as either Og, the king of Bashan who "escaped" the fate of the generation of the flood,[25] or as the angel Michael, who came

---

[20]This is the reading in Buber's MS Oxford Opp. 20. His n. 92 on p. 67 states that the "Rome" MS has פליט, yet Bietenhard (1. 72 n. 32) also reads פילוט.
[21]*Midrasch Tanchuma*, 67 n. 92, as well as Jastrow, 1180.
[22]For another case in the Eliezer narrative, see Saldarini, *The Fathers*, 100 n. 12. *Tanḥuma B* also offers an example of the vowels "oi" in Greek becoming "io" in Hebrew. See *Leviticus Tazri'a* 12 for πίθος as פוטיס (Bietenhard, 2. 62). *Tazri'a* 13a has the Latin *comes* as קמוס (Bietenhard, 2. 66), and *Emor* 6 κυνηγία as קינוני (Bietenhard, 2. 122).
[23]*Tanḥuma B*, 72 n. 32, which quotes S. Krauss, *Griechische und Lateinische Lehnwörter im Talmud, Midrasch und Targum* (Berlin, 1898; reprint, Hildesheim: Olms, 1964) 2. 425. See also LSJ 1434 on πολιτεύω B. IV, although the references are from the fourth century C.E.
[24]See below for additional influences of Genesis 14 on the Eliezer narratives.
[25]This was because of his extreme height as a giant. See *b. Nid.* 61a (Soncino 433), as well as *b. Zeb.* 113b (Soncino, 560). In *Deut. Rab. Debarim* 1/25 on Deut 3:2 (Soncino, 7. 26-27) this is said in the name of Bar Qappara, a fifth-generation Tanna (Strack and Stemberger, *Einleitung* 88). See also *Num. Rab. Chukkath* 19/32 on Num 21:33 (Soncino, 6. 781); *Tanḥuma B Numbers Chukkath* 55 (Bietenhard, 2. 360); and *Tanḥuma Chukkath* 25.

and told Abraham all the secrets of the world.[26] Although the meaning of פילוט in the *Tanḥuma* context cannot be ascertained with certainty, the meaning "fugitive/escapee" is the best suggestion, since both the father Hyrcanus and the son Eliezer are also shortly hereafter described as "fleeing."

The following sentence in *Tanḥuma B Lech Lecha* 10 states that Eliezer's father was "close to the government" and to affairs of the "army." The latter is איסטלטיוטין, of which the ל is corrupted from a ר.[27] The word most probably derives from στρατιώτης, "soldier," "officer," of the army.[28] This is important, for it shows that, at least in this narrative, which would appear to be for the most part fictional, Eliezer's father is pictured as one of those Jews who collaborated with the Roman occupational power. The situation is described in pre-66 C.E. terms. Tension was high in regard to Jewish-Roman relationships, particularly because of the growing Zealotic movement.[29] Anyone who was "close to the government" automatically made himself susceptible of his fellow Jews' criticism of collaboration with the enemy, or of the Romans' criticism of his not properly representing their interests.[30] This delicate situation is indicated by the continuation of the narrative.

After a certain period of time Eliezer's father went to another place. When he perceived that "they" were coming, he told his sons: "Get up! Let us flee (נברח) from 'them'." Who "they" are here is not clear. One possibility is the Roman army, which may have considered Eliezer's father to be betraying its interests. Another is that the local Jewish civilian population accused him of collaboration with the Romans and sought immediate revenge. The situation is pictured as dangerous; it called for drastic measures. "Immediately" the father called his slaves and servants and told them to bring him the cattle and camels. The

---

[26] See *Bereshit Rabbati* in C. Albeck, *Midraš Berešit Rabbati* (Jerusalem: Mekize Nirdamim, 1940) 70, where this is tannaitic; *Pirqe R. El.* 27 (Friedlander, 193); and *Midrash Haggadol* on Gen 14:13, in M. Margulies, *Midrash Haggadol on the Pentateuch, Genesis* (Jerusalem: Kook, 1975) 234. Friedlander's suggestion that פליט used for Michael is an abbreviation of פרקליט, is far-fetched (194 n. 5).
[27] As J. Goldin of the University of Pennsylvania points out to me, ל may also be a variant of ר. He compares לבלר from *librarius* (Jastrow, 689).
[28] Krauss, *Lehnwörter*, 84.
[29] See the mention of the Zealots' destruction in Jerusalem in *'Abot R. Nat. B* 13 (Saldarini, 102).
[30] See the situation of danger described in *t. 'Abod. Zar.* 3:5: "They permitted the house of Rabban Gamaliel to look at themselves in the mirror [when getting a haircut from a Samaritan], for they are close to the government." English in J. Neusner, *The Tosefta: Neziqin* (New York: Ktav, 1981) 319. See also *t. Soṭa* 15:8. Gamaliel I is meant here, a first-generation Tanna active before the war with Rome (Strack and Stemberger, *Einleitung* 74-75).

servants then put the (household) vessels upon the cattle. Hyrcanus and his sons "fled." However, Eliezer did not go with his father and brothers, but instead "fled" to Jerusalem. That the situation was desperate is shown in the later remark made by Eliezer's brothers to their father: "We risked our lives for you and did not leave you, but he did not come to look after you in your distress!"

The above motif of "fleeing" most probably derives from Gen 14:10 and 13, part of the biblical text commented upon by *Tanḥuma B Lech Lecha* 10 and *Gen. Rab.* 42/1.[31] The author(s) of the *Tanḥuma B* variant rather clumsily expanded the motif of flight into a "historical" setting for Eliezer's departure to Jerusalem, also called his "fleeing" there. Kagan and Neusner, however, are certainly correct in maintaining that the earliest ascertainable form of the *beginning* of the Eliezer narrative is now found in (a) *Gen. Rab.* 42/1, where the brothers of Eliezer are described as plowing (their father's land) in the plain while he plows on the mountain and then "flees" to Jerusalem, and in (b) *'Abot R. Nat.* A 6, where Eliezer must plow an entire furrow before leaving for Jerusalem.[32] I shall further discuss the chronological relationship between the various Eliezer traditions below in section III.

The *Tanḥuma B* narrative continues by relating that Eliezer does not tell his father or brothers what he intends to do in Jerusalem.[33] He simply flees there, taking neither a talent (= 3000 shekels)[34] nor a maneh (= 100 shekels).[35] Indeed, he arrives in Jerusalem like a "poor man" (עָנִי).

The motif of severe poverty now becomes the main one and moves the narrative further along. Having come to Jerusalem, Eliezer joins the disciples of Rabban Yoḥanan ben Zakkai. After two or three weeks, they smell the bad breath emanating from his mouth. Yoḥanan b. Zakkai knows that it is not due to something bad in Eliezer's mouth, but to hunger. He had not eaten anything. The teacher assigns his disciples to investigate the matter, and they finally ascertain at which inn he is staying. His only possession is a sack in which there is dust/earth.

---

[31] See n. 24.
[32] See Kagan, "Divergent Tendencies," 168-69; Neusner, *Eliezer*, 1. 446.
[33] Elsewhere Eliezer purposely goes up to Jerusalem in order to study with R. Yoḥanan b. Zakkai, in part against his father's wishes; see *'Abot R. Nat.* A 6 (Goldin, 43). In the later traditions of *Pirqe R. El.* 1 (Friedlander, 2) and *'Abot R. Nat.* B 13 (Saldarini, 99), it is Elijah who tells Eliezer to go to Ben Zakkai in Jerusalem.
[34] See Jastrow, 638, on כִּכָּר, 3. "Loaf" (of bread) is also possible, as Neusner translates (p. 439), but in the context much less probable. The emphasis is on how much he could have taken along if he had wanted to do so, since he was of a well-to-do family.
[35] See Jastrow, 797, on מָנֶה. Here Neusner (p. 439) does translate "money."

Eliezer would insert his head into it and suck as from a wine bag. Informed of this, Yoḥanan b. Zakkai is surprised. He recognizes Eliezer's "uprightness" (צדק), for he had not asked anyone to give him anything.

The other traditions also emphasize Eliezer's new abject poverty. *'Abot R. Nat. A* 6 relates that he put a stone from the road in his mouth; other rabbinic interpreters say it was cattle dung. Eliezer refuses twice to answer Ben Zakkai's question of whether he had eaten that day, and the innkeepers believe he is eating with his teacher.[36] *Gen. Rab.* 42/1 relates that in Jerusalem he ate clods of earth until his mouth began to stink.[37] In *Pirqe R. El.* 1, Eliezer first fasts two weeks until Elijah appears to him and directs him to study with Ben Zakkai in Jerusalem. There he fasts for another eight days before Ben Zakkai requests him to leave his presence because of the foul odor. Later asked by his teacher to eat with him, Eliezer even lies, saying he has already eaten at his host's.[38] The last two statements are also found in *'Abot R. Nat. B* 13, where Ben Zakkai reacts to discovering that Eliezer has not eaten by arising and tearing his clothes.[39]

Tanḥuma B continues by stating that Yoḥanan b. Zakkai in that hour/immediately arranged for Eliezer a large banquet (משתה רבה),[40] so that he could eat of good foods, as he was accustomed to do in his father's house,[41] until his bad breath was cured. The expression "large banquet" is biblical, found both in Gen 21:8[42] and in Esth 2:18 as מִשְׁתֶּה גָדוֹל; in Dan 5:1 as לְחֶם רַב; in Jesus' parable of the Great Banquet in Luke 14:16 as δεῖπνον μέγα; and in Rev 19:17 of the great supper of God at the end of time (τὸ δεῖπνον τὸ μέγα). Here in the Eliezer narrative it has no eschatological overtones.

---

[36] Goldin, 43.
[37] Soncino, 1. 340.
[38] Friedlander, 2-4.
[39] See Saldarini, 99-100 and his n. 15.
[40] This is the reading of the Rome MS, followed by Bietenhard, and is to be preferred to the Oxford MS's "much money." It is probably also somehow related to the "festival" (יום טוב) held by Ben Zakkai in Jerusalem, at which all the magnates were dining with him; see *Pirqe R. El.* 2 (Friedlander, 5) and *'Abot R. Nat. B* 13 (Saldarini, 101).
[41] See the statement regarding an orphan bride in *m. Ket.* 6:6 (English in H. Danby, *The Mishnah* [London: Oxford, 1933] 254): "if there was [more] in the poor-funds they should provide for her according to the honour due to her," as well as *Lam. Rab.* 1:16 §§ 47-48 (Soncino, 7. 128-129), and *b. Ket.* 65a-66b. In *b. Ket.* 67b (Soncino, 410-411) a formerly wealthy man applies to a rabbi for maintenance from the community poor-funds and informs him he is used to "force-fed chicken," as another is accustomed to "fat meat." I thank J. Goldin for the talmud references.
[42] Cf. *Gen. Rab. Vayera* 53/10 on this verse (Soncino, 1. 468-69).

In this episode Yoḥanan b. Zakkai shows that he is the true father of Eliezer.[43] He even takes the initiative to find out whether his new disciple is eating properly. Since the result is negative, he provides him with especially good food until his malady is healed. In contrast, Eliezer's father had not given him any money with which to support himself when all had to flee.

After the motif of severe poverty comes the second main emphasis in the narrative: Eliezer's inheritance and final reconciliation to his father. After Eliezer spent three years studying with Yoḥanan b. Zakkai in Jerusalem, his father returned to his "place," that is, to the original home from which he and his sons had fled. There he waited a month or two, yet Eliezer did not return to see him. He was distressed/grieved (היה רע לו)[44] and said: "Because[45] I abandoned him, he went to Jerusalem." Here the father begins to have a bad conscience. He realizes his own conduct at the time of their mutual flight was not that of a loving father.

At this stage Eliezer's brothers attempt to assuage their father's bad conscience. They tell him: "See what your son Eliezer did! He (it was who) abandoned you, went off to Jerusalem, and eats there 'force-fed meat'" (פטומות). The latter term derives from פָּטַם, "to be fat," *piel* "to fatten."[46] The form פטומות, fem. pl., can mean "crammed poultry/birds," yet also simply meat derived from force-fed/fattened animals.[47] The Mishna in ʿErub. 10:9 states that there was a street of those who force-fed animals for sale in Jerusalem.[48]

The brothers continue: "You left your home and went after him!" This sentence is out of place here, which betrays the fact that it has been incorporated from an older source. If Hyrcanus had indeed earlier

---

[43]Cf. *b. Sanh.* 19b (Soncino, 102): "He who teaches the son of his neighbour the Torah, Scripture ascribes it to him as if he had begotten him."
[44]Not "he was angry," as Neusner translates (*Eliezer*, 1. 440). For the meaning "distressed," see Jastrow, 1485, on רַע: "weak, sick, bad"; BDB, 948, on רַע, 2; and Bietenhard's "er war betrübt" (p. 73). "He felt bad about him/it" would be colloquial English. Kagan translates "he was loth to say to himself that he had abandoned him and let him go to Jerusalem" ("Divergent Tendencies," 157).
[45]See Jastrow, 1505, on -שֶׁ: "that, for."
[46]See J. Levy, *Wörterbuch über die Talmudim und Midraschim* (Berlin and Vienna, 1924; reprint, Darmstadt: Wissenschaftliche Buchgesellschaft, 1963) 4. 26, as well as Jastrow, 1156.
[47]Because the term is usually associated with cattle (oxen, calves), Kagan translates "fatted calves" here ("Divergent Tendencies," 157). In *Tanḥuma B Vayesheb* § 13 Bietenhard translates the same form of the noun as a general term, "Gemästetes" (p. 210). Perhaps עֲגָלוֹת, "calves," "heifers" (Jastrow, 1041, under עֵגֶל) is assumed, or it dropped out of the text. See τὰ σιτιστά in Matt 22:4 as a technical term for "fatted calves," eaten at a festive dinner.
[48]Danby, *The Mishnah*, 135, who paraphrases.

gone after Eliezer, he would not have been "distressed," as above. The brothers' knowledge of Eliezer's eating rich, force-fed meat in Jerusalem is also out of place. Nowhere is there an indication that they had had contact with him in the meantime. This segment, thus, also appears to belong to an earlier form of the Eliezer material.

The brothers now maintain that if something bad happened to their father, Eliezer would jump to collect his inheritance (ירושה). They argue: "See what a difference there is between us and your son![49] We risked our lives for you and did not abandon you, but he did not come to look after you in your distress. Now, if he hears that something bad happens to you, he will come to us to share (חלק) with us!" The father immediately maintains that Eliezer will not inherit (יורש) anything from him. The brothers counter by suggesting that he should rather disinherit him (מרחקו), Eliezer, now before he dies. They tell him it makes no sense to call for a notary, since Rabban Yoḥanan ben Zakkai, a patriarch in Jerusalem, would then help Eliezer and ask who it is who maintains that the father disinherited him (שרייחקו). This argumentation of the sons leads the father to resolve: "Since you say this to me, let Rabban Yoḥanan ben Zakkai become famous/gain his praise through representing my son (מתהלל בו).[50] I shall disinherit him (מרחקו)!"

His sons put Hyrcanus on a litter/palanquin.[51] He arrived in Jerusalem on Sabbath eve and resolved to disinherit Eliezer (מרחקו) publicly, before the assembled congregation. He then entered the academy, where "all Israel"[52] was present on the Sabbath to hear Eliezer's public teaching. The father then immediately realized (who the lecturing scholar was);[53] he thought Eliezer had (instead) gone off to a degenerate life (תרבות רעה).[54] The father is thoroughly amazed to see his own son as a famous rabbi, whom all Israel comes to hear and admire.

---

[49]Cf. *Num. Rab. Shelach* 16/23 on 14:21 (Soncino, 6. 690; parallel in *Tanḥuma B Numbers Shelach* 25 [Bietenhard, 2. 291]): "Come and observe the difference 'Between the righteous and the wicked, between him that serveth God and him that serveth Him not' (Mal. III,18)." This biblical verse well fits the situation of serving/not serving the father described in the Eliezer and Prodigal Son narratives.
[50]See Jastrow, 353, on הלל, hithpael. The phrase is open to various interpretations.
[51]On בסטרנא, from βαστέρνα = *basterna*, see Krauss, *Lehnwörter*, 2. 160. Only the rich could afford a litter; see the tannaitic statement in *Sipre Deut. 'Ekeb* § 37 on Deut 11:10, in L. Finkelstein, *Sifre on Deuteronomy* (New York: Jewish Theological Seminary of America, 1969) 71.
[52]The Rome MS reads "all Jerusalem."
[53]I here follow Neusner's interpretation in *Eliezer*, 1. 441.
[54]Jastrow, 1694.

The clause concerning Eliezer's ostensibly degenerate life makes little sense in the context. In an earlier form of the narrative it more probably belonged to Hyrcanus's remark: "Because I abandoned him, he went to Jerusalem," as well as to the brothers' accusation that Eliezer eats rich, force-fed meat in Jerusalem. That would be a better association with a "degenerate life." If, however, the sentence does belong here, it may be intended to emphasize Hyrcanus's shock. He had gone up to Jerusalem not knowing where Eliezer lived. In order to shame his son, Hyrcanus wanted to disinherit him publicly, in the place where most of the influential people of Jerusalem would be found. To his amazement it is his own son who is expounding the Torah this Sabbath morning, and underneath the prayer shawl and head phylacteries[55] he unexpectedly discovers his own flesh and blood. His fear had been that Eliezer had "fallen into bad ways" in the big city.[56]

The inheritance motif finds its culmination in Hyrcanus's next action. He now stands on a bench in the academy and says before the inhabitants of Jerusalem: "I only came up to Jerusalem to ban/excommunicate you (לנדותך),[57] Eliezer, my son, and also to disinherit you (לרחקך מירושה). Now I will give you two portions (חלקים) more than your brothers."

At this point in the *Pirqe Rabbi Eliezer* tradition, the father witnesses "all this praise" in the academy,[58] resolves to disinherit (נדה) Eliezer's brothers completely, and to give their portion to him as a gift. The now famous son replies, however: "Behold, I am not equal (שוה) to one of them."[59] Eliezer says he could have asked God for land, or silver and gold, and God could have given it to him, yet he instead asked God that he might be "worthy" (שאזכה) of the Torah alone.[60] Here Eliezer is

---

[55]As J. Goldin informs me, wearing phylacteries on the Sabbath was against later standard practice. Cf. for example m. *'Erub.* 10:1 and the relevant notes in Danby, 134. See, however, the remark of R. Meir in *b. Šabb.* 62a (Soncino, 289) and *b. Sanh.* 68a (Soncino, 461), both discussed in Str-B 4. 268 "f."
[56]This is approximately how Kagan interprets the clause in "Divergent Tendencies," 158.
[57]See Jastrow, 878, on נדה, נדי.
[58]The parallel in *'Abot R. Nat. B* 13 (Schechter, 32; Saldarini, 103) inserts here: "I have come and seen and rejoiced (ושמחתי) in the study of your teaching." See Jastrow, 1593, on שָׂמַח, "to be merry," "rejoice."
[59]See Jastrow, 1529, on שָׁוֶה, bottom. See *Pirqe Rabbi Eliezer* 7; Friedlander, 8. In *Gen. Rab.* 42/1 (Theodor and Albeck, 398; Soncino, 1. 340) Eliezer says: "I will take only an equal share (שוה) with my brothers."
[60]Cf. *Pirqe R. El.* 2 in the A. Epstein MS used by Friedlander, 8. This tradition and the citation of the Hebrew word are also found in S. Buber, *Jalkut Machiri ... zu den 150 Psalmen* (Berdyczew: J. Scheftel, 1899) 228-29, § 77 on Psalm 119, where, however, "Torah" is lacking (reference from Friedlander, 8 n. 2).

portrayed as the humble, modest person he was from the very outset, even now after he has become famous. Regarding his reputation, *'Abot R. Nat.* A 6 has Yoḥanan tell him earlier: "Even as a bad breath rose from thy mouth, so shall fame (שׁם טוב) of thee travel for thy mastery of the Torah."[61]

Two other details from the reunion scene in the parallel traditions are noteworthy. In *'Abot R. Nat.* A 6 Hyrcanus hears that his son is studying Torah with Yoḥanan b. Zakkai, so he goes to Jerusalem to disinherit him.[62] Once inside the academy, he "leaps" (מדלג) up in order to sit near the great ones of Israel, who are there to listen to Eliezer expounding the Torah.[63] After Eliezer does so, Yoḥanan b. Zakkai rises to his feet and kisses him on his head, calling him "master."[64] Then Hyrcanus delivers his short "inheritance" speech.

B. The Scriptural Background of the Eliezer Narratives

Tanḥuma B Lech Lecha 10 concludes its account, after the reconciliation of father and son, by asking which Bible verse R. Eliezer was interpreting at that moment. "Our teachers" said Gen 14:1, "In the days of Amraphel king of Shinar." R. Eliezer began his lecture/homily on this verse by saying: "This is what Scripture says: 'Their sword shall pierce their own heart'" (Ps 37:15).[65] At first sight there is no connection between these verses. The content of Genesis 14, however, aids in understanding the connection. Four eastern kings, including Amraphel, made war on the kings of Sodom and Gomorrah and three other neighboring kings in the Dead Sea valley. Defeated, the kings of Sodom and Gomorrah "fled" (נָסוּ, 14:10 twice). The enemy took all the

---

See also *'Abot R. Nat.* B 13 (Saldarini, 104, where he employs the alternate translation, "acquire"; see Jastrow, 398, on זכי, זכה).

[61] Goldin, 43; Schechter, 31; see also *'Abot R. Nat.* B 13 (Saldarini, 101), an interpretation of Exod 18:4.

[62] This also may show that an older tradition has been reworked here. In rabbinic thought any normal father would instead have rejoiced in his son's becoming a scholar.

[63] See Schechter, 31; and Goldin, 44, who calls attention to the strange expression in 184 n. 22. On דלג, "leap," "skip," see Jastrow, 308, and BDB, 194.

[64] See Schechter, 31; and Goldin, 44. The same kissing motif is also found in *Pirqe R. El.* 2 (Friedlander, 7). On the three kinds of rabbinic kisses, including that of reunion, see Str-B 1. 995-96. An example is given of Yoḥanan's kissing another disciple after an excellent lecture.

[65] By omitting this verse in his translation, Neusner does not allow the various Eliezer narratives to be connected in this important way (*Eliezer*, 1. 439). On Jewish interpretation of Genesis 14, the "war of the kings," see the many sources cited in L. Ginzberg, *The Legends of the Jews* (Philadelphia: Jewish Publication Society of America, 1968) 1. 227-34, 5. 223-26.

kings' goods and provisions, but also Lot, Abram's nephew who was living in Sodom, along with his goods (v 12). One who escaped (הַפָּלִיט, v 13) informed Abram, who then with his own forces smote the enemy (fatally, by the sword)[66] and rescued his nephew and the latter's goods (vv 14-16). The king of Sodom then went out to meet Abram at the Valley of שָׁוֵה, directly next to Jerusalem (v 17).[67] The famous encounter of Melchi*zedek*, king of Salem, with Abram followed (vv 18-20). Then the king of Sodom told Abram to give him those taken prisoner whom Abram had now brought back, but to take the goods for himself. However, Abram refused, saying that he would not take a thread or a sandal-thong or anything that was his, so that he could not say, "I have made Abram rich." Abram will take only what the young men have already eaten, as well as the share (חֵלֶק) of the men who accompanied him. The allies of Abram, among whom he was living (v 13), however, should also take their share (חֶלְקָם, vv 23-24).

This reveals that the six motifs and verbal associations of "flight,"[68] שׁוה, פליט, (Melchi-)*zedek*, the refusal to take anything at all from another person for oneself,[69] and חֵלֶק, all found in the *Tanḥuma B* Eliezer narrative and parallel accounts, derive from Genesis 14, which is the section of scripture in *Tanḥuma B* in which the Eliezer narrative is

---

[66]See BDB, 645, on נכה, *hiphil*. See, for example, 2 Sam 20:10 on fatally striking with the sword.
[67]Cf. Absalom's pillar being erected in the "King's Valley" in 2 Sam 18:18. Today it is a part of Jerusalem and contains the beginning of the old road to Jericho. For rabbinic wordplay on "Shaveh" in connection with the "king" Abraham, see the tradition found in *Gen. Rab. Lech Lecha* 42/5 on 14:3 (Soncino, 1. 347); 43/5 on 14:17 (Soncino, 1. 355); *Num. Rab. Beha'alothecha* 15/14 on 10:1 (Soncino, 6. 656-57); *Tanḥuma Lech Lecha* 13 on Gen 15:1; and *Tanḥuma B Numbers Beha'alotheca* 17 (Bietenhard, 2. 266).
[68]Rabbis Judah and Nehemiah, two third-generation Tannaim (Strack and Stemberger, *Einleitung* 83), comment on this motif of flight from Gen 14:10 in *Gen. Rab. Lech Lecha* 42/7 (Soncino, 1. 349), which shows that rabbinic consideration of this passage was early. The two deal with much of Genesis 14.
[69]In *Sipre Deut. Vaethchanan* § 33 on Deut 6:6 (Finkelstein, 59-60), the righteous Abraham's refusal to be greedy in Gen 14:22-23 is cited as an example of those who adjure their (evil) inclination. This is related by R. Josiah, a third-generation Tanna (Strack and Stemberger, *Einleitung* 82). Extensive comment on this motif is also found in *b. Ḥull.* 89a (Soncino, 496; parallel in *b. Soṭa* 17a, Soncino, 89-90); *Gen. Rab. Lech Lecha* 43/9 on Gen 14:21-23 (Soncino, 1. 359); *Tanḥuma Lech Lecha* 13 on Gen 15:1; *Tanḥuma B Lech Lecha* 17 on Gen 15:1 (Bietenhard, 5. 78-79); and *Eliyyahu Rabbah* (25) 23, p. 128 (English in W. Braude and I. Kapstein, *Tanna dēḇe Eliyyahu* [Philadelphia: Jewish Publication Society of America, 1981] 318). Josephus calls this Abraham's "virtue" (*Ant.* 1.10.3 § 183).

found.⁷⁰ This is corroborated by *Gen. Rab.* 42/1, where various expressions in Ps 37:14, the verse before 15, are also applied to Amraphel and his companions, Lot and Abram. Then Gen 14:15 is quoted.⁷¹

Finally, in Gen 15:1-6 Abram is afraid that his servant Eliezer (of Damascus) will become his heir (יוֹרֵשׁ), a motif repeated four times.⁷² One rabbi in *Gen. Rab.* 43/2 equates the numerical value of the Hebrew letters in the name Eliezer (318) with Abram's 318 trained men in Gen 14:14, which would mean that Eliezer alone helped Abram in battle.⁷³ The name Eliezer, and the motif of the danger of an inheritance being given to the wrong person⁷⁴ may also have influenced the development of the R. Eliezer narratives.⁷⁵

The above discussion of Genesis 14 and 15:1-6 points to the scriptural background of a number of motifs and verbal associations now found in the various accounts of R. Eliezer's "rise to fame." Except for the issue of inheritance, these can be removed from the Eliezer narratives. It will then be easier to compare the remaining material to Jesus' parable of the Prodigal Son and the Forgiving Father.⁷⁶

---

⁷⁰It also shows that the various traditions are more interrelated than it appears at first sight. The שׁוה motif, for example, appears in *Gen. Rab.* 42/1 (see also 42/5 and 43/5), but also in *Pirqe R. El.* 2 and *'Abot R. Nat. B* 13, the latter two generally thought to be the most recent of the Eliezer traditions.
⁷¹See Theodor and Albeck, 398-99; Soncino, 1. 340.
⁷²Except for *Onqelos,* all the targums on Gen 15:2 note that Eliezer "expected" to become Abraham's heir.
⁷³See Soncino, 1. 353 n. 3. D. Damrosch called attention to this in "Scripture and Fiction," 96.
⁷⁴Isaac, yet to be born, will be the true son.
⁷⁵I would also suggest that Ps 110:1-5 was the reading in the "writings" for the Torah text Genesis 14, the *haftarah* or reading from the prophets being Isa 41:2-13 in the ancient triennial lectionary system of the synagogue. "My lord" of Ps 110:1 was interpreted of Abraham's servant *Eliezer* addressing him, and the "kings" of v 5 were thought of as being shattered by Abraham in Genesis 14. Cf. *Mek. R. Ish. Shirata* 6 on Exod 15:7 on these three texts, in J. Lauterbach, *Mekilta de-Rabbi Ishmael* (Philadelphia: Jewish Publication Society of America, 1933) 2. 42, lines 33-41; *Midrash Haggadol* on Gen 14:20 (Margulies, 238); K. Kuhn, *Sifre zu Numeri* (Stuttgart: Kohlhammer, 1959) 787-92, "Exhurs II"; *b. Sanh.* 108b (Soncino, 747); *Midr. Ps.* 110/1-4, in W. Braude, *The Midrash on Psalms* (Yale Judaica Series, 13; New Haven: Yale University Pres, 1959) 2. 205-6; and Str-B 4. 453-56.
⁷⁶Flusser calls attention to the fact that not one of Jesus' parables explicitly cites an OT verse as its basis (*Die rabbinischen Gleichnisse,* 1. 27, 22). According to him, the same is true of the older rabbinic parables.

II.

Jesus' parable in Luke 15:11-32 has many parallels to, yet also differences from the present rabbinic narratives of R. Eliezer's rise to fame. It begins in v 11, after Luke's introductory words, by stating that there was a "man who had two sons." It is striking that the mother is never mentioned, nor are there any sisters. Like the *Tanḥuma B* narrative, the parable is completely male-dominated.[77]

Jesus' story is set on a farm. The older brother in Luke 15:25 returns to the house from (working in) the field. In what is considered to be one of the earliest ascertainable versions of the beginning of the Eliezer narrative, both the future rabbi and his brothers are represented as plowing their father's land (*Gen. Rab.* 42/1).

In contrast to Eliezer, who in *Tanḥuma B* never said תן לי כלום, "Give me something," the younger of the two brothers in Jesus' story at the very outset in v 12 says δός μοι, give me the share (μέρος) of property that falls to me. This μέρος corresponds to the share (חלק) of the inheritance Eliezer's father first wants to take away from him, and at the end of the story wants to increase. The inheritance motif dominates Jesus' parable from the very outset,[78] as it does the rabbinic story, where it is also coupled with abject poverty. Verse 12 states that the father divided his living between the two sons, that is, the older son also received his share, which was twice as much as that of the younger brother.[79]

Unlike Eliezer at the time of the family flight, the prodigal "shortly thereafter" gathers all he has, including his inheritance, which in

---

[77]Only in *'Abot R. Nat. A* 6 (Schechter, 30; Goldin, 43) is there mention of Eliezer's father-in-law, which implies that he is married. Yet the wife is alluded to nowhere else in this story. In *Pirqe R. El.* 1 (*Pirqe Rabbi Eliezer* 5; Friedlander, 2) and *'Abot R. Nat. B* 13 (Schechter, 30; Saldarini, 99), Hyrcanus encourages his son to marry and sire children rather than to study Torah.

[78]On a younger man's bidding Jesus to intercede with his older brother in regard to dividing the inheritance with him, cf. Luke 12:13b-14. The motif was apparently well known in the first century C.E.

[79]On the firstborn as receiving a double share of the inheritance in tannaitic times, see the rabbinic passages cited in Str-B 3. 545-53 on Gal 3:15; L. Schottroff, "Das Gleichnis vom verlorenen Sohn," in *ZTK* 68 (1971) 39-44; W. Pöhlmann, "Die Abschichtung des Verlorenen Sohnes (Lk 15, 12f) und die erzählte Welt der Parabel," in *ZNW* 70 (1979) 194-213; and *Sipre Num. Pinchas* § 134 on Num 27:7 (Kuhn, 542; see also 541 n. 5, referring to *t. B. Bat.* 7 and 10). See especially *t. Ketub.* 8:5, which deals with a situation in which a father has written over his property to his son: "If the son sold off the property or the father died ...." English in J. Neusner, *The Tosefta: Nashim* (New York: Ktav, 1979) 85.

contrast to his brother's share is now in cash form,[80] and departs εἰς χώραν μακράν, "into a far/distant country." "Not many days later" (RSV) in the Greek is μετ' οὐ πολλὰς ἡμέρας, and corresponds to Hyrcanus's going "after some days" (לימים) to a "far country." The latter in *Tanḥuma B* is למקום אחר, to a "different place," which in the Rome MS at another point in the story means going "abroad."[81] In Jesus' parable it is the son who goes abroad; here in the *Tanḥuma B* variant of the rabbinic story it is the father. The son takes πάντα with him; Hyrcanus has (all) his vessels put on the cattle, then departs with them and his camels.

In one of the earliest versions of the Eliezer narrative, it is also he who abandons father and brothers on the family farm. In *Gen. Rab.* 42/1, when his cow falls down and is injured while plowing, Eliezer irresponsibly leaves the maimed animal in the field. Without consulting either father or brothers, he simply flees (to Jerusalem).

In the far country in Luke 15, the younger son "squanders his property in loose living" (v 13). The Greek ζῶν ἀσώτως here is a direct parallel to Hyrcanus's thinking that Eliezer had gone off to Jerusalem to a "life of depravity" (תרבות רעה) in *Tanḥuma B*. The older brother in v 30 emphasizes this motif. He accuses his younger brother of devouring the father's living with harlots.[82]

Having spent his entire share of the inheritance, the penniless younger brother is now in want, especially because there is a great famine in his new country (v 14). Forced to work in order to eat, he as a Jew even takes on the despised task of being a swineherd for a πολίτης of that country.[83] This is the nadir of religious degradation, for he now cannot practice his own religion. Because he is too disgusted to eat carobs, swine fodder,[84] and because no one gives him anything to eat (v

---

[80] Jeremias, *Parables*, 129.
[81] See the Rome MS variant regarding the other sons' remarks to their father: He eats force-fed meat, while "you had to leave your house and go abroad." See the translation of Kagan, 157, as well as Bietenhard, 73: "ins Ausland gegangen," for לאכסניא (Buber, 68 n. 113) and LSJ, 1188, "II. *foreign*, ἐπὶ ξενίας (sc. γῆς)." The same expression is found in *Tanḥuma B Numbers Pinchas* 16 (Bietenhard, 2. 393).
[82] It is not stated where the older brother gets his specific information; compare Eliezer's brothers' maintaining that he ate rich, force-fed meat in Jerusalem. Their source of information is not given.
[83] Another expression such as "farmer" could have been used here. Could πολίτης reflect the same tradition that lies behind Hyrcanus as a פולים?
[84] See *Lev. Rab.* 35/6 (Soncino, 4. 450): "R. Aḥa commented: Israel needs carobs [poverty] to lead them to repentance." Reference from Str-B 2. 214. See also *t. 'Abod. Zar.* 4:1 for carobs eaten in a year of famine (English in Neusner, *The Tosefta: Neziqin*, 324).

16),⁸⁵ he comes to himself and recalls that while he is perishing of hunger, his father's hired servants (μίσθιοι) have bread enough and to spare (v 17).⁸⁶

This is parallel to Eliezer's having absolutely nothing to eat in Jerusalem, where he is forced to suck dust/earth out of a wine bag or, as other traditions have it, suck on a stone, eat clods of earth or even cattle dung. His mouth emits a terrible odor because the stomach has nothing in it. Yet at the same time, while he has nothing to eat, his father Hyrcanus's slaves and (hired) servants⁸⁷ (ולשמשיו לעבדיו) have enough to eat, even if they fled to a different place with Hyrcanus and Eliezer's brothers. Both fathers have slaves and hired servants, and both sons are on the verge of perishing from hunger.

In Jesus' parable the prodigal son resolves to confess before his father that he has sinned against both God and him (v 18). He will tell the father: "I am no longer worthy (ἄξιος) to be called your son; treat me as one of your hired servants" (v 19).⁸⁸ This emphasis on worthiness recalls Eliezer's statement to his father in some traditions: "Behold, I am not equal (שוה) to one of them (his brothers)." He wants to be "worthy" (שאזכה) of the Torah alone.

The prodigal in v 17 "comes to himself," he confesses his sins before God and humanity (vv 18 and 21). This is true repentance, as the underlying Semitic expression shows.⁸⁹ In the Eliezer narrative it is not the son but the father who "comes to himself." Confronted with his son's greatness as a scholar in Jerusalem, he makes a public confession before "all Israel/Jerusalem" that he had intended to do evil to his son, yet now he has changed his mind and will give him two more portions of the inheritance than his brothers.

---

⁸⁵Jeremias, *Parables,* 129, in part dependent on A. Fridrichsen. Yet J. Schniewind's suggestion that the prodigal son then had to steal his food, adopted by Jeremias (*Parables,* 130), is strained. It is more probable that the Gentile owner of the swine herd paid only a subsistence wage to his day laborer. The young man could not even get half full on his earned wages; thus, he would have been grateful if strangers had supplemented his diet.
⁸⁶It is important to note that the father not only has μίσθιοι; he also has δοῦλοι, house slaves (15:22), also called παῖδες (v 26) (see the next note). In Luke 17:7-10 a less wealthy farmer can afford only one slave, who must do both field work and housework; see Jeremias, *Parables,* 193.
⁸⁷Since the servants are contrasted to the slaves, they are paid wages; see Jastrow, 1602, on שמש as "attendant," "servant," "waiter."
⁸⁸The first half of the sentence is repeated in v 21. The father there interrupts the repentant son and does not allow him to humiliate himself.
⁸⁹See Str-B 2. 215, as well as 1. 162-72. See also the "repentance" or "change of mind" (μεταμέλομαι) of the son who first said no to his father in Matt 21:29.

The prodigal son returns home from the far country, and while he is still at a distance the father sights him and has compassion on him. He runs and embraces and kisses the son. Jeremias, quoting L. Weatherhead, correctly remarks on δραμών: "a most unusual and undignified procedure for an aged oriental even though he is in such haste."[90] I suggest that the "running" here derives from a common oral tradition, which is also still observable in the description applied to Hyrcanus's reunion with Eliezer in the Jerusalem academy. The father strangely "leaps" (מדלג) in order to sit near the great ones of Israel, who then with him listen to his son Eliezer expounding the Torah. At this point Yoḥanan b. Zakkai "kisses" Eliezer on his head. Gen 33:4, Esau's encounter with his brother Jacob, may also have influenced the terminology here,[91] as well as Gen 18:7.[92]

The prodigal son's father publicly restores him to his previous status. The robe, ring, and shoes of 15:22, as well as the banquet in v 23, attest this.[93] A similar action is undertaken by Eliezer's father. Though Eliezer fled to Jerusalem and remained there over three years, the father, first having intended to ban/excommunicate and disinherit his son, finally wants to grant Eliezer a double share of, or even the entire, inheritance publicly before "all Israel/Jerusalem." As the father of the prodigal at the reconciliation scene now publicly calls him "my son" before the servants (Luke 15:24), so Hyrcanus at the reconciliation

---

[90]*Parables*, 130.

[91]This is correctly seen in regard to Luke 15:20 by O. Hofius, "Alttestamentliche Motive im Gleichnis vom verlorenen Sohn," in *NTS* 24 (1977-78) 242, 245. He is not aware, however, of the Eliezer tradition. In Gen 29:13 it is Laban who runs (LXX ἔδραμεν) to meet his nephew Jacob, to embrace and kiss him, and to bring him to his house. In *Kallah Rabbathi* 3:19 (53a; Soncino, 456), Gen 29:13 and 33:4 are associated.

[92]Here Abraham "runs" (LXX ἔδραμεν) to give a "tender and good" calf to his servant, who then "hastens" (LXX ἐτάχυνεν) to prepare it for the unexpected guests. This verse is connected to Solomon's magnificent daily banquet, including fat oxen and fatted fowl, in *b. B. Meṣ.* 86b-87a (Soncino, 497-500). Other early comment on Abraham's running is found in *Mek. R. Ish. Beshallaḥ* 1 on Exod 13:21 (Lauterbach, 1. 84).

[93]On this "reinvestiture," see K. Rengstorf, *Die Re-Investitur des Verlorenen Sohnes in der Gleichniserzählung Jesu Luk. 15, 11-32* (Arbeitsgemeinschaft für Forschung des Landes Nordrhein-Westfalen, Geisteswissenschaften 137; Köln/Opladen: Westdeutscher Verlag, 1967). Rengstorf takes up the suggestion by D. Daube of a קְצָצָה (Jastrow, 1407), a legal severing of family relations, as involved in the parable (*Re-Investitur*, 22). Rengstorf's OT and Jewish sources for robe and ring as symbols of royal authority are convincing (p. 38), yet he overemphasizes the father as a royal figure (pp. 39, 51), even considering the father's embracing and kissing his son as very similar to a royal act of adoption (p. 54).

scene in Jerusalem again calls Eliezer "my son" before the great men of the city.[94]

After the reunion encounter, the prodigal's father orders his house slaves "quickly" to bring the "fatted calf" (τὸν μόσχον τὸν σιτευτόν) and slaughter it.[95] All are to eat and "make merry" (εὐφρανθῶμεν, v 23). The fatted calf is mentioned again in v 27 and v 30, which shows its important place in the narrative. In the Eliezer story "force-fed meat" also plays a role. His brothers accuse Eliezer of eating such choice meat in Jerusalem. The Semitic root of the expression is certainly the same, as pointed out above.

Slaughtering a fatted calf means a great deal, even for a man with hired servants and slaves, as the remark of the older brother in v 29 indicates: "not (even) a kid." It is a real banquet, a festal dinner, which the forgiving father provides for his repentant son, who was dead, but is again alive, who was lost, but is now found (vv 24, 32). This banquet for the son, "perishing of hunger," corresponds to the large banquet (משתה רבה) which Yoḥanan b. Zakkai, the spiritual father of Eliezer, "in that hour/immediately" arranges for him after his extensive fasting.[96]

The older brother of the prodigal, like a faithful son, has been out working in the field. When he approaches the house, he notes the music and the dancing and is informed by a house slave of the reason for this (vv 25-27). The reply angers him, and he refuses to enter the banquet room. Again it is the father, who (upon hearing that the son has returned from the field) takes the initiative and goes out to "comfort" him repeatedly (imperfect, v 28).[97] He well understands the older son's feelings. He does not contradict his statements, but addresses him as τέκνον, "My (dear) son!" (v 31).[98] In spite of this the older son, who knows he has a double share of the inheritance, cannot accept comfort at this point. He justifies his anger by stating: "Lo, these many years I have served you, and I never disobeyed your

---

[94] See all five Eliezer accounts for Hyrcanus's use of "my son" at this point.

[95] Hofius calls attention to the witch of Endor's "quickly" slaughtering a fatted calf for hungry Saul in 1 Sam 28:24 ("Alttestamentliche Motive," 243). See also Gen 18:7 in n. 92.

[96] There may be overtones of the eschatological banquet in Jesus' parable. Cf. the feast of "fat things" the Lord will make for all peoples and nations, a time when "death" will cease, a time of "being glad and rejoicing" in Isa 25:6-9, all motifs found in Jesus' parable. See also the sources cited by J. Behm, art. δεῖπνον in *TDNT* 2. 234-35, as well as J. Derrett, "The Parable of the Prodigal Son: Patristic Allegories and Jewish Midrashim," in *Studia Patristica*, 10 (TU 107), pp. 219-24, especially p. 221.

[97] See BAG, 622, on παρακαλέω, 4. The aspect of "inviting," "exhorting" him to join the festivities is also included.

[98] See BAG, 816, on τέκνον, 2a.

command; yet you never gave me (even) a kid, that I might make merry with my friends. But when 'this son of yours' came, who has devoured your living with harlots,[99] you killed for him the fatted calf!" (vv 29-30). The father acknowledges that the older son has always remained with him, and all that is his is also the son's (v 31).[100]

This speech corresponds very closely to that made by the other brothers to Hyrcanus in *Tanḥuma B* regarding their brother Eliezer, who did not flee with the rest of the family but went off alone to Jerusalem: See what Eliezer "your son" (בנך) did! He (it was who) abandoned you, went off to Jerusalem, and eats there force-fed meat .... See what a difference there is between us and "your son" (בנך)! We risked our lives for you and did not abandon you, but he did not come to look after you in your distress. Now, if he would hear that something bad happened to you, he would come to share with us!

The prodigal's older brother and Eliezer's brothers have all been hard-working, faithful sons who have never left their father's side. They are upright and well behaved. But they are also self-righteous/hardhearted. In the one case the older brother cannot accept the father's granting forgiveness to someone who formerly led a dissolute life and repents of it. In addition, he is outrightly jealous of the attention paid to his brother. In the other case, the brothers of Eliezer do not even know what he is doing in Jerusalem, yet they accuse him not only of having avoided the mortal danger attached to their father's flight, but also of amusing himself with choice food in Jerusalem, which means reveling at banquets (while they continued to work at home). The brothers cannot speak of "our" or "my brother" to the father. Instead they scornfully say he is "your son" or "this son of yours."

These two very similar speeches of the brothers are the most compelling evidence that Jesus' parable and the Eliezer narrative are somehow connected.

At the end of the parable the father tells the older son that he actually should also make merry and "be glad" (χαρῆναι, v 32) because of the return of his brother, just as the father was joyful and wanted to make merry by preparing a large banquet with music and dancing (vv 20, 22-24, 27). The motif of the father's joy at his reunion and reconciliation to Eliezer is also found in *'Abot R. Nat. B* 13, where Hyrcanus says that although he originally came to disinherit Eliezer

---

[99]Hofius compares Prov 29:3, "one who keeps company with harlots squanders his substance" ("Alttestamentliche Motive," 244). The verse had already been noted in the margin of Nestle's Greek NT.
[100]Cf. similar terminology in *Sipre Num. Korach* § 119 on Num 18:20 ("I am your portion and your inheritance"): "My son! I have given you no gift, yet you eat at my table and you drink at my table" (see Kuhn, 402 and n. 8a).

from his possessions, now that he has come and seen him in Jerusalem he "rejoices" (וישׂמחתי)[101] in the son's study and teaching.

It is interesting that after Eliezer's reconciliation to his father in Jerusalem the narrative stops. We are not told how he and his brothers will react to each other in the light of the new situation. The same is true for Jesus' parable. The question remains open in Luke 15:32 whether the prodigal and his older brother will become reconciled to each other.

III

From the comparisons just made in section II it is clear that Jesus' parable of the Prodigal Son and the Forgiving Father in Luke 15 and the rabbinic traditions regarding Eliezer's rise to fame have many similarities. Elements in the basic structure resemble each other. (1) The setting of both stories is a family farm, where field work/plowing is done by the brother(s). (2) A son voluntarily leaves his father and brother(s) for another place. The relationship of these persons to one another is then disturbed. (3) The son experiences in a different location abject poverty and hunger. (4) At the reunion scene of father and son there is public reconciliation between the two. (5) This reconciliation causes the jealousy of the older brother/other brothers.[102] (6) Both narratives close with an open end. It is not related how Eliezer and the prodigal son, reconciled to their fathers, will now get along with their brother(s).

In addition to common elements in the basic structure, there are too many motif parallels and similar verbal associations in the two narratives not to assume a relationship of some kind. The following summary presents a maximal picture. (1) Both narratives, although they deal with family situations, are completely male-dominated. (2) The fathers are both wealthy: Eliezer's father in one tradition is close to the government and is connected with the army; Eliezer could have taken a talent with him to Jerusalem; the son is accustomed to good

---

[101]See Schechter, 32; Saldarini, 103. Again, Prov 29:3 aptly describes this situation: "He who loves wisdom makes his father glad (ישׂמח), but one who keeps company with harlots squanders his substance." See also 23:24, "The father of the righteous will greatly rejoice; he who begets a wise son will be glad (וישׂמח)." Eliezer's father, Hyrcanus, states: "I am blessed, since he came from my loins" (Saldarini, 103).

[102]In *Tanḥuma B* the brothers' self-righteous speech to their father regarding Eliezer is out of place. It logically belongs *after* the reconciliation of father and son, as in Jesus' parable. A later development made this jealousy into the *reason* for Hyrcanus's going up to Jerusalem. For other inconsistencies in the speech, see section I above.

food; the father is taken by litter to Jerusalem; Hyrcanus has cattle and camels, hired servants and slaves. In another tradition, the father has many plowmen. The father of the prodigal son has property, hired servants, and slaves; he can afford to let the younger son receive his share of the family estate now; he can afford to keep force-fed animals. (3) In both narratives the motif of inheritance plays a major role. The term "portion/share" occurs in both. The older brother of the prodigal is concerned that the latter has devoured the father's living; Eliezer's brothers are concerned about keeping their father's possessions intact. (4) A "degenerate life" is associated with the major figure of the absent son in both stories. (5) A large banquet, to be prepared quickly/immediately, is provided for the sons in both accounts. (6) "Force-fed meat" and a "fatted calf" have the same Semitic root. (7) Both fathers strangely "leap/run" at the reunion scene with the son who has been absent for a long period of time. (8) The sons are kissed at the reunion scene. (9) At this point both fathers publicly speak of "my son." (10) On this occasion both fathers also express joy. (11) The jealous, hardhearted brothers emphasize that they have never left their father. They speak scornfully of "your son" or "this son of yours."

The cumulative effect of the above similarities in structure, motifs, and verbal associations is impressive. Yet the *Tanhuma B* variant of the Eliezer narrative, from which a number of the above parallels derive, is in some respects closer to later accounts of Eliezer's "rise to fame." The question of the chronological relationship of the five Eliezer traditions to each other must now be raised before the validity of comparing their content to Jesus' parable can be conceded.

In his extensive study of Eliezer, J. Neusner agreed with Z. Kagan's conclusion that *'Abot R. Nat. A* 6 and *Gen. Rab.* 42/1 in general belong to an earlier period than *'Abot R. Nat. B* 13 and *Pirqe R. El.* 1-2.[103] The latter two, for example, introduce the additional figures of Elijah, who encourages Eliezer to go to Yoḥanan b. Zakkai in Jerusalem, and Moses, whom Eliezer now exceeds in regard to words of the Torah; Eliezer now rejects *all* earthly wealth; he wants only to be worthy of the Torah. Nevertheless, in the light of these patently later developments one cannot simply state that *'Abot R. Nat. A* 6 and *Gen. Rab.* 42/1 "preserved a more realistic view of the figures, the plot and numerous details" because they were "told closer to the time when the events took place," as Kagan maintains.[104] Neusner correctly criticizes her for too easily jumping to historical conclusions.[105] The fact is that *'Abot R. Nat. A* 6

---

[103]*Eliezer*, 1. 446.
[104]See "Divergent Tendencies," 168.
[105]*Eliezer*, 1. 446.

and *Gen. Rab.* 42/1 themselves also clearly show signs of the incorporation of various earlier traditions. In *'Abot R. Nat.* A 6, for example, Eliezer's father tells him that he will get no food until he has plowed an entire furrow. However, this granting of food has nothing at all to do with the son's going to study Torah with Yoḥanan b. Zakkai in Jerusalem. In addition, the repetition of the phrase "some [commentators] say" shows that this narrative was definitely influenced by various earlier sources.

In *Gen. Rab.* 42/1, the other "earlier" account, there is first no logical connection between Eliezer's fleeing to Yoḥanan b. Zakkai (who is in Jerusalem, as the double mention of the father's "coming up" implies and the other narratives explicitly state) and his cow's falling and injuring itself. The latter is proverbial for having good fortune.[106] Eliezer could just as well have then procured a new cow for plowing or have left for Jerusalem before even beginning to plow that day. Leaving an injured cow alone in the field represents him to the modern reader as irresponsible, yet this was certainly not the intention of the earlier source from which this motif came. Here it is reproduced only in part and therefore makes a strange impression. Second, Eliezer's father (he is nowhere called Hyrcanus here) strangely knows that he must "go up" (to Jerusalem) to find his son. It is nowhere indicated how he ascertains where his son is. Indeed, Eliezer simply fled from the field, leaving an injured cow there. This is another sign of an older tradition being incorporated into a larger narrative. Third, Eliezer's interpretation of Gen 14:15 and Ps 37:14 "is certainly nothing which would deserve to be retold by later generations of rabbis," as D. Damrosch correctly observes.[107] As I pointed out above, one must be well acquainted with the contents of Genesis 14 in order adequately to understand the connections Eliezer makes in his exposition.[108] This shows that later rabbis presupposed that the reader was acquainted with other "insider" or school material. The present account would read more smoothly if Eliezer's exposition were omitted. Then the father's "disinherit" speech would logically follow his coming (to Jerusalem) in order to disinherit Eliezer and his finding his son lecturing before the greatest of the land. Fourth, *Gen. Rab.* 42/1 begins with an implied tension between Eliezer's brothers, who together plow in the more easily tilled ground of the plain,

---

[106] J. Goldin calls my attention to *Sipre Num. Korach* § 119 on Num 18:20 (Kuhn, 404); *Lev. Rab. Vayyikra* 5/4, commenting on Prov 18:16 (Soncino, 4. 66-67); and *Eliyyahu Rabbah* 117 (Braude and Kapstein, 296). Cf. the German "Hals- und Beinbruch!"
[107] "Scripture and Fiction," 93.
[108] Damrosch calls attention to Kagan's weakness in this respect ("Scripture and Fiction," 93). She does not analyze the scriptural connections whatsoever.

while he alone plows on the mountain (which is stony). This tension, however, is not made explicit for the reader. The narrative also concludes with Eliezer's relationship to his brothers. The father is so impressed by Eliezer's lecturing as a rabbi before the greatest of the land that he wishes to give his now famous son "all his property." Yet Eliezer only wishes to take a share of the inheritance equal to that of his *brothers*. The narrative thus begins and ends with Eliezer's relationship to his brothers. It is only in the middle section that the figure of the father is developed, together with the inheritance motif. This is important to notice because it points to an earlier tradition informing the Eliezer narrative in which the tension between the brothers was not at the beginning implicit, but rather explicit. Because *'Abot R. Nat. B* 13 and *Pirqe R. El.* 2 have the other brothers encourage Hyrcanus to go to Jerusalem and disinherit Eliezer/vow that he will not enjoy any of the father's possessions, Kagan maintains that there is here a "shift of gravity from father to sons," and that in this respect *Tanḥuma B* is closer to these later accounts.[109]

This, however, is not tenable for *Tanḥuma B,* which Kagan herself calls a "unique variant," which in general is closer to the earliest accounts.[110] As in Gen. Rab. 42/1, in *Tanḥuma B* the other brothers are also mentioned at the very outset. Hyrcanus tells all the sons to rise and flee with him, "and his sons fled." Yet because Eliezer decided not to go with his father (and brothers), but instead fled to Jerusalem, the same tension as in *Gen. Rab.* 42/1 appears here at the outset between the brothers who stay at home with their father and the one brother who irresponsibly leaves the bonds of family – in this tradition not while plowing but during a time of danger from outside. When the brothers later encourage their father to disinherit Eliezer, this is only an elucidation of the tension already present from the very outset. No real "shift of gravity" occurs, for within their speech to the father an element of an earlier tradition shines through. They reproach him by saying: "You left your home and went after him [Eliezer]." This is illogical at this point because Hyrcanus has not yet been in Jerusalem seeking his wayward son. Before this the father is even distressed because *he* left Eliezer.

As pointed out above, other elements in *Tanḥuma B* also indicate diverse earlier traditions being employed here – for example, the "large banquet" given impoverished Eliezer by Yoḥanan b. Zakkai; the brothers' strange knowledge that Eliezer has settled in Jerusalem; the father's fear that Eliezer had gone off to a degenerate life. All of these,

---

[109]"Divergent Tendencies," 159.
[110]Ibid., 158.

plus the relatively large number of foreign loan words, point to the *Tanḥuma B* variant as incorporating several traditions that appear to be at least as early as (or even older than) those found in *'Abot R. Nat. A* 6 and *Gen. Rab.* 42/1, which in general show less development than *'Abot R. Nat. B* 13 and *Pirqe R. El.* 1-2. As noted, *'Abot R. Nat. A* 6 and *Gen. Rab.* 42/1 themselves have numerous literary seams and layers, which indicates that they too have incorporated various earlier traditions.

In the light of the above consideration of all five Eliezer narratives, including the motifs and terms deriving from Genesis 14, the biblical text commented upon in *Gen. Rab.* 42/1 and *Tanḥuma B Lech Lecha* 10, it seems very plausible that a well-known, and thus "floating," oral haggadic tradition, a folk tale, with the basic structure and the various motifs enumerated on pp. 68-75 above, was applied within the school of R. Eliezer at Lydda by devoted disciples to their master within decades after his death, that is, in the first half of the second century C.E. *Gen. Rab.* 42/1, containing the Eliezer narrative, begins, for example, with a quotation by his son Joshua in the name of R. Levi (bar Sisi), a fifth-generation Tanna.[111] R. Joshua b. Levi was a well-known haggadist active at the beginning of the third century C.E. at Lydda, the same location where R. Eliezer had his school.[112] The more the tradition developed within the Eliezer school, the more glorification of the master occurred – for example, his face shining like the sun and his "effulgence beaming like that of Moses" when he expounded the Torah in Jerusalem, so that one could not tell the difference between night and day.[113] A parallel phenomenon can be seen in the rapid development of the legendary material concerning R. Akiba's rise to fame from extreme poverty,[114] as well as in the same rapid development of legendary material concerning Jesus (for example, the "birth stories") now found in the four canonical Gospels, all completed within about seventy years after Jesus' death,[115] and in the apocryphal Gospels of the second and later centuries.

---

[111] See Strack and Stemberger, *Einleitung* 89-90 and 88 respectively.
[112] Ibid. 89. For Eliezer, Strack refers to *b. Sanh.* 32b (Soncino, 204). See also *Pesiq. Rab Kah.* 18/5 on Isa 54:12 for R. Joshua b. Levi as sitting on the teacher's chair in the great academy of Lydda. He is called the greatest man of his generation. See also *Pesiq. R.* 32/ 3.4.
[113] See *Pirqe R. El.* 2 (Friedlander, 7); and *'Abot R. Nat. B* 13 (Schechter, 32; Saldarini, 103).
[114] As Saldarini points out (98 n. 3), this may in part explain why stories regarding R. Akiba and R. Eliezer are adjacent to each other in *'Abot Rabbi Nathan B*.
[115] See, for example, R. Bultmann's discussion "Historical Stories and Legends" in *The History of the Synoptic Tradition* (New York: Harper & Row, 1963) 244-

Jesus' parable is special Lucan material, and the usual dating of this Gospel is between 70 and 90 C.E.[116] The overwhelming majority of scholars now maintain that, in spite of very minor Lucan stylistic changes, Jesus himself told this parable.[117] If this is true, Jesus' narrative dates at the latest to ca. 30 C.E.

Jesus' story of the Prodigal Son and the Forgiving Father is definitely not dependent on the presently known rabbinic traditions regarding R. Eliezer's rise to fame. Nor do the latter betray any dependence on Jesus' narrative. Thus, they most probably both borrow from a common oral folk tale containing the basic structure and the various motifs enumerated above, which then must have developed in different directions.[118] An original "fatted calf," for example, still found in Jesus' parable, has become a general term, "force-fed meat," or even "crammed poultry," in the *Tanhuma B* Eliezer story. In addition to the "degenerate life" of the Eliezer narrative, Jesus' story has a specific reference to "harlots." As noted above, Kagan, Neusner, and Saldarini have also called attention to specific inconsistencies and literary "seams" in the various Eliezer narratives,[119] and I have also commented on a number of others. All of these point to the haggadic material as being applied *later* to the famous head of the Lydda school. The rabbis borrowed from an earlier common oral tradition as well as from motifs and terminology found in Genesis 14, and they at once began to develop the original material in new directions based on the exigencies of the Eliezer "biography," for example the young man's studying in Jerusalem under Yoḥanan b. Zakkai. A new point was then made in the story: one who forsakes wealth and studies the Torah under adverse conditions (poverty, bad breath due to little food) not only attains fame as a rabbinic exegete but also (re-)gains riches. An even further development is that a scholar spurns silver and gold altogether; his only goal is to become worthy of learning and expounding the Torah.[120]

---

317. I do not deny that some or even much of the legendary material can have a historical basis.
[116]W. Kümmel, *Introduction to the New Testament* (14th ed.; Nashville: Abingdon, 1966) 106.
[117]See the discussion in section IV below.
[118]Jesus' parable is definitely not based on Deut 32:6-26, Mal 1:6a, and Deuteronomy 21-22, a suggestion made by J. Derrett in "Law in the New Testament: The Parable of the Prodigal Son," *NTS* 14 (1967-68) 56; see also 71 n. 11.
[119]See Kagan, "Divergent Tendencies," 158-70; Neusner, *Eliezer*, 1. 403-5, 441-42 (here Neusner speaks of "other stories" that appear to lie behind the *'Abot R. Nat. A* account), 445-46; and Saldarini, *The Fathers* 98-104 notes.
[120]See also Kagan, "Divergent Tendencies," 170; Neusner, *Eliezer*, 2. 404.

IV

If the above thesis is basically correct, we learn little about the historical Eliezer from the rabbinic traditions cited here concerning his becoming a scholar; they are basically fictional. At the most, they may indicate that he came from a wealthy family and that he was an illustrious disciple of Yoḥanan b. Zakkai in Jerusalem prior to 70 C.E. Thus, they could only corroborate what is maintained in other rabbinic sources.[121]

From the Eliezer traditions, however, we do learn several important things about Luke 15:11-32. Although C. Schöttgen in the eighteenth century had called attention to one similar motif in a rabbinic source,[122] and P. Billerbeck had commented on a number of individual expressions,[123] up till now no one had noted a specific rabbinic narrative with a significant number of structural, motif, and verbal connections to the parable of the Prodigal Son.

Taking up a suggestion of A. Adam, K. H. Rengstorf proposed that Luke 15:11-32 is closely related to the third-century Gnostic Hymn of the Pearl, now found in the *Acts of Thomas* – indeed, that they derive from a common source.[124] It cannot be denied that certain similarities do exist in plot and individual motifs, yet the differences by far outweigh these.[125] A much larger number of motif and verbal similarities are found in the rabbinic narrative of Eliezer's rise to fame.

---

[121]The almost total skepticism of J. Neusner, (*Eliezer* 2. 296), however, is unwarranted. He considers it unlikely that Eliezer was Yoḥanan's disciple (p. 405).

[122]See his *Horae hebraicae et talmudicae,* which refers to *Exod. Rab. Ki Thissa* 46/4 on Exod 34:1 (Soncino, 3. 530-31). Here the mercy of a physician father is stirred for a wayward son who later, when ill, acknowledges him as his true father. Yet a father's compassion is only one of a number of motifs in Luke 15:11-32. Schöttgen's volume is cited in *Exégesis: Problèmes de méthode et exercises de lecture (Genèse 22 et Luc 15)* (ed. F. Bovon and G. Rouiller; Bibliothèque Théologique; Neuchâtel and Paris: Delachaux & Niestlé, 1975) 52.

[123]See Str-B, 2. 212-17.

[124]*Re-Investitur,* 57-60. An English translation of the Hymn is offered in E. Hennecke and W. Schneemelcher, *New Testament Apocrypha* (Philadelphia: Westminster, 1965) 2. 498-504. For the dating, see G. Bornkamm's preface, 436 and 441.

[125]In the Hymn of the Pearl the parents of the little child deliberately make a covenant with him, sending him from the East to Egypt to bring home the one pearl in the midst of the sea in the abode of the loud-breathing serpent. Only if he performs this task, the fulfillment of his father's commands, will they return his splendid robe to him. The inhabitants of Egypt then deal treacherously with him, yet he receives so much food from them that he becomes sleepy. A letter from his family and the great ones of the East awakens him and reminds him of his task, which he then fulfills. The Joseph story has influenced this narrative in

In his recent commentary on Luke, W. Schmithals maintains that Hellenistic rhetoric is employed in Luke 15:11-32.[126] L. Schottroff, for example, had pointed out a very general similar motif regarding the redemption of sons captured by pirates in a declamation of (Pseudo-) Quintillian.[127] Yet this is, indeed, only very general. The rabbinic Eliezer sources offer much closer similarities.

Relying on H. Conzelmann, Schottroff also asserts that the parable of the Prodigal Son does not stem from Jesus, but from Luke himself. She believes it in part illustrates Luke 15:7, which she considers a statement by Luke the redactor.[128] The large number of motif and verbal parallels still found in the Eliezer narratives rather point to a Semitic, Jewish origin to the parable, and make it very improbable that the Hellenist Luke composed it. There are no indications that he knew either Hebrew or Aramaic. The parable more probably reached the evangelist via Greek-speaking Jewish Christianity.

Although J.T. Sanders finds major marks left by Luke the redactor in 15:11-32,[129] in the light of my own study I agree with the large majority of scholars who maintain that Luke made only minor changes in the language of the parable.[130]

It cannot be proved with absolute certainty that Jesus himself, and not some Aramaic-speaking Jewish Christian, told the parable of the Prodigal Son. Here too, however, I agree with the great majority of scholars in considering Jesus as the author. Under this assumption, in the light of the Eliezer narratives, the following remarks can also be made in regard to Jesus' emphases in the parable.

---

several places, for example in the motif of the boy's splendid robe of glorious colors.
[126]*Das Evangelium nach Lukas* (Züricher Bibelkommentare, 3.1; Zurich: Theologischer Verlag, 1980) 165.
[127]"Das Gleichnis," 45 n. 80.
[128]Ibid., 34.
[129]"Tradition and Redaction in Luke XV. 11-32," *NTS* 15 (1968-69) 433-38.
[130]See J. Jeremias's rebuttal of Sanders in "Tradition und Redaktion in Lukas 15," *ZNW* 62 (1971) 172-89; C.E. Carlston, "Reminiscence and Redaction in Luke 15:11-32," *JBL* 94 (1975) 368-90; F. Schnider, *Die verlorenen Söhne: Strukturanalytische und historischkritische Untersuchungen zu Lk 15* (Orbis biblicus et orientalis, 17; Göttingen: Vandenhoeck & Ruprecht, 1977); and I. Broer, "Das Gleichnis vom Verlorenen Sohn und die Theologie des Lukas," *NTS* 20 (1974) 459-60.

If Jesus addressed the Pharisees through the figure of the older brother, as maintained for example by A. Loisy[131] and E. Ellis,[132] he decisively modified a motif found in the oral folk tale available to him. There, as still reflected in Hyrcanus's offer to Eliezer in Jerusalem to give him a double portion or even the entire inheritance, excluding the other brothers, no effort is made on the part of the father also to placate and comfort the well-behaved and faithful son(s) who stay at home with their father. As I noted above, in Jesus' parable the opposite is true. In Luke 15:28 the father purposely leaves the banquet room in order to comfort/entreat the older brother, whom he later warmly calls "my son." He can understand his anger, his hurt feelings; yet he nevertheless takes the initiative in trying to make him understand that God is joyful not only over faithful people who never depart from his ways but also over those who sin and then "come to themselves," that is, who repent. In spite of the vehement condemnation of the Pharisees now found in stylized form in Matt 23:1-36 and Luke 11:37-52, Jesus refused to abandon these "religious zealots." Rather, he sought to win them over to a wider understanding of God's grace,[133] which was for all men and women, even for the "pious" people.

It has also been proposed that the two halves of the parable (15:11-24 and 25-32) did not originally belong together.[134] This is improbable in the light of the same division in the original folk tale, now still reflected in the *Tanḥuma B* Eliezer narrative.

On the basis of the Eliezer narratives, where the terms (although not the motif) are lacking, it also appears that the robe, ring, and shoes of Luke 15:22 are Jesus' own addition made to accentuate the father's joy. This is also indicated by 15:27, where the house slave informs the older brother, who has just returned from the field, only of the fatted calf slaughtered for the banquet. The robe, ring, and shoes are no longer mentioned.[135]

---

[131]*L'Evangile selon Luc* (Paris, 1924; reprint, Frankfurt am Main: Minerva, 1971) 403.
[132]Well stated in his *The Gospel of Luke* (New Century Bible; London: Oliphants, 1977) 198: "He does not judge the Pharisees but entreats them to appreciate the meaning of his associations."
[133]In the Gospels, a partial female counterpart of the older brother is Martha, who dutifully served while her sister sat and listened to Jesus; cf. Luke 10:38-42 and John 12:2-3. See also the remarks of those who bear the burden of the day and the scorching heat, who cannot understand the owner's generosity, in Jesus' parable of the Laborers in the Vineyard, Matt 20:1-15.
[134]See most recently Sanders, "Tradition," 438.
[135]As noted above, Jesus may have added them to emphasize the public nature of the father's reconciliation to his son, which would correspond to Hyrcanus's public reconciliation to Eliezer in the academy of Yoḥanan ben Zakkai before

It is also very questionable whether Luke 15:21-24 reflects a rite of readmittance, with confession of sins and absolution, as practiced by the early church.[136] The opposite is more probable: this was one of the NT passages that influenced the development of such a rite.

Whereas in one strand of the Eliezer tradition Hyrcanus at the end "rejoices" over his son, now found in Jerusalem, in Jesus' parable all should not only "be glad – rejoice" (15:32) but also be "merry." The repetition of the latter term in vv 23, 24, 29, and 32 shows Jesus' own accentuation of the motif of rejoicing. The repetition of all the father's words in Luke 15:23b-24 in v 32 also shows Jesus' own emphasis on the (earthly and divine) joy inherent in the lost becoming found, the spiritually dead becoming alive again. It is noteworthy that there are ten known parables by Jesus concerning the theme of God's mercy for sinners. Only regarding the motif of imminent judgment do more occur.[137]

This is how Jesus understood his own mission. He sought to proclaim God's joy not only over those who were not sick, who needed no physician because they were *already* righteous, but also over those who were spiritually sick and needed to be brought to repentance, to reconciliation with a forgiving and merciful Father. God's "amazing grace" was meant for *all*, even for prostitutes and tax collectors, who, like the prodigal son, associated with Gentiles. But it was also meant for the hardhearted, self-righteous righteous, who frowned upon such associations. It is for this reason that Jesus' parable even today speaks to our human situation, for all are addressed.[138]

Jesus was a good storyteller in spite of, and in part because of, the fact that he at times made use of contemporary popular material such as that still recognizable behind present rabbinic traditions on R. Eliezer's rise to fame. He was himself like a "householder who brings out of his treasure what is new and what is old" (Matt 13:52).[139]

"all Jerusalem." In contrast to K. Rengstorf (*Re-Investitur*, 57-60), I do not believe the three items derive from a common *Vorlage*, now ostensibly still observable in the Hymn of the Pearl.
[136]This is proposed by W. Schmithals, *Das Evangelium nach Lukas*, 166.
[137]See Jeremias, *Parables*, 124-46, and 160, middle. See also Flusser, *Die rabbinischen Gleichnisse*, 1. 58.
[138]This is well stated in a different way in regard to Luke 15 by L. Goppelt, *Theologie des Neuen Testamentes* (Göttingen: Vandenhoeck & Ruprecht, 1975) 1. 181.
[139]The imagery of "treasuring up new and old" derives from Cant 7:14. See Str-B, 1. 677, citing *b. 'Erub.* 21b (Soncino, 149), which has the "new" of this verse as the words of the scribes. See also *m. T. Yom.* 4:6 and *t. T. Yom.* 2:14 on the innovations of the scribes. For a further study of Jesus' parable of the Prodigal Son, cf. "Die Rückkehr des verlorenen Sohnes. Motive aus der

Josefsüberlieferung in Lukas 15, 11-32" in my *Weihnachtsgeschichte, Barmherziger Samariter, Verlorener Sohn.* Studien zu ihrem jüdischen Hintergrund (ANTZ 2; Berlin: Institut Kirche und Judentum, 1988) 126-73.

4

The Magi at the Birth of Cyrus, and the Magi at Jesus' Birth in Matt 2:1-12

The first scholarly book on the NT I laid hands on as a college freshman was *Understanding the New Testament,* by Howard Clark Kee and Franklin W. Young.[1] In gratitude for "heading me off in the right direction" so many years ago, I present the following study to Professor Kee with the hope that it will help elucidate one of the most popular, yet puzzling narratives in the NT, the visit to Jerusalem and Bethlehem of Magi (the "wise men" of the RSV) from the East in Matt 2:1-12.

As most commentators agree, the major background to all of Matt 2:1-23 is found in Jewish haggadic traditions on the endangered birth of Moses, Israel's first redeemer, in Exod 1:15-2:10. There Pharaoh, like Herod the Great, causes the death of innocent children so that he can retain the throne. Yet the baby Moses, like the baby Jesus, who is later to "save" Israel, miraculously escapes.[2] Another, though minor, part of the background may lie in the story of Balaam in Numbers 22-24, especially the "star of Jacob" in 24:17.[3]

---

[1] My copy was that of Englewood Cliffs, N.J.: Prentice-Hall, 1959.
[2] These traditions also provide the motif of the "census" at the time of Jesus' birth in Luke 2:1-7. See the chapter "Die Weihnachtsgeschichte im Lichte jüdischer Traditionen vom Mose-kind und Hirten-Messias (Lukas 2, 1-20)" in my *Weihnachtsgeschichte, Barmherziger Samariter, Verlorener Sohn.* Studien zu ihrem jüdischen Hintergrund (ANTZ 2; Berlin: Institut Kirche und Judentum, 1988), 11-58. The Matthean and Lucan birth stories are more closely related than generally thought.
[3] Cf. especially Leqaḥ Ṭob on Num 24:17, where the King, the Messiah, is this star, and Isa 60:6 is cited, a verse which also informs Matt 2:11 (see the margin of the Nestle Greek NT). It is translated by A. Wünsche as "Messias-Haggada" in *Aus Israels Lehrhallen* (Leipzig: 1907; reprint Hildesheim: Olms, 1967) 3.103-106, and in *Str-B* 2.298-99 and 1.96-97. In *The Birth of the Messiah* (Garden City, N.Y.: Doubleday, 1977) 190-96, R. Brown places special emphasis on the Balaam narrative. Yet U. Luz correctly points out that there is no clear reminiscence of the story in Matt 2:1-12. See his *Das Evangelium nach Matthäus (Mt 1-7)* (EKK 1/1; Zurich, etc., Benziger; Neukirchen-Vluyn: Neukirchener, 1985) 115. For recent and older secondary literature on Matt 2:1-12, see Luz 111 and 86.

However, "the motif of the Magi is the most difficult one," as E. Lohmeyer has stated."[4] Elsewhere in the NT a *Magos* is a negative figure, connected with magic.[5] Yet here in Matthew 2 the Magi are "wholly admirable," as R. Brown has aptly noted.[6]

How did they get into the Matthean birth narrative? I suggest that this was due primarily to their intimate connection with the birth of Cyrus of Persia, called by (Second) Isaiah the Lord's "Anointed One" or מְשִׁיחוֹ in 45:1. Indeed, the section Isa 44:24 to 45:25 was in many ways in the mind of "Matthew" when he composed 2:1-12 sometime at the end of the first century C.E.[7] Along with many other scholars, I consider Matthew to have been bilingual, or to have had at least a reading, working knowledge of Hebrew, as shown in his quotations of the "Old" Testament and in his Semitisms.[8] His familiarity with the Hebrew Bible also decisively influenced his knowledge of the Anointed One and Shepherd Cyrus, and thus also the content of Matt 2:1-12.

I shall begin this study by analyzing the Isaiah passage on Cyrus. After a brief portrait of the Persian king in Josephus, the rabbis and the pseudepigrapha, I shall point out the motif of Magi present at his birth. Finally, I shall note an event at the end of the sixties which most

---

[4]*Das Evangelium des Matthäus* (Meyer; Göttingen: Vandenhoeck & Ruprecht, 1962³) 20.
[5]Cf. Acts 13:6 and 8, as well as 8:9 and 11. See also the art. "Magos," etc. by G. Delling in *TDNT* 4.356-59. The work by G. Messina cited by him on 356 was a 1930 Berlin dissertation: *Der Ursprung der Magier und die zarathustrische Religion.* In addition, see S.V. McCasland, art. "Magi" in *IDB* 3.221-23.
[6]*The Birth* 168, after his statement that "There is not the slightest hint of conversion or of false practice in Matthew's description of the magi."
[7]For the dating, see W. Kümmel, *Einleitung in das Neue Testament* (Heidelberg: Quelle & Meyer, 1983²¹) 90, who maintains 80-100 C.E. See also F.W. Beare, *The Gospel According to Matthew* (Oxford: Blackwell, 1981) 7-8, and Luz, *Das Evangelium nach Matthäus (Mt 1-7)* 76 (not long after eighty). As Luz points out on p. 114, one can no longer get back to an earlier form of the content of Matt 2:1-12. I see no major obstacle to the gospel writer's having composed it himself on the basis of Jewish and non-Jewish traditions available to him.
[8]See, for example, Beare, *The Gospel* 10, who also posits a Greek- and Aramaic-speaking community, perhaps in Syria or Phoenicia, as the recipient of the gospel. In *Das Evangelium nach Matthäus* (NTD 2; Göttingen: Vandenhoeck & Ruprecht, 1956⁸) 17, J. Schniewind even maintained that Matt 2:1-12 was part of a section originally written in a Semitic language. There is, however, no proof of this. On possible Semitisms in 2:1-12, see the lack of the article in *en hēmerais* in v 1; *poreuthentes* in v 8; *akousantes tou basileôs* in v 9 (the Magi do not simply "hear" Herod, they "obey" his order, as in the Hebrew וַיִּשְׁמַע; thus "they obeyed the king and went their way"); and "they rejoiced with exceedingly great joy" in v 10. For Matthew's knowledge of the Hebrew text of Mic 5:1,3 and 2 Sam 5:2 in v 6, see below.

probably provided the decisive impetus for Matthew's use of Magi in his birth narrative.

I. Cyrus as Messiah and Shepherd

In 587 B.C.E. Jerusalem was captured and many Jews exiled to the Babylonia of Nebuchadnezzar. Yet at the latter ruler's death in 562, the empire's decline was rapid. During the reign of Nabonidus (556-39), Cyrus the Persian conquered the Medes (550), as well as Lydia in western Asia Minor (547/6). He thereby captured the tremendous amount of gold owned by Lydia's king, Croesus, in the capital of Sardis.[9]

It was in this setting that the unknown author of Isaiah 40-55 issued his words of consolation and new hope to the exiles of Babylonia. At the time of his writing 44:24-45:25, the defeat of Babylon by Cyrus was imminent. In fact, it occurred very shortly thereafter, in 539.[10] It was the prophet's firm belief that a new age, the eschatological period, was now dawning, Cyrus would play a pivotal role in it, and the nations would convert to belief in the one God, bringing their wealth to Jerusalem.

The form of the "Cyrus Oracle" in 44:24-45:13 is that of the Near Eastern royal oracle, which borrows its imagery from the ritual of a king's enthronement. Psalms 2 and 110, also applied by early Jewish Christians in the NT to their own Anointed One, Jesus, reflect the same pattern.[11]

In Isa 45:1, the author employs an image which was shocking for the Babylonian exiles. He labels Cyrus, a Gentile, the Lord's "Anointed One," the same term later used by Jews for the "Messiah." The LXX even states that he is "My [the Lord's] Anointed One."[12] This is the only occurrence in the Hebrew Bible of a Gentile being so designated. The

---

[9]For these dates, cf. J. Bright, *A History of Israel* (Philadelphia: Westminster, 1959) 324 and 334-35. On Croesus' gold and other great wealth, see Herodotus 1.30,51-52,92-93,153-54; 6.125; and 8.35.

[10]Bright, *A History* 342.

[11]C. Westermann, *Das Buch Jesaja. Kapitel 40-66* (ATD 19; Göttingen: Vandenhoeck & Ruprecht, 1981[4]) 125, 128. He limits the royal oracle itself to 45:1-4. J. Muilenburg in "The Book of Isaiah, Chapters 40-66," in *The Interpreter's Bible* 5 (New York: Abingdon, 1956) has 44:24-45:13 as the extent of the entire Cyrus oracle, yet notes (p. 528) that "Many scholars consider vv 14-25 a continuation of 44:28-45:13." He states (p. 529) that Jerome, Ibn Ezra, Grotius, Skinner, Mowinckel and others see Cyrus addressed in 45:14, the importance of which will be shown shortly. Of course, Matthew was unburdened by present-day scholarship's division of Isaiah; he read it as a whole. Isa 45:23 is alluded to in the pre-Pauline hymn in Phil 2:10-11; see also Rom 14:11.

[12]*Isaias*, Göttingen Septuaginta 14, ed. J. Ziegler (Göttingen: Vandenhoeck & Ruprecht, 1967[2]) 290.

Lord has grasped Cyrus' right hand, subduing nations before him, and conquering other kings. This decision of God, although greatly unusual, should not be questioned by the skeptical Babylonian Jews (45:9-13). Cyrus is indeed God's chosen instrument, as expressed in different terms elsewhere.[13]

In 45:3 the Lord promises to give Cyrus the "treasures of darkness and the hoards in secret places," perhaps a reference to future booty like the captured gold and other wealth of King Croesus of Sardis.[14]

God will employ Cyrus to rebuild the ravaged Temple (44:28) and the city of Jerusalem (45:13). The Persian will also set free the Lord's exiles in Babylon (also v 13). Yet through Cyrus' activity *all men,* "from the rising of the sun and from the west," are to know that there is no other God than the Lord (45:6; cf. vv 22-23). Second Isaiah's vision is truly universalistic, including both Jews and Gentiles. Indeed, he even has God speak of the Gentiles as "my children," "the work of my hands" (v 11).

In 45:14 the prophet employs the fem. sing. for the addressed subject, the city of Jerusalem. Egypt's wealth, Ethiopia's merchandise, and the Sabeans, from southwest Arabia,[15] on their way from Africa and Arabia along the coastal plain of Palestine, shall come over to Jerusalem and be hers.[16] They shall come over to her, "bow down to her," and "make supplication to her," acknowledging Israel's God as the only God.

This Isaianic verse influenced Matt 2:1-12 in a major way. First, I suggest Matthew read the Hebrew אנשי מדה not as "men of measure," meaning "of stature," "tall," from מִדָּה. Rather, he employed the common form of exegesis: "Read not מדה, but" אנשי מדי, "men of Media," "Medes,"

---

[13]Cf. "one from the east whom victory meets at every step" in 41:2; "a bird of prey from the east, the man of my counsel from a far country" in 46:11; and "The Lord loves him" in 48:14.

[14]In Est. Rab. 2/1 on Est 1:4 (Soncino English 9.33-34), God reveals all the money in the world, which Nebuchadnezzar had amassed and hidden in the Euphrates, to Cyrus on the day he decrees the Temple should be rebuilt. Isa 45:3's "treasures of darkness" and "hidden riches" are so interpreted. This is said by R. Tanḥuma, a fifth generation Palestinian Amora. See H. Strack and G. Stemberger, *Einleitung in Talmud und Midrasch* (Munich: Beck, 1982⁷) 100.

[15]Cf. G. Van Beek, art. "Sabeans," in *IDB* 4.144-46, who notes the intimate relationship with Sheba/Seba. See also D. Harvey, art. "Sheba, Queen of," in *IDB* 4.311-12. Interestingly, in his "Dialogue with Trypho" 77-78, Justin Martyr says five times that the Magi come from Arabia. Could he have had Isa 45:14 in mind?

[16]In Isa 43:3, these three nations had been given to Cyrus by God as a ransom for the Babylonian exiles. For this interpretation of 45:14, I follow G. Fohrer, *Das Buch Jesaja. 3. Band, Kapitel 40-66* (Zurich: Zwingli, 1964) 92.

from מִדַּי.[17] That is, not only the Arabian Sabeans are to bring Cyrus, the Anointed One, presents. The Medes, who come from the home of the Magi, as to be seen below, also are to come with their gifts to Jerusalem. While this may seem far-fetched to the modern reader, it was not then. It was a standard method of Jewish exegesis, and Matthew does the same type of thing in his use of Mic 5:1 in Matt 2:6. I shall point out the latter below.

Secondly, C. Westermann notes the "exact correspondence" of Isa 45:14 to Isaiah 60, where the nations bring their treasures to Zion and bow down at her feet (v 14).[18] Following not only the general similarities of these two chapters from the end of Isaiah, but also the catchword Seba/Sheba, Matthew appropriated from 60:6 the gold and frankincense to be brought by all those of Sheba to Jerusalem. The LXX may have encouraged him to do so, for it then reads: "they shall proclaim as good news *(euangeliountai)* the salvation of the Lord." In addition, the Greek form of "your" *(sou)* is not feminine, as in the Hebrew, but applied to all genders, allowing the addressee to change from Jerusalem to Jesus.[19] Matthew's Magi from the east bring gold and frankincense as two of their three gifts to the king of the Jews (Matt 2:11).[20] They also expect him in Jerusalem. Indeed, they must be told to seek him elsewhere (Matt 2:1,5).

Isa 60:6 is also connected with the coming of the Messiah in the late Midrashim Bereshit Rabbati on Gen 25:19,[21] and Leqaḥ Ṭob on Num 24:17.[22]

---

[17]For a different wordplay on *middah,* see m. Ber. 9:5 in H. Danby, *The Mishnah* (London: Oxford University, 1964) 10. "The Medes" and "the men of the East" are also variants of the same saying by Rabban Simeon b. Gamaliel II, a third generation Tanna (Strack and Stemberger, *Einleitung* 84). See, for example, Gen. Rab. Vayetze 74/2 on Gen 31:4 (Soncino English 2.677), and Eccl. Rab. 7:23 §1 (Soncino 8.203). Matt 2:1 speaks of magi "from the East," a motif repeated in vv 2 and 9. For a Jewish-Christian with knowledge of Hebrew, they thus could be thought of as Medes.
[18]*Das Buch Jesaja* 138.
[19]This applies, of course, also to Isa 45:14.
[20]The third gift, myrrh, is used to scent the robes of God's anointed one, his king, in Ps 45:8. It is thus also a gift fit for a king. For myrrh and frankincense together, see Cant 3:6; 1 Enoch 29:2; and Tanḥuma B Vayera on Gen 18:1. I have an extensive discussion of rabbinic and other Jewish sources on the gifts to be made to the Messiah, at the time the nations flock to Jerusalem, in "Paul's Travel Plans to Spain and the 'Full Number of the Gentiles' of Rom. XI 25" in *NT* 21 (1979) 232-62, here pp. 163-191.
[21]Ch. Albeck, ed., *Midrash Bereshit Rabbati* (Jerusalem: Mekize Nirdamin, 1940) 102-03. Here the Sabeans are descendants of Abraham via Jokshan in Gen 25:3.
[22]See n. 3 above.

Thirdly, Isa 45:14 also speaks of the nations "bowing down" and "making supplication" to Jerusalem. The Hebrew of "bowing down" is the Hithpa. of שָׁחָה, translated by the LXX as *proskyneô*. The same Greek verb is found in Matt 2:2 and 11 of the Magis' "doing obeisance" to the newborn king, Jesus, and in v 8 of King Herod's deceitful desire to do the same. This threefold mention of the motif of obeisance shows how important it was for Matthew.

The RSV translates *proskyneô* here in Matthew 2 with "to worship," yet the baby Jesus is not worshiped by the Magi as a god. He is for them a king (v 2), and in the Near East one "does obeisance" primarily to kings. For example, 2 Sam (2 Kgdms) 9:6 says Mephibosheth came to King David "and fell on his face and did obeisance." He did not "worship" David; only God is worshiped.[23] The Magi also "fell down" and "did obeisance" to Jesus in Matt 2:11, who is the king of the Jews (v 2), as well as the son of David (1:2; v 6–the king).

Something else which was probably also influential here is the fact that in rabbinic Hebrew, the Messiah is usually designated "the King, the Messiah" (מלך המשיח). Considered by his followers to be the Messiah, Jesus was thus almost automatically also thought to be a "king."

This scene of obeisance in Matthew 2 stands in intentional contrast to the crucifixion in chapter 27, the only other place in the gospel where Jesus is described as King of the Jews (vv 11,29,37) and King of Israel (v 42).[24] There, like the Magi, Gentiles also "fall on their knees" before him (v 29). Yet Pilate's soldiers merely mock the "King of the Jews" before their whole batallion (vv 27-31).[25]

Finally, Cyrus is not only designated the Lord's "Anointed One" by Second Isaiah in 45:1. The prophet also has God say: "He is my shepherd" (רעי; 44:28). The targum translates: "that saith of Cyrus that he will give to him the kingdom" (מלכו).[26] This emphasizes the shepherd's rule, as elsewhere.[27] The LXX also avoids the term "shepherd," translating: "He who says to Cyrus, 'Be wise.'" To my knowledge there is not one single rabbinic citation of this verse, which is

---

[23]Against H. Greeven, who in his art. *proskyneô* etc. in *TDNT* 6.763 states: "When the NT uses *proskynein*, the object is always something – truly or supposedly – divine."

[24]Matt 21:5 also applies the term king to Jesus, yet it is a quotation of Zech 9:9.

[25]Mark 15:19 has *proskyneô*. Here the RSV translates better: "they knelt down in homage to him."

[26]J. Stenning, *The Targum of Isaiah* (Oxford: Clarendon, 1949) 152-53.

[27]See, for example, Jer 23:1-5. The "shepherds of Israel" in Ezekiel 34 are also its kings.

very probably due to Christian emphasis on Jesus as the "good shepherd."[28]

It is also worthwhile noting that the only other example of a shepherd king G. Fohrer gives in his commentary on Isa 44:28 is 2 Sam 5:2. There the Israelite tribes tell David at Hebron: "The Lord said to you, 'You shall be shepherd (תרעה) of my people Israel, and you shall be prince (נָגִיד) over Israel."

It is precisely this biblical verse which Matthew quotes in slightly modified form in 2:6. First he took the LXX's *hēgoumenos* (leader, guide, ruler) from 2 Kgdms 5:2b and added to it Mic 5:1's "Out of you shall come." He could have employed the term *archōn* (ruler) from Micah, but purposely chose the 2 Kgdms 5:2b expression. He then rewrote the LXX's "You shall shepherd" to "who shall shepherd," and continued on with "my people Israel."

I suggest that bilingual Matthew selected imagery from 2 Kgdms 5:2 precisely because he had the Cyrus oracle in mind for all of 2:1-12. In Second Isaiah the Persian is not only the Lord's "Anointed One," he is also God's "Shepherd." Matthew knew his Hebrew (and Greek) Bible just as well as modern-day commentators do with the aid of their concordances, and he, like them, naturally thought of 2 Sam 5:2 in regard to the "shepherd" king, David.

Matthew's modifications of Mic 5:1 (Eng. 2) in 2:6 have often been adequately described elsewhere. It suffices to note here that they also betray his knowledge of how the Hebrew text can be read in various ways through different vocalization.[29] There is thus no compelling reason to posit a collection of "messianic testimonies" here, as proposed by some commentators.[30] Via the catchword "shepherd," Matthew associated Isa 44:28 and 2 Sam 5:2. Since the ruler of Israel, to come forth from Bethlehem, also shall "shepherd" (וְרָעָה) his flock in Mic 5:3 (Eng. 4), Matthew could also easily employ imagery from the neighboring v 1 (Eng. 2). He knew that Jesus grew up in Galilean Nazareth (Matt 2:23).[31] Yet the messiah, the son of David, according to

---

[28]See J. Jeremias, art. *poimēn* etc. in *TDNT* 6.489.
[29]See, for example, Klostermann, *Das Matthäusevangelium* 15, and Lohmeyer, *Das Evangelium des Matthäus* 23. One instance is אַלְפֵי, "thousands," "families," read as אַלֻּפֵי "chiefs," "princes." See *BDB* 49 on both.
[30]A. McNeile, *The Gospel According to St. Matthew* (New York: St. Martin's, 1965; original 1915) 16; Lohmeyer, *Das Evangelium des Matthäus* 23; and W. Grundmann, *Das Evangelium nach Matthäus* (THKNT 1; Berlin: Evangelische Verlagsanstalt, 1975⁴) 78.
[31]See 13:53-58, where *patris* can also mean "home town" (BAGD 636-37). Nazareth is clearly meant, as in Luke 4:16.

strong Jewish traditions was to be born in Bethlehem of Judea.[32] Mic 5:1 helped the evangelist get Jesus there.

* * *

If the above suggestions are basically correct, this means that Isa 44:24-45:25 provided Matthew with his motifs of the messianic king and shepherd, to whom gifts would be made, also by Medes, and to whom Gentiles would do obeisance in Jerusalem.

Before analyzing the other major motif in Matt 2:1-12, the Magi, it is helpful first to see how Cyrus is viewed in other Jewish writings.

II. Cyrus in Josephus, the Rabbis and the Pseudepigrapha

A. Josephus

In *Bell.* 5.389 (9.4) Josephus urges the Jerusalemites to surrender in their war with the Romans in 70 C.E. One episode he recalls to them from Israel's history is that of Cyrus: "You know, moreover, of the bondage in Babylon, where our people passed seventy years in exile and never reared their heads for liberty *(eleutheria)*, until Cyrus granted it in gratitude to God...." Through Cyrus the Jews were allowed to reestablish their Temple worship in Jerusalem.[33]

In *Ant.* 20.233 (10.2) most of this statement is repeated; here Cyrus "freed" *(apolyô)* the Jews from Babylon.

Cyrus' "gratitude to God" in Josephus is based on Ezra 1:1-2 (= 2 Chr 36:22-23), where the Lord stirs up the Persian king to make a proclamation throughout all his kingdom: "The Lord, the God of heaven, has given me all the kingdoms of the earth, and he has charged me to build him a house at Jerusalem...." In v 3 the Jews of Babylonia are encouraged to go up to Jerusalem and rebuild the Temple.

Thus according to both scriptural and Jewish tradition it was God himself who commissioned Cyrus, his Anointed One and Shepherd, to free the Jews from their Babylonian captivity and to rebuild the Temple.

Josephus paraphrases this Ezra passage in *Ant.* 11.4 (1.1):

> Since the Most High God has appointed me king *(basileus)* of the habitable world, I am persuaded that He is the god whom the Israelite nation worships, for He foretold my name through the prophets and that I should build His temple in Jerusalem in the land of Judea.[34]

---

[32]See John 7:42 and the rabbinic and targumic passages cited by T. Zahn, *Das Evangelium des Matthäus* (Leipzig: Deichert, 1910³) 96.
[33]I employ the *LCL* edition of Josephus, here translated by H. St. J. Thackeray.
[34]English translation by R. Marcus.

Josephus then comments on this statement of Cyrus:

> These things Cyrus knew from reading the book of prophecy which Isaiah had left behind two hundred and ten years earlier. For this prophet had said that God told him in secret, "It is my will that Cyrus, whom I shall have appointed king *(basileus)* of many great nations, shall send my people to their own land and build my temple" (11.5; 1.2).

Here Josephus, or the source he employs, interprets the Shepherd and Anointed One of Isa 44:28-45:1 to mean that Cyrus is the king commissioned by God to carry out his purpose. This is buttressed by the continuation of Josephus' remarks: "And so, when Cyrus read them [Isaiah's prophecies], he wondered at the divine power and was seized by a strong desire and ambition to do what had been written" (11.6; 1.2). He then summoned the leading Babylonian Jews and allowed them to return to Judea and rebuild the Temple.

Writing at the end of the first century C.E., and thus as a contemporary of Matthew, Josephus in his description of Cyrus thus positively associates the Persian with "liberating" the Jews from their Babylonian captivity. He also connects this liberation event with the Cyrus oracle of Isa 44:24-45:13.

B. The Rabbis

With the exception of b. Meg.12a, where Isa 45:1 is interpreted of God's raising a complaint with the Messiah against Cyrus,[35] rabbinic sources generally give a very positive portrait of the Persian king.[36] In Eliyyahu Rabbah 20 it is stated, for example: "The Holy One brought the kingdom of Media into the world and put up with it only as a reward for Cyrus, who wept and sighed when the heathen destroyed the Temple."[37] In b. Roš. Haš. 3b a tannaitic tradition says that "Cyrus" was so called because he was a "worthy" king, a wordplay on "Koresh" and

---

[35] Soncino English 67. This is said in the name of R. Naḥman b. R. Ḥisda, a third generation Babylonian Amora (Strack and Stemberger, *Einleitung* 96).

[36] This agrees with Herodotus 3.89, where in contrast to the huckster Darius and the imperious Cambyses, Cyrus is labeled by the Persians "the father," "for he was kind and always brought about good things for them."

[37] Hebrew in M. Friedmann, *Seder Eliahu and Seder Eliahu Zuta (Tanna d'be Eliahu), Pseudo-Seder Eliahu Zuta* (Jerusalem: Wahrmann, 1969³; original Vienna, 1904) 114. The same Hebrew consonants appear in "as a reward for" and "Cyrus." English in W. Braude and I. Kapstein, *Tanna debe Eliyyahu* (Philadelphia: Jewish Publication Society of America, 1981) 289.

"kasher," which have the same consonants.[38] In Cant. Rab. 2:13 §3, R. Joḥanan, a second generation Palestinian Amora,[39] comments on v 12: "The turtle-dove (תּוֹר) is heard in our land." He says this is Cyrus, the good "explorer" (תָּיָּר).[40] Shortly after this, in §4 on "the voice of the turtle-dove," it is stated that this is the voice of the King Messiah, who calls out and says: "How beautiful upon the mountains are the feet of the messenger of good tidings" (Isa 52:7).[41]

In the latter passage we see how Cyrus, who according to Josephus was to "liberate" the Jews from Babylonia, could be described with the same imagery as the Messiah. Other rabbinic passages corroborate this. In Pirqe R. El. 11, ten kings are mentioned who have ruled or will rule from one end of the world to the other. On the basis of Ezra 1:2 (= 2 Chr 36:23), Cyrus is listed as the seventh king. The ninth, before God's final rule, will be the King Messiah, as Ps 72:8 and Dan 2:35 are interpreted.[42]

In Mek. Pisḥa 7 on Exod 12:11 ("And ye shall eat it in haste"), R. Eliezer (b. Hyrcanus), a second generation Tanna,[43] says this haste at the Exodus event is that of the Shekinah, the divine presence. To buttress this, he quotes Cant 2:8-9. Then he asks: One could think that in the time to come it [the deliverance] will be in haste. He then cites Isa 52:12 to disprove this.[44]

This Mekilta text shows that Cant 2:8-9 was associated with the future redemption at a very early date. Cant. Rab. 2:8 §3 states that

---

[38]Soncino English 9. See also the similar statement before this by R. Abbahu, a third generation Palestinian Amora (Strack and Stemberger, *Einleitung* 94); Soncino English 8.
[39]Strack and Stemberger, *Einleitung* 91.
[40]Soncino English 9.125. The Hebrew is found in S. Donski, *Midrash Rabbah, Shir ha-Shirim* (Heb.) (Jerusalem: Dvir, 1980) 70. A parallel is found in Pesiq. Rav Kah. 5/9. English in W. Braude and I. Kapstein, *Pesikta de-Rav Kahana* (Philadelphia: Jewish Publication Society of America, 1975) 108. The Hebrew is found in B. Mandelbaum, *Pesikta de Rav Kahana* (New York: Jewish Theological Seminary of America, 1962) 1.96. The same tradition is also found in Pesiq. R. 15/13. English in W. Braude, *Pesikta Rabbati* (New Haven: Yale University, 1968) 1.325. The Hebrew is found in M. Friedmann, *Pesikta Rabbati* (Vienna, 1880; reprint Tel Aviv, 1962/63) 74b.
[41]Donski, 71; Soncino English 9.125-26. Parallels are found in Pesiq. Rav Kah. 5/9 (Braude and Kapstein 109; Mandelbaum 97, also in the name of R. Joḥanan), and Pesiq. R. 15/14.15 (Braude 1.326; Friedmann 75a).
[42]English in G. Friedlander, *Pirke de Rabbi Eliezer* (London: 1916; reprint New York: Hermon, 1970) 82-83. See also the relevant notes. The translation is based on a MS which belonged to A. Epstein of Vienna (xiv).
[43]Strack and Stemberger, *Einleitung* 77.
[44]See the Hebrew and an English translation in J. Lauterbach, *Mekilta de-Rabbi Ishmael* (Philadelphia: Jewish Publication Society of America, 1976) 1.52-53.

"my beloved," who "comes," is the Messiah.⁴⁵ Other comment on 2:9 compares the Exodus redemptive event and the future redemption, as well as the first deliverer of Israel (Moses) and the future or final deliverer (the Messiah).⁴⁶

In Cant. Zuta 2:9 it is stated that the Messiah is he who "looks through the windows." For him the gates of the east will open as soon as he comes, as it is written, "Who stirred up one from the east, on his step righteousness will follow" (Isa 41:2).⁴⁷ The Messiah is of the descendants of David, for which Ps 89:37 (Eng. 36) is quoted. When the final time (קץ) will have arrived, God will stir him up from the north and east (Isa 41:25). Finally, Isa 45:1 is interpreted to mean that the gates of the east and the south (in Jerusalem) will be opened to him.⁴⁸

This midrashic comment cannot be dated. However, it follows the same line of interpretation of Cant 2:(8-)9 as found in the tannaitic Mekilta, applying the verse(s) to the future redemption and the Messiah. Most importantly, it applies imagery employed of Cyrus in Isa 45:1 and elsewhere to the Messiah. This shows that Matthew, a Jewish Christian, could have done the very same thing.⁴⁹

C. The Pseudepigrapha

Chapter fifteen of "The Lives of the Prophets," a work according to D. Hare most probably Palestinian and from the beginning of the first century C.E.,⁵⁰ deals with Zechariah. In v 4 it is stated regarding the prophet while he is still in Chaldea: "And concerning Cyrus he gave a portent of his victory, and prophesied regarding the service which he

---

⁴⁵Soncino English 9.117. Parallels are found in Pesiq. R. 15/7 (Braude 1.316), and Pesiq. Rav Kah. 5/7 (Braude and Kapstein 101).
⁴⁶Cf. Cant. Rab. 2:9 §§ 1, 3-4 (Soncino 9.118-21). See also Num. Rab. Naso 11/2 on Num 6:23 (Soncino 5.412-13).
⁴⁷In the original setting, צדק meant victory; here it more probably stresses the Messiah's righteousness.
⁴⁸See S. Buber, *Midrasch Suta*. Haggadische Abhandlungen über Schir ha-Schirim, Ruth, Echah und Koheleth (Berlin: 1893/94; reprint Tel Aviv 1963/64) 24.
⁴⁹See also Yalqut Shem'oni § 1085 on 2 Chr 36:23, which states on the basis of a "midrash": "In this world you were saved by flesh and blood [Cyrus] and return and do service, but in the world to come you will be saved by God with an eternal redemption." In Midr. Ps. 7/17 on Ps 7:1, the redemption under Cyrus (2 Chr 36:22-23) is compared with the future redemption (Isa 63:4). English in W. Braude, *The Midrash on Psalms* (New Haven: Yale University, 1959) 1.115-16. The Hebrew is found in S. Buber, *Erläuterungen der Psalmen Haggada* (Vilna: Romm, 1891; reprint Jerusalem, 1965-66) 71.
⁵⁰J. Charlesworth, ed., *The Old Testament Pseudepigrapha* (Garden City, N.Y.: Doubleday, 1985) 2.380-81. Chapter fifteen is on p. 394.

was to perform for Jerusalem, and he blessed him greatly." Then in v 5 Zechariah's "twofold judgment" is mentioned. As Hare notes in the margin, this can only refer to Zech 9:12.

Yet nowhere in our texts of Zechariah does the prophet refer to Cyrus. I suggest that the author(s) of "The Lives of the Prophets" knew of a Jewish tradition which applied 9:9-10 to him, verses adjacent to v 12, which is definitely alluded to. Here Jerusalem is told: "Lo, your king comes to you; triumphant (צַדִּיק) and victorious is he.... He shall command peace to the nations; his dominion shall be from sea to sea, and from the [Euphrates] River to the ends of the earth."

This well-known passage was applied by the rabbis to the Messiah, and by the gospel writers to the Messiah Jesus at his entry into Jerusalem.[51] It is indeed a "great blessing," which could have been interpreted as a portent of Cyrus' victory, including worldwide dominion.

If this is true, it again shows how a biblical text usually applied to the Messiah could also be applied to the Lord's "Anointed One," Cyrus.

Sib. Or. 3.285-86 also states:

> And then the heavenly God will send a king and will judge each man in blood and the gleam of fire. There is a certain royal tribe whose race will never stumble. This, too, as time pursues its cyclic course, will reign, and it will begin to raise up a new temple of God. All the kings of the Persians will bring to their aid gold and bronze and much-wrought iron. For God himself will give a holy dream by night and then indeed the temple will again be as it was before.[52]

J. Collins dates book three of the Sibylline Oracles as written ca. 160-50 B.C.E.; it was definitely composed by Egyptian Jews.[53] He believes that Cyrus is most probably meant here, and the "royal tribe" is the Jews. He also calls attention to Isa 44:27-45:1 in the margin.[54]

"A holy dream by night" most probably refers to Daniel 7, the vision which this official of Cyrus (6:28; 10:1; Bel 1-2) had "by night": vv 1, 2, 7 and 13. In Cant. Rab. 3:4 §2,[55] regarding the Babylonian kingdom's being given over to the Medes and Persians (Dan 5:28), it is related that the Israelites ask Daniel when the seventy years of Jer 29:10 are to be accomplished. At that time they are to return to Jerusalem (and rebuild

---

[51] See *Str-B* 1.842-44 on Matt 21:5, as well as John 12:15.
[52] J. Charlesworth, *The Old Testament Pseudepigrapha* (1983) 1.368.
[53] Charlesworth 1.355-56.
[54] Charlesworth 1.368. See also his reference to Sib. Or. 5.108 (p. 395) on Cyrus as "a certain king sent from God." In 1.355, n. 11, reference is made to an article by J. Nolland, who considers Sib. Or. 3.282-94 to refer to a Davidic messiah.
[55] Soncino English 9.145.

the Temple with Cyrus' permission). Daniel asks for a copy of Isaiah and reads until 21:1, including the word "sea." Since Isa 21:1-10 is an oracle regarding the fall of Babylon, it is connected here by the rabbis to the night vision of the rise and fall of the four world kingdoms, including the Babylonian, by the catchword "sea" in Dan 7:2-3. Dan 7:3 and 15 are then quoted in this midrash.[56]

A variant of this tradition is found in Midrash Panim Aḥerim 2 on Est 1:12.[57] There Darius, in phraseology dependent on Isa 21:5, tells Cyrus: "Arise and take the kingdom. You are worthy of it because Daniel says regarding you that you should take it." Daniel had told Cyrus, who was on the official staff[58] of Belshazzar, that in the future God would give him the kingdom. In addition, Isaiah had already prophesied regarding Cyrus that he would reign and give permission to rebuild the Temple, as Isa 45:1 is interpreted.[59]

The above midrashim, connecting the rebuilding of the Temple under Cyrus, Isa 45:1, and the night vision of Daniel 7, provide a probable explanation of the above passage from the Sibylline Oracles, where after a "night dream" the Temple will be rebuilt. If so, Josephus' statement in *Ant.* 11.4 that God foretold Cyrus' name through the prophets (pl.) would include not only Isaiah and Zechariah, but also Daniel. Although the book of Daniel in the Hebrew Bible is found in the hagiographa and not with the prophets, he was definitely considered a prophet by Josephus[60] and the Palestinian rabbis.[61]

III. The Magi at the Birth of Cyrus

The Greek historian Herodotus of Halicarnassus, born at the beginning of the fifth century B.C.E.,[62] writes in his first book of the very unusual birth of Cyrus. At the very end of his life, for example, the king was eager to lead his army against an enemy for many weighty reasons,

---

[56]Ibid., and 147.
[57]S. Buber, *Aggadic Books on the Scroll of Esther* (Hebrew; Vilna: Romm, 1886) 60.
[58]See S. Krauss, *Griechische und lateinische Lehnwörter in Talmud, Midrasch und Targum* (Berlin: Calvary, 1898-99) 2.1 on אאפיקין as *officium*, "der Beamtenstab."
[59]For part of this discussion, see also Est. Rab. 3/4 §2 in Soncino 9.148.
[60]Cf., for example, *Ant.* 10.246, 249, 266-67 (his books, probably the "additions" to Daniel).
[61]See the sources cited in L. Ginzberg, *The Legends of the Jews* (Philadelphia: Jewish Publication Society of America, 1968) 6.413, n. 76. In the LXX the Daniel writings follow the prophet Ezekiel.
[62]Cf. the *LCL* edition of his nine books, translated by A. Godley. For the dating, see I, vii.

the first among them being "his birth, whereby he seemed to be something more than mortal man" (1.204).

Herodotus relates Cyrus' birth as follows. His grandfather, the Median king Astyages, had a dream about his daughter Mandane. Enough water flowed from her to fill his city and overflow all Asia. Having asked those Magi who interpret dreams to ascertain its meaning, he was terrified *(phobeomai)*. When his daughter grew old enough to marry, he still "feared" *(deidô)* the vision. Instead of marrying her to a Mede, he therefore chose a Persian named Cambyses as his son-in-law.

In the first year of his daughter's marriage, Astyages saw a second vision:

> He dreamt that there grew from his daughter a vine, which covered the whole of Asia. Having seen this vision, and imparted it to the interpreters of dreams, he sent to the Persians for his daughter, then near her time, and when she came, kept her guarded, desiring to kill whatever child she might bear: for the interpreters declared that the meaning of his dream was that his daughter's offspring should rule in his place.

In order to prevent the grandson's usurpation of his kingship, Astyages then summoned his most faithful servant and steward Harpagus to take the newborn son, kill it, and bury it. However, Harpagus instead gave the infant to a cowherd in the mountains. His wife had just given birth to a stillborn child, which they then substituted for Cyrus, placing the infant in an *angos,* a cradle/coffin, and exposing it in the most desolate part of the mountains.

Having discovered that he was tricked by Harpagus, Astyages in revenge had the latter's own son slaughtered and cunningly made him eat of the flesh. Then he again called the Magi and asked them to repeat their interpretation of his vision. "They answered as before, and said that the boy must have been made king *(basileusai)* had he lived and not died first." Astyages then informed the Magi that Cyrus was indeed alive, and his boyfriends had made him king in a game, which role he played very well. Concerned that Astyages' rule *(archê)* should continue, the Magi declared their prophecy fulfilled in this game. Thereupon the king released his grandson. Cyrus, however, later became head of the Persian army and defeated that of the Medes. Because the Magi who interpret dreams had persuaded Astyages to let Cyrus go free, he at this point impaled them.

Referring to the above events in his speech to the Persians in order to get them to join his army and fight the Medes, Cyrus argued: "For I think that I myself was born by a marvelous providence to take this work in hand."⁶³

The above narrative resembles that of King Herod and the Magi in Matt 2:1-12 (and 13-23) in many respects. Magi inform the ruling king that a child to be born soon will become king (Matt 2:2). In order to prevent this, the terrified king (2:3) orders the child to be killed (2:13). Yet it miraculously escapes (2:14), whereupon the king takes terrible revenge (2:16).

Herodotus admits in 1.95 (cf. 214) that already in his time there were three other accounts of Cyrus which he could have given, presumably also including the future king's miraculous birth. Other early writers seem to have known additional, or different, sources.⁶⁴

Elsewhere (7.37) Herodotus notes that the Magi not only interpreted dreams. They also concerned themselves, for example, with celestial phenomena for King Xerxes. The Greek historian states that while the sun is the prophet of the Greeks, for the Magi it is the moon. That is, they deal primarily with the nocturnal heavens. When the Magi from the east in Matt 2:2 state that they have seen (at night) the star of him born king of the Jews and then follow it (at night) to Bethlehem in vv 8-9, it thus belonged to a normal realm of their concern.

I suggest that Matthew was aware of the account of the Magi present at (the Anointed One) Cyrus' birth. Josephus, for example, quotes Herodotus a number of times, even by book.⁶⁵ Matthew's Greek is quite good, and as an educated person of the time he may have read the famous historian's works himself.

Yet another possibility also exists, that Matthew became aware of the Magi at Cyrus' birth from another source. Herod the Great appointed Nicolaus of Damascus as his official court historian. This historian-philosopher was also his counselor in family difficulties and his

---

⁶³Herodotus 1.107-28. For the Magis' predicting at the birth of Alexander the Great that he would become (king of all of) Asia, see Cicero, *De Div.* I.23 (47). He calls them "wise and learned men among the Persians" (46). See the *LCL* translation of W.A. Falconer.
⁶⁴See G. Binder, *Die Aussetzung des Königskindes. Kyros und Romulus* (Beiträge zur klassischen Philologie, 10; Meisenheim am Glan: Hain, 1964) 17-28, with a list of sources on p. 175: Ktesias, Deinon, Ephoros, Aelian, Xenophon, Plutarch and Strabo. Binder has nothing on Matt 2:1-12. Many of these sources are analyzed in G. Messina, *Der Ursprung der Magier,* and in the art. "Kyros II" by F.H. Weissbach in PWSup 4 (1924) 1129-77. In his *Das Evangelium nach Matthäus,* Luz has a special chart between pp. 84-85 summarizing the motif of the persecuted and rescued child of the king. To it could be added Herodotus 5.92 on the birth of a future ruler of Corinth.
⁶⁵See, for example, *Ant.* 10.18, as well as *Ap.* 1.168.

ambassador to, and advocate with, Augustus in Rome.[66] Because of his non-Davidic, Idumean lineage, Herod even had Nicolaus make him a distinguished Jewish genealogy.[67] In addition, the historian wrote a special history of the world for Herod, certainly also containing an account of Cyrus.[68] Nicolaus, however, from whom Josephus borrows a number of times, also wrote a work in which he recounted Cyrus' birth, primarily drawing on the "Persika" of Ktesias.[69] This too may have been available and known to Matthew, whom many scholars would place in nearby Syria.[70]

IV. The Obeisance Done by Magi from the East to Emperor/King Nero

The decisive impetus for Matthew's employing Magi from the east, who do obeisance to the newborn king of the Jews, Jesus, probably derived from a spectacular event of the year 66 C.E.[71] Dio Cassius relates in his "Roman History," composed ca. 200-220 C.E.,[72] that the Armenian King Tiridates traveled by horseback from the Euphrates to Naples in what was like a triumphal procession. Together with his relatives, servants, 3000 horsemen and numerous Romans, he was received in festively decorated cities all along the route of his journey, which took nine months in one direction. The emperor, Nero, paid for his daily expenditures of 800,000 sesterces. Arriving in Naples, Tiridates knelt upon the ground, called Nero "master" *(despotês)* and "did obeisance" to him *(proskyneô)*. Nero then took him to Rome, which had been festively decorated especially for this occasion. There

---

[66]A. Schalit, *König Herodes. Der Mann und sein Werk* (Studia Judaica 4; Berlin: de Gruyter, 1969) 412, with the relevant references to Josephus.
[67]Schalit 476, citing *Ant.* 14.9. According to 2 Kgs 24:14, only the poorest people remained in Judea; the rest were taken to Babylon. Perhaps Nicolaus wanted to imply that Herod was a descendant of the "princes" of Jerusalem *(ibid.)*, i.e., that he was of Davidic descent. See also Schalit's article "Die frühchristliche Überlieferung über die Herkunft der Familie des Herodes" in *ASTI* 1 (1962) 109-60, which deals primarily with Jewish sources such as b. B. Bat. 3b-4a (Soncino 10 and 12). Interestingly, Schalit also considers the birth of Cyrus in Herodotus 1.107-08 as closest to Matthew 2 of all non-Jewish sources. Yet he mentions this only in a footnote (148, n. 29), and does not develop it.
[68]Schalit, *König Herodes* 412, with the sources given in notes 929-30.
[69]See Nicolaus' Frg Hist 90F66, cited by Binder, *Die Aussetzung* 19, 25 and 175; Weissbach, "Kyros II" 1131 and 1134; as well as Messina, *Der Ursprung* 82.
[70]See Kümmel, *Einleitung* 90, as well as Luz, *Das Evangelium nach Matthäus* 73-75.
[71]This has been known since A. Dieterich, "Die Weisen aus dem Morgenlande" in *ZNW* 3 (1902) 1-14, who notes the relevant sources.
[72]Cf. the *LCL* English translation by E. Cary on LXIII 1.1-7.1. For the dating, see vol. I, xi.

Tiridates and his entire entourage passed by the emperor, members of the senate and the Praetorians, "doing obeisance" to Nero again. Calling the emperor "Master," Tiridates says he is his slave. "And I have come to thee, my god, to worship *(proskyneô)* thee as I do Mithras." Nero then declared him king of Armenia, placing a diadem on his head. Afterwards there was a celebration in the theatre, which was completely covered with gold for the occasion, having the effect that people "gave to the day itself the epithet of 'golden.'"[73] After other festivities, Tiridates and his immense following returned home by a different route from the one taken in coming.[74]

Suetonius, probably born in 69 C.E., notes in his "Lives of the Caesars" that Nero had lured Tiridates to Rome through great promises. He also mentions the Armenian's "falling at his feet" and "doing obeisance" to Nero, who was then hailed as "imperator."[75]

In his "Natural History" XXX.6, Pliny, who died at the eruption of Mt. Vesuvius in 79 C.E., also describes the above event, calling Tiridates a *Magus*. He notes that the Armenian king also brought Magi with him and initiated Nero into their banquets.[76]

Matthew, living within the Roman Empire and probably close to the route taken westward by Tiridates and the Magi, certainly knew of this event, which occurred only some years before the writing of his gospel. Magi from the east, who fall on their knees and do obeisance to the king/emperor of the entire empire on a "day of gold," returning home by a different route, most probably gave him the idea to relate his birth narrative of the King of the Jews, Jesus, in a similar way. In contrast to the despotic and immoral Nero, whom Tiridates and the Magi actually despised and rejected,[77] Jesus, and not Caesar, is the true king. In order to fill out his narrative, Matthew also borrowed imagery and motifs from the Lord's Anointed One and Shepherd, Cyrus, in Second Isaiah, at whose marvelous birth the Magi were also present.

---

[73] This may have influenced Matthew's choice of gold as the first gift the Magi present to the newborn king of the Jews, Jesus (Matt 2:11).
[74] This motif of returning home by a different route was probably decisive for Matt 2:12, and not 1 Kgs 13:9-10, as some commentators note.
[75] Cf. the *LCL* English translation by J.C. Rolfs, "Nero" XIII.1 and XXX.2. For the dating, see vol. I, ix.
[76] I employ the *LCL* translation of W.II.S. Jones. For the dating, see vol. I, vii.
[77] See Dio Cassius, LXIII 6.4 and 6, and Pliny XXX.6, respectively.

5

Three Pillars and Three Patriarchs: A Proposal Concerning Gal 2:9

In his letter to the churches of Galatia Paul provides us with some invaluable first-hand information concerning the early situation of the Jerusalem church, about which we unfortunately know precious little from other sources. Among other things the Apostle to the Gentiles relates in Gal 2:9 that at a meeting in Jerusalem James, Cephas and John, "reputed to be pillars" (οἱ δοκοῦντες στῦλοι εἶναι), gave him and Barnabas the right hand of fellowship. The latter two were to go to the Gentiles; the "pillars," on the other hand, were to missionize among the circumcised.

The commentators speak only in general terms of this non-Pauline phrase, "reputed to be pillars"[1]; nor are the two special studies of this expression entirely satisfying.[2] Rabbinic and intertestamental sources concerning the pillars of Israel, however, offer new insights into the self-understanding of the early Jerusalem church, including how it conceived its three leaders, James, Peter and John. They also provide us with a better understanding of Paul's relationship to the Jerusalem church as expressed in the theology of the "Magna Charta of Christian Liberty," Galatians, and offer a probable explanation of the connotation (negative, positive or neutral) of the adjective δοκοῦντες in 2:9.[3]

---

[1]Instead of the noun "pillars," Paul himself would probably have employed an adjective such as ἐπίσημος, as he described Andronicus and Junias in Rom 16:7 as "men of note among the apostles," men who were in Christ before him.
[2]Cf. the essay by C.K. Barrett, "Paul and the 'Pillar' Apostles," in *Studia Paulina in honorem Johannis de Zwaan*, (Haarlem 1953), 1-19, to which I am at times indebted, as well as the article on στῦλος in *TDNT* 7, 732-36, by U. Wilckens, which cites other secondary literature up to 1964.
[3]Unfortunately it cannot be ascertained whether the three "reputed" to be pillars in Gal 2:9 are the same as "those who are of repute" in 2:2 and 6 (twice). Against G. Klein, "Galater 2, 6-9 und die Geschichte der Jerusalemer Urgemeinde," in *ZThK* 57 (1960)) 288, n. 3, who equates them. The term οἱ δοκοῦντες in Hebrew would probably be either חֲשִׁיבֵי (cf. the examples cited in M. Jastrow, *A Dictionary of the Targumim, the Talmud Babli and Jerushalmi, and*

Within the Dream Visions of Enoch, which R.H. Charles considers to stem from the middle of the second century B.C.E.,[4] chapter ninety relates concerning the new Jerusalem of the end time that before its arrival the old house (= present Jerusalem)[5] will be folded up. All its *pillars,* beams and ornaments will be carried off (v 28). The lord of the sheep (= God) will then bring a new house larger and loftier than the first and set it up in its place. The new building is to have *new pillars* and ornaments, and all the sheep will be within the house (v 29). Later follow the resurrection (v 33) and the Messiah (v 38). This text from the Jewish pseudepigrapha shows that the idea of "new pillars" in the eschatological Jerusalem was an important element in Jewish thinking even before the ministry of Jesus and the birth of the Christian church.

In the NT the twelve disciples/apostles are intimately connected with the new covenant community and with the new Jerusalem. In both of the latter the motif of pillars plays an important role. At the outset of his public ministry Jesus chose twelve disciples,[6] a reconstituting of the twelve tribes of Israel, and at the "Last Supper" he inaugurated a new covenant with the twelve, indicating a "new" Israel.[7] In the covenant ratification ceremony of Exodus 24, Moses at the foot of Mt. Sinai erected twelve "pillars" (Heb. מַצֵּבָה), according to the twelve tribes (v 4). He then threw the "blood of the covenant" upon the people of Israel (v 8).[8] Since in rabbinic sources the Messiah is often viewed as the final redeemer, the first being Moses,[9] the connection between Moses' twelve pillars and the blood of the covenant, and Jesus the Messiah, the twelve disciples and the blood of the "new" covenant, is striking. Also, according to one "Q" tradition in the Synoptics, the twelve disciples are to participate in the eschatological judgment of the twelve tribes of

---

the Midrashic Literature (New York 1950) 510, as well as the pass. part. of חָשַׁב, 508) or גְּדוֹלִי (Jastrow, 211, to which Git. 56a and 56b may be added). F. Delitzsch in ספרי הברית החדשה (London 1958), 348-49 has חָשַׁב in Gal 2:2, 6, 9.

[4]Cf. his *APOT* 164 and 170-71 for the dating 165-61 B.C.E. See also O. Eissfeldt, *The Old Testament. An Introduction* (Oxford 1966), 618-19 for the second century B.C.E.

[5]Not the Jerusalem Temple, which Barrett emphasizes in his consideration of this passage ("Paul," 10-12). Cf. Str-B 4.920 and *APOT* 259.

[6]The election of Matthias as successor to Judas in Acts 1:15-26, even before Pentecost, shows how much importance was attributed to maintaining the continuity of the twelve in the Jerusalem church. According to Luke, Peter says that one who accompanied Jesus during his entire ministry *must* become a witness of the resurrection along with the eleven (1:21).

[7]Cf. Mark 14:24, Matt 26:28 and Luke 22:20, as well as 1 Cor 11:25 ("the new covenant in my blood"). See also 2 Cor 3:6, 14; Heb 8:8; 9:15.

[8]For rabbinic sources regarding this, cf. L. Ginzberg, *The Legends of the Jews* (Philadelphia 1968), 6.34, n. 194.

[9]Cf., for example, the sources cited in Str-B 1. 69-70.

Three Pillars and Three Patriarchs 115

Israel.[10] Rev 21:12 relates that on the gates of the holy city, the new Jerusalem coming down from heaven in the eschatological age, the names of the twelve tribes of the sons of Israel are inscribed. V 14 states that the names of the twelve apostles of the Lamb are on the twelve foundations of the wall of the city. Here the twelve disciples of Jesus support the new Israel, the Christian church.[11] They function as its foundations, a term parallel to and at times interchangeable with "pillars."[12]

As indicated above, all the twelve disciples/apostles can be thought of in apocalyptic contexts of the NT as supporting the community of the new covenant, the new Israel. Yet in Gal 2:9 there are not twelve members of the early Jerusalem church who are "reputed to be pillars," but rather three: James, Cephas (Peter) and John. Was this number merely due to the fact that these men gradually evolved as the community leaders? There are strong reasons to think that this was not the case. Although rabbinic writings can at times speak of twelve pillars supporting the world,[13] or of seven,[14] or of one,[15] they much more

---

[10]Cf. Matt 19:28 and Luke 22:30. Is Paul's remark in 1 Cor 6:2, that (all) the saints are to judge the world, against this emphasis on the twelve?

[11]Cf. the fact that in b. Ḥag. 12b the sages say that (the world) rests on twelve pillars (עמודים), meant as the twelve tribes of Israel, as the quotation of Deut 32:8 shows. See also the parallel tradition in Midr. Pss. 136/5; English in W.G. Braude, *The Midrash on Psalms* (New Haven 1959), 2.325-26. For the cosmological significance of pillar imagery applied to humans, see S. Aalen, *Die Begriffe 'Licht' und 'Finsternis' im Alten Testament, im Spätjudentum und im Rabbinismus* (Oslo 1951), 285-87.

[12]Cf., for example, Gen. Rab. Vayyishlach 75/11, in the Soncino English translation, London 1961, 2.697, regarding the third of the Patriarchs, Jacob: he "was a pillar and a foundation of the world": משתותו ויסודו. I am grateful to Dr. N. Oswald of Berlin for aid in verifying a number of the Hebrew/Aramaic references I cite.

[13]Cf. the references in n. 11.

[14]This is usually based on the seven pillars (עמוד) of wisdom of Prov 9:1. Cf. not only b. Ḥag. 12b, but also Pesiq. R. 8/4 (English in W.G. Braude, *Pesikta Rabbati* [New Haven 1968] 1.151; מצוק is also employed here); 5/7 (Braude 1.106); and Lev. Rab. 29/11 (Soncino 4.378). In addition to Abraham, Isaac and Jacob, who are always mentioned first, Kohath, Amram, Moses, and Levi or Aaron are the other four.

[15]Cf. b. Ḥag. 12b, which has one pillar (עמוד), the righteous person, as in Prov 10:25 (יסוד). This is said by R. Eleazar b. Shammua, a third generation Tanna (see H. Strack and G. Stemberger, *Einleitung in Talmud und Midrasch* [Munich: Beck, 1982⁷] 83). Midr. Pss. 11/2 (Braude 1.159), employing both the "foundations" of Ps 11:3 (שתות) and Prov 10:25, also speaks of the righteous as the foundation of the world, yet the term is plural here. The same midrash (1.160) also records another tradition, that the world is established upon the foundation stone of the (Jerusalem) Temple. A parallel tradition to the numbers listed in b. Ḥag. 12b is found in Midr. Pss. 136/5 (Braude 2.325-26).

frequently speak of three.[16] These in turn can at times also be thought of as three entities or virtues.[17] Later traditions concerning three human beings can list the three sons of Korah; Daniel's three friends Hananiah, Mishael and Azariah; and Adam, Noah and Abraham as the three pillars of the earth.[18] Yet by far the strongest and earliest tradition as far as three humans is concerned is that of the three Patriarchs, who are always mentioned *before* the above alternatives.

Rabbinic sources show that in a Jewish community there were always three judges for non-capital cases,[19] and some traditions state that there were three witnesses or assistants in the baptism of a proselyte (which may in part have served as the model for Christian baptism).[20] Nevertheless, I would suggest that the number three in Gal 2:9 is due to a deliberate selection by the Aramaic-speaking Jerusalem church of three disciples/apostles as community leaders on the basis of the model of the three Patriarchs, Abraham, Isaac and Jacob,[21] thought of in rabbinic sources as the three pillars of Israel, indeed, of the entire world.

---

[16]For the very late and singular tradition that the world rests on four pillars, which in turn rest on Leviathan, cf. Ginzberg, *Legends* 5.45, n. 127.

[17]For the world being sustained by three things, the Law, the (Temple-) service, and deeds of loving-kindness, cf. m. 'Abot 1:2, said in the name of Simeon the Just from the third century B.C.E.(Strack and Stemberger, *Einleitung* 72). Three virtues: truth, judgment/justice, and peace, are mentioned in 1:18, a saying transmitted in the name of Rabban Simeon b. Gamaliel, probably a first, possibly a third generation Tanna (*Einleitung* 75 and 84). For the latter listing, see also Deut. Rab. 5/1 (Soncino 7.102).

[18]For the three sons of Korah and Daniel's friends, cf. Midr. Pss. 1/15 (Braude 1.22) and Cant. Rab. 7/8.1 (Soncino 9.295). For Adam, Noah and Abraham, see Midr. Pss. 34/1 (Braude 1.408).

[19]The general rule is found in m. Sanh. 4:1: "Non-capital cases [are decided] by three and capital cases by three and twenty [judges]." Translation H. Danby, *The Mishnah* (London 1933), 386. Cf. also 1:1-3; 3:1; 8:4. Dr. M. Krupp of Jerusalem kindly called my attention to this fact, as to the number of witnesses at a baptism.

[20]Cf. the relevant sayings in b. Yebam. 46b, one of which makes the number three parallel to that required in a law court. For the number two, see b. Yebam. 47a Bar. All these sources are cited in Str-B 1.110-11.

[21]Cf. b. Ber. 16b, which states that "Our Rabbis taught: The term 'patriarchs' is applied only to three, and the term 'matriarchs' only to four." Translation from the *Hebrew-English Edition of the Babylonian Talmud* (London 1965). The three are Abraham, Isaac and Jacob, the four are Sarah, Rebeccah, Leah and Rachel. For this listing, see also 'Abot R. Nat. 37, an English translation of which is found in J. Goldin, *The Fathers According to Rabbi Nathan* (Yale 1955) 153.

Three Pillars and Three Patriarchs

While the three "Fathers" or "Patriarchs" can also be called or described as the fathers of the world[22]; the princes of the world[23]; the sureties or guaranties of Israel[24]; God's servants[25]; God's companions[26]; God's holy ones[27]; God's heavenly chariot[28]; the lintel and the two sideposts of a doorway[29]; the windows of Cant 2:9[30]; as conspicuous in the world as the waves of the sea[31]; three kinds of burnt offerings[32]; rocks[33]; and mountains[34]; what is more important for this inquiry is that they are described as the roots supporting Israel[35], and as a throne of three legs (supporting the world).[36]

The latter imagery appears to be very old. In a discussion of the three Patriarchs as being born in the month Tishri, R. Eliezer (ben Hyrcanus), a second generation older Tanna active at the end of the first century C.E.,[37] calls them not only the mountains, but also the "enduring foundations (מוסדי) of the earth," from Mic 6:2.[38] In *Migr. Abr.* 121 Philo speaks of the righteous man as the pillar (ἔρεισμα) on which

---

[22]Cf. the examples given in Str-B 1.284 and 918, as well as Tg. Ps.-J. and Frg. Tg. Gen. 40:12.
[23]Cf. Num. Rab. 19/26 (Soncino 6.775) as well as Frg. Tg. Num 21:18.
[24]Cf. Midr. Pss. 8/4 (Braude 1.125) as well as Cant. Rab. 1:4 § 1 (Soncino 9.41).
[25]Cf. Exod 32:13, quoted in Eccl. Rab. 4/1 (Soncino 8.112).
[26]Cf. Cant. Rab. 1:7 § 1 (Soncino 9.63) and Pesiq. R. 39/2 (Braude 2.696). See also the Essene writing CD 3:2-4.
[27]Cf. Midr. Pss. 16/2 (Braude 1.197).
[28]Cf. Gen. Rab. 47/6 (Soncino 1.403); 69/3 (2.631); 82/6 (2.757).
[29]Cf. Exod. Rab. 17/3 (Soncino 3.213-14).
[30]Cf. Num. Rab. 11/2 (Soncino 5.414), and Pesiq. Rab Kah. 5/8 (English in W.G. Braude and I.J. Kapstein, *Pesikta de Rab Kahana* [Philadelphia 1975] 104).
[31]Cf. Lam. Rab., proem 1 (Soncino 7.1).
[32]Cf. Num. Rab. 14/5 (Soncino 6.587).
[33]Cf. Est. Rab. 7/10 (Soncino 9.85) and Pesiq. R. 12/5 (Braude 1.227).
[34]Cf. Exod. Rab. 15/7 (Soncino 3.168-69); 15/26 (Soncino 3.198); 23/5 (Soncino 3.284); 28/2 (Soncino 3.332); Lev. Rab. 36/6 (Soncino 4.464); Num. Rab. 9/13 (Soncino 5.265); 20/19 (Soncino 6.810); Cant. Rab. 4:8 §3 (Soncino 9.209); Pesiq. R. 33/4 (Braude 2.637); Pirqe R. El. 48 (English translation in G. Friedlander, *Pirkê de Rabbi Eliezer* [London 1916; reprint New York 1970] 376); b. Sanh. 81a; b. Roš. Haš. 11a; Tg. Ps.-J. Gen. 49:26; Tg. Ps.-J., Frg. Tg. and Tg. Neof. on Num 23:9; Tg. Ps.-J. and Frg. Tg. Deut 33:15.
[35]Cf. Exod. Rab. 44/1 (Soncino 3.507-08); Lev. Rab. 36/2 (Soncino 4.459); Num. Rab. 13/14 (Soncino 6.530; Abraham is here called the "root of the genealogical tree"; see also Rashi on Num 23:9); Lam. Rab., proem 2 (Soncino 7.4); and Pesiq. Rab Kah. 15/5 (Braude and Kapstein, 280).
[36]Cf. Gen. Rab. 68/12 (Soncino 2.625). See also the sources cited in Ginzberg, *Legends* 6.97, n. 541, and 6.53, n. 275. In addition, Abraham is described as he who "bears the generations before and after him" in Gen. Rab. 14/6 (Soncino 1.114) and Koh. Rab. 3:11 § 2 (Soncino 8.89).
[37]Cf. Strack and Stemberger, *Einleitung* 77.
[38]Cf. b. Roš. Haš. 11a.

mankind rests. Abraham's faith is then mentioned in 122. In 124 the righteous man in the human race is like the (supporting) pillar (στῦλος) of a house. Abraham, Isaac and Jacob are then mentioned in 125. Thus Philo, an Alexandrian Jew contemporary with Jesus, is most probably also acquainted with the tradition of Abraham and the other two Patriarchs as pillars, even though he allegorizes in this passage, as elsewhere.

Another passage, Gen. Rab. Lech Lecha 43/8 on Gen 14:20 ("And Abram gave him [Melchizedek] a tenth of everything"), relates that R. Judah said in the name of R. Nehorai, a third generation Tanna[39]: "In virtue of that blessing the three great pillars of the world, Abraham, Isaac, and Jacob, enjoyed prosperity."[40] The early and almost interchangeable terms pillar/foundation/support must have been a customary way of designating the three Patriarchs, as two later sources show. Midr. Pss. 1/15 states that the earth's standing on three pillars (עמודים: Abraham, Isaac and Jacob)[41] is a "popular saying."[42] In addition, Cant. Rab. 7:8 § 1 has Abraham, Isaac and Jacob as the first, and thus probably oldest, explanation of the "popular oath": "By him who established the world on three pillars" (עמודים).[43]

The latter saying aids in understanding why James, Cephas (Peter) and John were thought of as pillars by the earliest Jerusalem congregation.[44] As God once "established the world," the covenant community Israel, on the basis of the three Patriarchs,[45] so in the messianic period, inaugurated by the resurrection of Jesus from the

---

[39]Cf. Strack and Stemberger, *Einleitung* 84.
[40]English translation in Soncino, 1.357. The Hebrew is יתדות, literally "(tent-) pegs," here in the sense of basic supporting elements, as in Zech 10:4.
[41]The other alternatives, Hananiah, Mishael and Azariah, as well as the three sons of Korah, are mentioned *after* the three Patriarchs and are most probably a later development of the tradition.
[42]Cf. Braude 1.22.
[43]English translation in Soncino 9.295. Cf. also Exod. Rab. 2/6 (Soncino 3.57) for Abraham as the "pillar" (עמודו) of the world." In Gen. Rab. 75/11 (Soncino 2.697) Jacob is a "pillar" (משתותו) of the world."
[44]For reasons of space I cannot elaborate here on the relationship of the "rock" Cephas to the "rock"/"pillar" Abraham (cf., however, below), nor on the association of James "the Just" with pillar imagery. This is done in an abbreviated manner by Barrett, "Paul", 14-15. For the Jerusalem apostles' giving a surname to Joseph, a Levite from Cyprus, see Acts 4:36 (Barnabas as "son of encouragement" is problematical; see Str-B 2.634 and the commentaries). If this surnaming is historical, it is a phenomenon parallel to the same Christian community's calling some from their own midst "pillars."
[45]Cf. Exod. Rab. 15/7 (Soncino 3.169), where the (three) Patriarchs are the "pillars of the earth" (Heb. מצקי ארץ) of 1 Sam 2:8, upon whom God will establish his world.

Three Pillars and Three Patriarchs

dead, God was thought of by Jewish Christians as having "established the world" anew, the new covenant community, the "Israel of God," to employ Paul's phrase from Gal 6:16, on the basis of three new pillars.[46]

Paul, to be sure, has a basically positive attitude to the three Patriarchs. Elsewhere, in a discussion of his hope that "all Israel will be saved," both Jews and Gentiles (Rom 11:26), he states that the Jews are beloved (of God) "for the sake of the fathers" (11:28)[47]; the latter belong to the Jews (9:5). Yet the idea of the "merit of the Fathers" (זכות אבות)[48]

---

[46]The sectarians at Qumran on the Dead Sea also believed they were members of the community of the "new covenant" of the final time (cf., for example, 1 QS 5:6; CD 6:19 in MS "A" and 1:33 in "B"; and 1 QHab 2:3). While 1 QS 8:1 states that there shall be twelve men and three priests in the Council of the Community; and CD 10:4 speaks of the ten periodically chosen judges of the Congregation; the closest parallel to the expression "pillars" of Gal 2:9 is that found in 1 QSa 1:12, 13, which speaks of the new recruit to Qumran or of a male child raised there: "Then at the age of twenty-five years he may take his place among the foundations of the 13) holy congregation (ביסודות עדה) to ensure the service of the Congregation." English translation in A. Dupont-Summer, *The Essene Writings from Qumran* (Cleveland and New York 1962) 105; see his n. 7 there, as well as p. 151, n. 2-3. Here the "foundations" appear to hold various leading offices in the community, yet they certainly are not modeled on the Patriarchs of the OT. In addition to other office holders, the Teacher of Righteousness, the priestly lay leader, is the "foundation (סוד) of truth and understanding" for the sect (1 QH 2:9; cf. 6:25; 7:8, 9 and 4 QpPs 37, 4:15, 16). For a special study of the image "foundation" at Qumran, see now H. Muszynski, *Fundament, Bild und Metapher in den Handschriften aus Qumran: Studie zur Vorgeschichte des ntl. Begriffes* ΘΕΜΕΛΙΟΣ *(AnBib 61, Rome 1975)*, who is wary of comparing 1 QSa 1:12 and Gal 2:9 (p. 203). G. Klinzing in: *Die Umdeutung des Kultes in der Qumrangemeinde und im NT* (StUNT 7, Göttingen 1971) expressly discusses Gal 2:9, maintaining that the Qumran texts offer no parallel to the idea of pillars as found in Gal 2:9; rather, a rabbinic title of honor is present here (p. 200). I agree with Klinzing's observation that it is difficult to imagine that the Christian community in Jerusalem viewed itself as the (new or true) Temple, since, in contrast to the Qumranites, it continued to frequent the Temple (p. 200).

[47]This, as E. Käsemann notes, is not causal ("because of the merit of the Patriarchs") but relates to the blessings and promises of v 29 (cf. his *An die Römer* [HNT 8a, Tübingen 1974³] 305).

[48]On the "merit of the Fathers," cf. A. Marmorstein, *The Doctrine of Merits in Old Rabbinic Literature* (London 1920); S. Schechter, *Aspects of Rabbinic Theology. Major Concepts of the Talmud* (New York 1961; original 1909) 170-98; C.F. Moore, *Judaism in the First Centuries of the Christian Era* (Cambridge, Mass. 1927) 1.541-45, and 3.164; and most recently E.P. Sanders, *Paul and Palestinian Judaism* (Philadelphia 1977) 90-92, 195-98. Sanders correctly emphasizes that God's covenantal promises to the Patriarchs often form the background for rabbinic sayings regarding the merit of the Fathers. The older Protestant view of Jewish thought on merit as legalistic "works-righteousness" is certainly a caricature. Yet the element of paradox inherent in such terms as

was so intrinsically bound up with these three pillars of Israel that Paul, in contrast to the Aramaic-speaking Christians of Jerusalem, would have been wary from the outset of calling three leaders of the new covenant community the "pillar apostles."

This concept of the merit of the three Patriarchs is already implied in Exod 2:24, where upon hearing their groaning, God delivers the Israelites from slavery in Egypt because he remembers his covenant with Abraham, Isaac and Jacob. In the first century C.E. the motif was already widespread. Philo writes that the (three) "founders of the race" "cease not to make supplications for their sons and daughters, supplications made not in vain, because the Father grants to them the privilege that their prayers should be heard."[49] Josephus has Nehemiah say to the Jerusalemites: "Fellow Jews, you know that God cherishes the memory of our fathers Abraham, Isaac and Jacob, and because of their righteousness does not give up His providential care for us."[50] In the gospels of the NT, John the Baptist and Jesus in prophetic fashion scold those who rely on descent from Abraham.[51] One summary rabbinic statement on this subject is that found in Tg. Ps.-J. Deut 28:15 regarding the Patriarchs, to whom a bath-kol says: "Fear not, ye fathers of the world; if the merit of all generations should fail, yours shall not."[52]

Several rabbinic passages show the direct implications of this idea of the Patriarchs' merit for the "rock" Peter and the other "pillar" apostles,

---

בזכות, בשכר, כדי, למען and על מעשה easily lent them to caricature and abuse. Because Paul had an exclusivist soteriology, i.e. for him only the crucified and resurrected Jesus as Lord at the right hand of God can intercede on behalf of men now, the merits of the Patriarchs or pious contemporaries, the "righteous," is by definition of terms ineffective.

[49]Cf. the English translation by F.H. Colson and the Greek text of *De Praemis et Poenis* 166 in the LCL edition 8.419, and note "d." For the intercession of the Patriarchs, see also Mek. R. Ish. Vayassa' 4 on Exod 16:14 (in the *Mekilta de Rabbi Ishmael*, ed. J.Z. Lauterbach [Philadelphia 1949] vol. 2.112) regarding manna as being sent to the Israelites in the desert because God accepts the prayer of the fathers who lay in the dust. This is spoken by R. Eleazar of Modi'im, an older second generation Tanna (Strack and Stemberger, *Einleitung* 78). See also 2 Bar 85:2.

[50]The English translation by R. Marcus, and the Greek text of *Ant.* 11.169, are to be found in the LCL edition, 6.396-97. I owe this reference to G. Schrenk's article πατήρ in *TDNT* 5.976.

[51]Cf. Matt 3:9 and Luke 3:8, "these stones" probably being a reference to Isa 51:1, 2 (see below). See the article λίθος in *TDNT* 4.271 by J. Jeremias, as well as John 8.

[52]Translation by J.W. Etheridge, *The Targums of Onkelos and Jonathan ben Uzziel on the Pentateuch, with the Fragments of the Jerusalem Targum* (London, 1862-65) 642. The basic idea here is that God does not forget the promises he made to the Patriarchs. Once made, they will be fulfilled.

James and John, in Gal 2:9. Pesiq. R. 12/5, commenting on Israel's battle with Amalek at Rephidim, states regarding the phrase "top of the hill" in Exod 17:9: "The next term, 'top,' intimates that Israel invoked the merit of the Patriarchs: 'From the peaks of the rocks I see him' (Num. 23:9), [for the merit of the Patriarchs is topmost in Israel]."[53] In rabbinic sources the Patriarchs are often the rocks of Num 23:9,[54] and because of his faith the pillar Abraham is *the* rock,[55] in one rabbinic source on Num 23:9 called not צור but *petra*,[56] as in the account of Peter's confession of faith in Matt 16:18. Another rabbinic reference can even call the merit of the Fathers "rock" (צור).[57]

The merit of the three Fathers and that of the four Mothers were thought to deliver from damnation after death. Tg. Ps.-J. Exod 40:8 speaks of "the merit of the mothers of the world, which spreadeth at the gate of Gehennam, that none may enter there of the souls of the children of Israel."[58] In Gen. Rab. 48/8 R. Levi says: "In the Hereafter Abraham will sit at the entrance to Gehenna, and permit no circumcised

---

[53]Cf. the English translation in Braude, 1.227, who has added the explanation in brackets. See also the merit of the Patriarchs and the rocks of Num 23:9 in Frg. Tg. (Etheridge 423) and Tg. Neof. on this verse.
[54]Cf. Exod. Rab. 15/7, with the Patriarchs as the "pillars of the earth" of 1 Sam 2:8 (Soncino 3.168-69); Num. Rab. 20/19 (Soncino 6.810); Est. Rab. 7/10 (Soncino 9.85); Pesiq. R. 12/5 (Braude 1.227); Pesiq. Rab Kah. 3 (Braude and Kapstein, 40); Mek. R. Ish. Amalek 1/118 on Exod 17:10 (Lauterbach 2.143-44); and Tg. Ps.-J., Frg. Tg., and Tg. Neof. on Num 23:9.
[55]Abraham is the rock (צור) of Deut 32:30 in Gen. Rab. 44/21 (Soncino 1.375), Exod. Rab. 51/7 (3.569), Pesiq. R. 15/2 (Braude 1.306), and Pesiq. Rab Kah. 5/2 (Braude and Kapstein 92; cf. Str-B 4.1065, with other parallels from Tanhuma). He is also the rock (צור) of Isa 51:1 (cf. v 2) in b. Yebam. 64a, Exod. Rab. 51/7, Pesiq. R. 15/2, Pesiq. Rab Kah. 5/2, Midr. Pss. 52/8 (Braude 1.483), and 53/2 (Braude 1.487). For Abraham and the rock (צור) of Ps 105:41 (cf. v 42), see Num. Rab. 19/26 (Soncino 6.775).
[56]Cf. Yalqut I § 766. The text, together with a German translation, is provided by K.G. Goetz, "Zwei Beiträge zur synoptischen Quellentradition," *ZNW* 20 (1921) 166-67. Excerpts are translated in Str-B 1.733 on Matt 16:18. Another early haggadic treatment of the Hebrew text of Num 23:9 is reflected in Josephus, *Ant*. 4.114, and in Ps.-Philo, *Bibl. Ant*. 18:10 (see also 23:4-5 for Abraham as derived from a rock; directly after this his faith in God is emphasized). Cf. the evidence presented by Ginzberg, *Legends*, 6.130, n. 764.
[57]Cf. Yalqut § 763, which comments on the texts Num 21:18 and Ps 105:41, 42. Reference from Schechter, *Aspects*, 173. Basically the same tradition is found in Num. Rab. 19/26 (Soncino 6.775).
[58]English translation of Etheridge, 577. The next verse in the targum speaks of the King Messiah. Can Paul's remark in Gal 4:26, "the Jerusalem above is free, and she is our mother," in part be directed against the idea of the merit of the four Matriarchs?

Israelite to descend therein."⁵⁹ Another of the three Patriarchs, Isaac, "goes and sits at the entrance of Gehinnom to deliver his descendants from the punishment of Gehinnom,"⁶⁰ according to R. Simeon b. Yoḥai, a third generation Tanna,⁶¹ a reference which shows that the tradition of the merit of the (three) Patriarchs delivering from the gates of Gehenna is early. This motif is directly related to the gates of Hades (Gehenna) in Matt 16:18 as not having power over "it," the church or the rock Peter, who in turn is modeled here after the rock Abraham because of the latter's being the first to believe in God (cf. Gen 12:1, 4; 15:6; and 22:12).

As seen in his remarks on Abraham in Galatians and in Romans 4, the Christian convert Paul emphatically rejects the idea of the merit of the Patriarchs.⁶² For him, just as uncircumcised Abraham was justified before God because of his faith, so the uncircumcised Gentile Christian must also be fully accepted by circumcised, "law-abiding" Jewish Christians on the basis of his faith in Jesus Christ as Lord. For Paul "no other foundation can any one lay than that which is laid, which is Jesus Christ" (1 Cor 3:11). The merit of Israel's three pillar Patriarchs is no longer significant, since the death of the crucified Messiah Jesus atones fully for man's sins.⁶³ It is Jesus Christ, now exalted at the right hand of God, who (alone) intercedes for men (Rom 8:34; cf. Heb 7:25). One rabbinic source regarding the Messiah sounds as if it could have been written by Paul: "By his merit all nations shall be blessed ...,"⁶⁴ a sentence reminiscent of the promise made to Abraham. While Abraham

---

⁵⁹English in Soncino 1.409. R. Levi was a third generation Palestinian Amora (Strack and Stemberger, *Einleitung* 94). Cf. also the numerous references cited in Ginzberg, *Legends*, 5.267, n. 318.

⁶⁰Cf. the English of Cant. Rab. 8:9 § 3 in Soncino 9.317, as well as the references noted in Ginzberg, *Legends*, 5.280, n. 69.

⁶¹Cf. Strack and Stemberger, *Einleitung* 82-83.

⁶²A number of later rabbis also warned against misinterpreting the merit of the Fathers. See the sources cited in Str-B 1.120, as well as Ps.-Philo, *Bibl. Ant.* 33:5.

⁶³One early tradition concerning the Patriarchs relates that there was neither sin nor iniquity in them (as Jesus' followers also maintained of him; on the sinlessness of the Messiah, see Ps Sol 17:41 and T. Juda 24:1). Cf. the saying by R. Eleazar of Modi'im in Mek. R. Ish. Vayassa' 3, 1.77 (Lauterbach 2.106) on Exod 16:10. See also Pr Man 8.

⁶⁴Tg. Pss. 72:17, as cited in S. Levey, *The Messiah: An Aramaic Interpretation* (Cincinnati 1974) 117. Midr. Pss. 21/5 (Braude 1.296) on Ps 21:7 interprets this verse as meaning "that all the nations shall bless themselves in the king Messiah." For the "merit of the Messiah," see also the saying by Resh Laqish, a second generation Palestinian Amora (Strack and Stemberger, *Einleitung* 91), in Str-B 3.506g, and Pesiq. R. 34/2 on Zech 9:9 (Braude 2.666 and 668).

Three Pillars and Three Patriarchs

can also be called the "great mountain,"[65] other rabbinic sources call the great mountain of Zech 4:7 the King Messiah, "For he is greater than the Patriarchs."[66] Paul would agree with the latter statement completely as far as the "merit" of the three pillars of Israel is concerned.[67]

Although Paul gave James the right hand of fellowship in Jerusalem (Gal 2:9), and later according to Acts 21:18 went in to confer with the same apostle at his last visit to Jerusalem, his relationship to the brother of the Lord, who like he had received a special resurrection appearance from Jesus, could only have been one of cautious restraint. There is no reason to doubt that the "certain men from James" who came from Jerusalem to Antioch belonged to the circumcision party of the Jerusalem Jewish Christians (Gal 2:12).[68] Even if the "false brethren secretly brought in," those who "slipped in to spy out" the freedom of the Gentile Christians at the Jerusalem meeting between Paul's followers and the Jewish Christians (Gal 2:4), were not commissioned or encouraged to do so by James,[69] the fact that Jesus' brother favored the circumcision of Gentile Christians could only have irked Paul. In addition, the Jewish Christians of Jerusalem had coined the term "pillars" for James, Cephas and John. This was not offensive to Paul because he thought it devalued his own apostleship to the Gentiles.[70] It was a very inappropriate term in his eyes because for him and many others it was clearly modeled on the three pillars of Israel, the Patriarchs, whose "merit" in turn was thought to be continually effective. Theologically Paul could no longer accept the latter, thus his reticence towards the term, as noted in the expression "reputed to be" pillars. In order not to break fellowship with James and the Jerusalem church, however, the Apostle to the Gentiles did not openly refute the

---

[65]Cf., for example, Pesiq. R. 3/3 in Braude 1.68, referring to Gen 19:17.
[66]Cf. Yalquṭ on Zech 4:7, as well as Tanḥuma B 70a on the same verse. The latter is cited with other parallels in Str-B 1.483. Tg. Neb. Zech 4:7 has the "top stone" of this verse as God's Messiah. See Levey, *The Messiah*, 98. For the Patriarchs as acknowledging that the Messiah is greater than they are, cf. also Pesiq. R. 37/1 (Braude 2.685). For Abraham as astonished that in the future the Messiah will sit at God's right (Ps 110:1), and he at God's left or less important side, see Midr. Pss. 18/29 (Braude 1.261). Other relevant sources are cited in Ginzberg, *Legends*, 6.142, n. 836, and 272, n. 129.
[67]The Apostle to the Gentiles' aversion to the merit of Israel's three Fathers was probably also in part due to the fact that according to Judaism Gentile proselytes have no share in this merit, even after becoming full Jews through circumcision. Cf. Num. Rab. 8/9 (Soncino 5.232-33). This and other similar references are cited in Str-B 1.119-20.
[68]Cf. the fact that the persecution of Acts 12:1-3 does not touch James.
[69]Cf. Acts 15:24, 25.
[70]Against Wilckens, art. στῦλος in *TDNT* 7.735.

idea of three new pillars. Instead, he presented a careful theological argument that since Abraham believed and was reckoned righteous by God even before he was circumcised, the Gentile does not need to be circumcised before he can become a Christian. Faith in Jesus as one's Lord suffices completely.

It is one of the ironies of early Christian history that the Apostle to the Gentiles, who now rejected all merit except that acquired through the atoning death of Christ on the Cross, only a few decades after his death was labeled one of the "greatest and most righteous pillars" (of the church).[71]

---

[71]Cf. 1 Clem 5:2, which names Peter in v 4 and Paul in v 5. For First Clement as probably written 90-100 C.E., see the LCL edition of the Apostolic Fathers, translated by K. Lake, 1.4-5. See also the Apocalypse of Paul 51, where Christ says: "Greetings, Paul, roof and foundation of the Church!" English in E. Hennecke and W. Schneemelcher, *New Testament Apocrypha* (Philadelphia 1965) 2.797.

6

The Relevance of Isaiah 66:7 to Revelation 12 and 2 Thessalonians 1

Isaiah 66:7-9

MT: Before she was in labor she gave birth;
before her pain came upon her she was delivered of a son.
8 Who has heard such a thing?
Who has seen such things?
Shall a land be born in one day?
Shall a nation be brought forth in one moment?
For as soon as Zion was in labor
she brought forth her sons.
9 Shall I bring to the birth and not cause
to bring forth? says the Lord;
shall I, who cause to bring forth, shut the womb?
says our God.[1]

Targum: Before stress shall come upon her she shall be delivered,
and before trembling shall come upon her,
as pangs upon a woman with child,
her king shall be revealed.
8 Who hath heard such a thing?
who hath seen such things?
Is it possible that a land should be made in one day?
shall its people be created at once?
for Zion is about to be comforted,
and she shall be filled with the people of her exiles.
9 I God created the world from the beginning
(Berēshīth), saith the Lord;
I created all mankind;

---

[1]The translation is that of the Revised Standard Version, also employed elsewhere unless stated otherwise.

> I scattered them among the nations;
> I also am about to gather together thy exiles,
> saith thy God.²

The latter chapters of the prophet Isaiah (56-66), who already in the second century B.C.E. was considered a kind of apocalyptic seer,³ deal with the question of why God's final theophany promised in chapters 40-55 did not take place.⁴ Haggai and his contemporary Zechariah shared the imminent expectation of Second Isaiah and led in the rebuilding of the temple, hoping that this would aid in ushering in the messianic age. Third Isaiah, however, said that a new temple would not suffice. In 66:1 the Lord prefers to throne in heaven;⁵ he prefers men who are humble and contrite in spirit, who tremble at his word (66:2), to those who put their entire stock in a building. Nevertheless, says the author of Isaiah, God *will* return to his temple, he will vindicate his faithful adherents (66:6, 15-16);⁶ Zion will be reborn-restored (vv 7-9); Jerusalem will again comfort her oppressed followers (vv 10-14), who will participate in her glory; the Lord will gather all nations and tongues to Jerusalem; all flesh shall worship before him (vv 18-23); and his people shall endure (v 22).⁷

It was to be expected that this grand eschatological vision of Isaiah 66 would become a favorite for later writers. In this article the messianic interpretation of Isa 66:7 in Rev 12:2 and 5-6, in a context of persecution, will first be discussed (I). Then Jewish messianic interpretations of Isa 66:7 will be examined, relating them to the general idea of the messianic birth pangs or "woes" (II). Finally, the use of

---

²Translation and text in J.F. Stenning, *The Targum of Isaiah* (Oxford: Clarendon, 1949) 218-21.
³See Sir 48:22-25, where it is said of this prophet "who was great and faithful in his vision": "By the spirit of might he saw the last things, and comforted those who mourned in Zion. He revealed what was to occur to the end of time, and the hidden things before they came to pass" (vv 24-25). O. Eissfeldt in *The Old Testament. An Introduction* (Oxford: Blackwell, 1966) 597, dates Ben Sira, the grandfather of the Greek translator, as active ca. 190 B.C.E.
⁴Cf., for example, 52:8 for this promise.
⁵He will reign over the entire earth as his kingdom. Note the motif of universal kingship, as in the similar passage Zech 14:9.
⁶For the Lord's executing judgment in v 16, cf. the OT idea of judgment as belonging to the king.
⁷For a discussion of the problem for Third Isaiah of God's final theophany not setting in, cf. H.-J. Kraus, "Die ausgebliebene Endtheophanie. Eine Studie zu Jes 56-66," *ZAW* 78 (1966) 317-32. On Third Isaiah see J. Muilenburg, "The Book of Isaiah, Chapters 40-66," in *The Interpreter's Bible,* 5 (New York, Nashville: Abingdon, 1956). It is clear that the NT writers did not divide Isaiah as most of modern scholarship does.

various verses from Isaiah 66 in 2 Thessalonians 1, a letter also set in a context of persecution, will be pointed out (III).

I. *Revelation 12* "has always been, consciously or not, considered as the center of and key to the entire book."[8] Before the King of kings, mounted on a white horse, triumphs over the beast and his allies (19:11-21); before the great judgment occurs (20:11-15); and before a new heaven and a new earth are created (Isa 65:17; 66:22) and the new Jerusalem descends from heaven, when God will be with his people and will comfort them from their sorrows (21:1-4), the writer of Revelation portrays in ch. 12 the conflict to be undergone before the final victory. In ch. 11 God's two witnesses, although apparently killed by the beast, are given God's breath of life and taken up to heaven in a cloud. Assurance is thereby given to afflicted Christians that, although they may be persecuted to death, they too will triumph in like manner. Then the seventh angel blows his trumpet,[9] and heavenly voices sound: "The kingdom of the world has become the kingdom of our Lord and of his Christ, and he shall reign for ever and ever" (11:15). This proleptic victory song is echoed in the words of the twenty-four elders in heaven, that God has taken his great power and *begun to reign* (v 17). Already at this point the final battle is envisaged as well as the resurrection and judgment of the dead; the time for rewarding God's servants, the prophets and the saints (the Christian church); and the time for vanquishing those who presently afflict the saints (v 18). The beginning of the end is thus here, as seen in the persecutions the Christians are enduring, probably thought of as part of the messianic woes.[10] In spite of their afflictions the final victory is assured. This is the addressees' present consolation.

In this setting the author describes in ch. 12 Satan's attempt to overcome the newborn child of the woman who appears in heaven.

---

[8]P. Prigent, *Apocalypse 12. Histoire de l'exégèse* (Tübingen: Mohr, 1959) 1.
[9]At this time the mystery of God (victory for his adherents in spite of what appears to them to be a loss of the battle against the beast) is to be fulfilled (10:7).
[10]Three woes *(Ouai)* are set in the context of the angels' trumpet-blowing; the first are indicated in 9:12 and 11:14. Since 11:14 states that the third woe is soon to come, the battle between the woman and the dragon of chapter twelve is probably this third and last woe. This is made more probable by the fact that the only occurrence of "woe" before the plural "woes" of the city of Babylon in chapter eighteen is found in 12:12. The only time *odinō*, the verb form of the birth woes, is used in Revelation is also in 12:2. Cf. also the association of *ouai* with the pregnant woman at the time of the messianic woes in Mark 13:17; Matt 24:19; Luke 21:13. A general discussion of these woes, relating them to the coming of the Day of the Lord, occurs in part II of this essay.

Failing in this, the dragon fights there with the archangel Michael. Failing here too, he pursues the woman on earth. Unable to catch her, he goes off "to make war on the rest of her offspring, on those who keep the commandments of God and bear testimony to Jesus" (v 17), in other words the Christian church, whose accused brethren witness to their faith even to the point of death (vv 10-11).

Isa 66:7 is employed by the author of Revelation to describe the birth of the Messiah here. In 12:1 he envisions a great "sign" in heaven. This is definitely the σημεῖον of Isa 7:14, a promise that a young woman from the house of David shall conceive and bear a son whose name will be Immanuel. This will take place "on that day" (v 18). The author of Revelation then proceeds to another Isaianic passage, 66:7, to develop his picture of the pregnant woman and her *son*, the Messiah.

In 12:2 the woman is with child, she cries out in her birth pangs, in anguish for delivery: καὶ κράζει ὠδίνουσα καὶ βασανιζομένη τεκεῖν. LXX Isa 66:7 reads: πρὶν ἢ τὴν ὠδίνουσαν τεκεῖν, πρὶν ἐλθεῖν τὸ πόνον τῶν ὠδίνων, ἐξέφυγεν καὶ ἔτεκεν ἄρσεν.[11] Since other OT texts also have the natural combination of *ōdinō* and *tiktō*,[12] the similarity pointed out by the underlining is not great enough to deduce that the author here is alluding to Isa 66:7.[13] However, the fact that in the adjacent verses of 12:5 καὶ ἔτεκεν υἱὸν ἄρσεν, and 12:6 καὶ ἡ γυνὴ ἔφυγεν[14] appear, both borrowings from the same verse in Isaiah, makes the use of Isa 66:7 also in Rev 12:2 certain.

---

[11] The best reading in the LXX and in Rev 12:5 is *arsen*. Cf. the LXX text in J. Ziegler, *Septuaginta*, 14 (Göttingen: Vandenhoeck & Ruprecht, 1967²). Symmachus reads διέσωσεν ἄρσεν.

[12] The closest other parallel to Rev 12:3 is found in Mic 4:9-10. For other, less direct parallels, see also Mic 5:2-3; Isa 26:17; Gen 3:14-15; and 1QH 3:6-18, a text to be considered below.

[13] The term "allusion" is used here of phrases from the OT which are definitely in the mind of an author, yet where no introductory formula is given by him such as the expression "as it is written" in Rom 1:17. If one substitutes "alluding" for "quoting," the following statement by L.P. Trudinger is applicable here ("Some Observations Concerning the Text of the Old Testament in the Book of Revelation." *JTS* N.S. 17 [1966] 82): "One can be said to be quoting when one uses word combinations in a form in which one would *not* have used them had it not been for a knowledge of their occurrence in this particular form in another source."

[14] For the eschatological motif of escape, cf. the flight of the Day of the Lord, when "the Lord your God will come, and all the holy ones with him," when "the Lord will become king over all the earth," in Zech 14:5,9. For the King Messiah associated with this flight, see Leḳaḥ Ṭob Num 24:17. Reference from P. Billerbeck, *Kommentar zum Neuen Testament aus Talmud und Midrasch* (Munich: Beck, 1922-61) 2.298-99. See also Mark 13:14.

Rev 12:5 reads: "she brought forth a son, a male, one who is to rule all the nations with a rod of iron." The Greek ὃς μέλλει ποιμαίνειν πάντα τὰ ἔθνη ἐν ῥάβδῳ σιδηρᾷ reflects LXX Ps 2:9: ποιμανεῖς αὐτοὺς[15] ἐν ῥάβδῳ σιδηρᾷ. This clear allusion not only clinches the identification of the "son, a male," as the Messiah, it also may help to explain why Isa 66:7 is alluded to here. In the psalm the nations and their kings plot against the Lord and his Anointed. Yet the Lord shatters their plan, saying: "I have set my *king* on Zion, my holy hill." He decrees to his Anointed: "You are my *son*, today I have begotten you. Ask of me, and I will make the nations your heritage, and the ends of the earth your possession." Then comes the passage alluded to by the author of Revelation, whereby the LXX turns the "break" (them with a rod of iron; Hebrew רעע) into "shepherd," "guide," "*govern*" *(poimainō)*, a term suitable for kings.[16] Sonship and universal kingship or rule by the Messiah over all the nations, from Zion, are thus the points of contact between Ps 2:9 and Isa 66:7, causing the author of Revelation to associate them here.

Although the above discussion has dealt with the use of two OT texts interpreted messianically in Revelation 12, it should be noted that the emphasis in this chapter is not primarily on what happens to the child, the Messiah, but on what happens to his mother, the church. It is a suffering, persecuted church which the author of Revelation addresses. It is this church, the Christian churches of Asia Minor, which he attempts to comfort and undergird through his visions. In one of these, Revelation 12, the author shows that although the church is afflicted and tried by evil again and again, each time it is nourished by God (vv 6, 14) or can escape (v 16). This is the consolation he offers until the bride marries the lamb, until a new heaven and a new earth are created, when there shall neither be mourning nor crying nor pain anymore. Part of this consolation is made up of the messianic interpretation of Isa 66:7.

II. Three *Jewish Interpretations of Isa 66:7* show that it was logical for the Jewish-Christian writers of Revelation and Second Thessalonians, to be examined shortly, to interpret the verse messianically. They are A) Midrash Rabbah Genesis 85; B) Leviticus

---

[15]The *autous* here are the *ethnē* of the preceding verse, making the allusion complete.
[16]As will be shown shortly, the targum on Isa 66:7 substitutes "King" (Messiah) for the "son" of the MT, making the association of imagery from Ps 2:9 and Isa 66:7 very suitable.

Rabbah 14/9; and C) Targum Jonathan on Isa 66:7.[17] The relevance of the messianic "birth pangs" to this Isaianic verse will then be discussed.

A) Genesis Rabbah 85 (Vayesheb) on Gen 38:1, "It happened at that time that Judah went down from his brothers," etc., shows how a rabbinic reference to Isa 66:7 is interpreted as referring to the King Messiah.[18]

>R. Samuel b. Naḥman[19] commenced thus: "For I know the thoughts that I think toward you, saith the Lord" (Jer. XXIX, 11). The tribal ancestors were engaged in selling Joseph, Jacob was taken up with his sackcloth and fasting, and Judah was busy taking a wife, while the Holy One, blessed be He, was creating the light of the Messiah:[20] thus, "And it came to pass at that time, etc."[21]

>"Before she travailed, she brought forth" (Isa. LXVI, 7). Before the last who shall enslave [Israel] was born, the first redeemer was born, as it says, "And it came to pass at that time."[22]

---

[17]In addition to the following Jewish messianic interpretations of Isa 66:7, the quotation of Isa 66:5-11 by Justin Martyr in his Dialogue with Trypho 85:7-8 should be noted (Greek Text in C. Otto, *Iustini Philosophi et Martyris Opera*, vol. 2 [Jena: Dufft, 1888] 308-10. Corpus Apologetarum Christianorum, 2), since it clearly interprets the text messianically. Justin's text of Isaiah betrays enough important variants from the LXX and MT to imply that he is probably dependent on an inherited tradition here. The Jewish interpretations of Isa 66:7 now to be discussed probably point to the ultimate source of the tradition informing his Greek text. My attention was called to this passage in Justin by the article ὠδίν by G. Bertram in *TDNT* 9, 667-74. See also Irenaeus, Demonstratio 54; Methodius of Olympus' Symposion, eighth discourse, ch. 7; and Eusebius, Eccles. Hist. I. 4:3.

[18]The English translation of Midrash Rabbah (London: Soncino, 1961) is employed here. The reference is from vol. II, Genesis II, translated by H. Freedman, 787-88.

[19]Samuel bar Naḥman was a third generation Palestinian Amora. Cf. H. Strack and G. Stemberger, *Einleitung in Talmud und Midrasch* (Munich: Beck, 1982[7]) 93-94.

[20]This should read "King Messiah." Cf. the critical edition of *Bereshit Rabba* by J. Theodor and Ch. Albeck (Jerusalem: Wahrmann, 1965) vol. II, p. 1030: של מלך המשיח. It is based on the reading of MS "ח," which has מלך משיחנו. P. Billerbeck in Str-B 1.15-16 also prefers "King Messiah."

[21]The translator H. Freedman remarks here: "From the union of Judah and Tamar of which this chapter treats the Messiah was ultimately to spring" (Genesis II, 787, n. 5).

[22]H. Freedman notes that the current editions are perhaps preferable here. According to him they read: "Before the *first* enslaver was born (sc. Pharaoh), the *last* redeemer was born (the Messiah, whose advent was already being prepared now)" (Genesis II, 788, n. 1). P. Billerbeck in Str-B 1.15-16 (cf. 2. 346) also prefers the latter reading. For our purposes it is immaterial which reading should be preferred. The same passage reappears almost as it is here in Yalkut Shim'oni (New York: Horeb, 1925/26; reprint Jerusalem 1959) vol. I 144 (p. 89). Here the phrase מלך המשיח is also found.

B) Leviticus Rabbah 14/9 (Thazria) on Lev 12:2, "If a woman conceives and bears a male child ...", also clearly relates Isa 66:7 to the messianic age, the "time to come." R. Abbahu states:[23]

> In this world a woman bears children with pain, but of the Time to Come [see] what is written! "Before she will travail, she will have brought forth; before her pain will come, she will have been delivered of a man-child" (Isa. LXVI, 7).

The birth pains now typical of a woman about to bear will thus miraculously be lacking in the messianic age.

C) The most important Jewish parallel to the Christian messianic interpretation of Isa 66:7, however, is that of Targum Jonathan on this verse.[24] To facilitate comparison, the English translations of the Hebrew and Aramaic of vv 7-9 have been placed at the beginning of this essay. Of the targum's many differences from the Hebrew of chapter 66, the most remarkable is the messianic interpretation of v 7. For the Hebrew "before her [Jerusalem's] pain came upon her <u>she was delivered of a son</u> (המליטה זכר)," the targum reads, "before trembling shall come upon her, as pangs upon a woman with child, <u>her king shall be revealed</u> (יתגלי מלכה)."[25]

That the "king" here is the Messiah and not God is shown first of all in the great improbability of a Jew conscious of the Hebrew text substituting King = God for the son to be born of Jerusalem. For the Jew God is never "born," yet according to OT prophecy the Messiah will be. Secondly, there is evidence for the Messiah as King in other passages from the Isaiah targum, where the Messiah's "kingdom" can also be mentioned.[26] Thirdly, the term "messianic King" or "King Messiah" is a

---

[23] The text used here is also the Soncino edition of Midrash Rabbah, Vol. IV, Leviticus, translated by J. Israelstam, 187. According to Strack and Stemberger, *Einleitung* 94, R. Abbahu was a third generation Palestinian Amora.
[24] The editions of J.F. Stenning, *The Targum of Isaiah*, and A. Sperber, *The Bible in Aramaic*. 3. The Latter Prophets According to Targum Jonathan (Leiden: Brill, 1962), are employed here.
[25] Stenning's translation, my underlining. A variant reading, "the king" (מלכא), does not change the sense.
[26] Targ Isa 11:1 (cf. the allusion to Isa 11:4 in 2 Thess 2:8) reads, for example: "And a king shall come forth from the sons of Jesse, and an Anointed One (or *Messiah*) from his sons' sons shall grow up." The Hebrew is: "There shall come forth a shoot from the stump of Jesse, and a branch shall grow out of his roots." In the targum of v 10 the messianic King's rule is also mentioned: "And it shall come to pass at that time, that the son of the son of Jesse, who is about to arise as a sign to the peoples, to him shall the kingdoms be subject ...." (Cf. 1 Cor 15:24-28,) In Targ Isa 53:10 the Messiah has his own kingdom: the remnant of God's people "shall look upon the kingdom of their Anointed One (or *Messiah*) ...." This is lacking in the Hebrew. David is also called "king" in Targ Isa 55:4:

common expression found in Jewish and Jewish-Christian writings. Examples from other passages in the targums,[27] midrashim[28] and other writings[29] clearly show this.

In light of the above arguments the "king" of Targ Isa 66:7 must be taken to refer to the Messiah. The targum places the birth of the King Messiah in the future. The Hebrew, in contrast, has the past (perfect) tense for Jerusalem's delivering a son, who is clearly Israel, as shown by

---

"Behold, I have appointed him for a prince to the peoples, a king and a governor over all the kingdoms."

[27]Fragment Targum and Neofiti 1 on Num 11:26 read: "At the very end of the days Gog and Magog (will) ascend on Jerusalem and by the hands of King Messiah they fall" (translation by M. McNamara, *The New Testament and the Palestinian Targum to the Pentateuch* [Rome: Pontifical Biblical Institute, 1966] 236). Here the messianic King, as in Targ Isa 66:7, will triumph over evil in the final period, in Jerusalem. Targ 1 Chr 3:24 reads: "ענני: This is the King Messiah who shall reveal himself." He who comes with the "clouds" of Dan 7:13, in other words the Son of man, is meant here. For the Aramaic, see Sperber, *The Bible in Aramaic*, IV A, 6. Cf. the same connection of King Messiah and Son of man in Midrash Psalm 21 (W.G. Braude, *The Midrash on Psalms* [New Haven: Yale, 1959] 1.296) and in Tanḥuma B תולדות § 20 (70b). For the latter reference, see Str-B 1.486. Targ Jon Jer 30:21 states: "Their king shall be anointed from their midst, and their Messiah from among them."

[28]The midrash on Psalm 21 states that "God will call the king Messiah after His own name, for it is said of the king Messiah, 'This is his name whereby he shall be called: The Lord our righteousness (Jer 23:6)'" (translation W.G. Braude, *The Midrash on Psalms*, 1. 294. For the parallel traditions, see Str-B 3. 796 and 4. 922-23). In Tanḥuma שופטים 19a the King Messiah will destroy the godless with the breath of his lips, imagery borrowed from Isa 11:4. Reference from Str-B 3. 148; the parallel passage is found in 4. 880. Cf. the same imagery in 2 Thess 2:8. In the Fathers According to Rabbi Nathan, ch. 34, the King Messiah is inferred from Zech 4:14 and Ps 110:4 (Melchizedek). This is spoken by Rabban Simeon ben Gamaliel, active ca. 66-70 C.E. Cf. *The Fathers According to Rabbi Nathan*, trans. and ed. J. Goldin (New Haven: Yale, 1967) 138. For the dating of this rabbi, see Strack and Stemberger, *Einleitung* 75. Targ Jon Zech 4:12 has the Messiah.

[29]Ps Sol 17:21 speaks of "their king, the Son of David," who in v 24 is described as destroying the godless nations in terms of Ps 2:2 and Isa 11:4. In v 32 he is "their King, the Anointed of the Lord." This writing probably stems from 80-40 B.C.E. Cf. *The Apocrypha and Pseudepigrapha of the Old Testament*. Vol. II, Pseudepigrapha. Ed. R.H. Charles, Oxford: Clarendon, 1913, 625-30, and A.-M. Denis, *Introduction aux Pseudepigraphes Grecs d'Ancien Testament* (Leiden: Brill, 1970) 62. In the NT the triumphal entry of Matt 21:5; Luke 19:38; and John 12:13-15 is important, as well as the trial scene with its emphasis on Jesus' kingship, and Matt 25:34, 40. In the latter verses it is the Son of man, sitting on his throne, who as the King (Messiah) will judge the nations when he comes. In Mart Pol 9:3 and 17:3 Jesus is also described as King.

"a land," "a nation" and the plural (Zion's) "sons" in v 8.³⁰ The targum also omits the past (perfect) reference in v 8 of the MT to Zion's *having* brought forth her sons. For this it substitutes: "she shall be filled with the people of her exiles." This stresses the eschatological motif of gathering,³¹ which is part of Zion's comfort, a motif also lacking in v 8 of the MT.³² In all probability the tradition behind the targum has not only the "eastern" (former Assyrian and Babylonian) exiles in mind, but also the "western" exiles of the Hellenistic diaspora. It seeks to include all Israelites.

Why did the authors of the traditions found in Genesis Rabbah 85, Leviticus Rabbah 14/9, and the targum interpret the Hebrew of Isa 66:7 messianically?³³ They did so because, of the relatively few occurrences of חבל in the sense of "birth pang" in the OT, one is found here in the Isaianic vision of the final theophany of the Lord. Jerusalem's "pang(s)" were taken to mean the birth pang(s) or woe(s) of the Messiah, the חבלו של משיח, a well-known eschatological motif in Judaism, primarily signifying for God's people the persecution and oppression to come upon

---

³⁰It is also possible that the targum had as its basis the reading המליטה, without the waw, as found in the Qumran Isaiah Scroll. This would make it a better parallel in the Hebrew to ילדה. My former colleague at the Genezarethkirche in Berlin, the Rev. P. Baess, kindly informs me that the future (imperfect) tense is also found, as in the targum, in the Peshitta, which, however, does not interpret messianically.

³¹Note the addition in v 9 of the targum of "to gather together my exiles." God's promise in the MT of v 9, to complete what he has begun, is intended as assurance to his people that he will indeed come again. That time will be one of new birth, when new heavens and a new earth will be created and his people will endure (v 22). For the King Messiah as coming precisely to gather the exiles of Israel, cf. the saying of R. Ḥelbo cited by Str-B 1. 599 (see also the parallel in 4. 907).

³²For Isaiah 40-66 as employed by the Jews as passages of comfort, cf. their being read on the so-called "Consolation Sabbaths" of the Jewish liturgy. See my 1971 Yale dissertation, *Comfort in Judgment: The Use of Day of the Lord and Theophany Traditions in Second Thessalonians* 1, 264-66. The remark found in ch. 40 of *The Fathers According to Rabbi Nathan* (Goldin, 167) regarding the fate of a man seeing a particular book in a dream, is indicative of the Jewish estimation of Isaiah: "If Isaiah, let him look forward to consolation."

³³The verse is also quoted in Bereshit Rabbati on Gen 30:41 (ed. Ch. Albeck, Jerusalem: Mekize Nirdamim, 1940) 131 in connection with the birth of the Messiah in Bethlehem of Judah, associated with the destruction of the Temple. This is also found in Panim Aḥerim 2 on Est 2:7 in S. Buber, *Aggadic Books on the Scroll of Esther* (Vilna: Romm, 1886) 39b. Cf. also y. Ber. 2:4, 5a and Lam. Rab. 1:16 § 51 (Soncino English 7. 135-36). In the article "Haftarah" in *J.E.* (1904) 6.137, Isa 55:6-66:8 is the prophetic reading for the Ninth of Ab, commemorating the destruction of the Temple.

them before their Messiah arrives.³⁴ The origin of this idea lies with Dan 12:1, which states that before the time of the end, with the general resurrection of the dead and the judgment, "there shall be a time of trouble,³⁵ such as never has been ...."³⁶

This tradition of the Messianic Woes is found, for example, in A) rabbinic writings, B) the pseudepigrapha and the NT, and C) the Qumran writings.

A) R. Eliezer, a second generation Tanna,³⁷ stated that "If you will succeed in keeping the Sabbath you will escape the three visitations: The day of Gog, the suffering preceding the advent of the Messiah [חבלו של משיח], and the Great Judgment Day."³⁸

---

³⁴The Hebrew and Aramaic of Isa 66:7 emphasize a miraculous aspect. The pangs inevitably to be expected at the time of birth do not set in. For the targum this means that the King Messiah will be revealed without the customary "woes" or tribulations. That the writers of Revelation and Second Thessalonians chose not to consider this miraculous element of painlessness but employed the passage precisely in a situation of persecution, means that they chose those elements of Jewish tradition in and concerning this verse which best fit their own situation.

³⁵The Hebrew is עת צרה, the LXX ἐκείνη ἡ ἡμέρα θλίψεως. That צרה and חבל can both mean "birth pang" is shown in Jer 49:24, where they are used together of a woman in travail. The LXX's "that day of tribulation" in Dan 12:1 is eschatological and points to the Day of the Lord. LXX Hab 3:16 also reads: "I shall rest in the day of tribulation," making the unclear Hebrew, probably present, into an eschatological future. The references to Dan 12:1 and Hab 3:16 are from H. Schlier, article θλίβω κτλ. in *TDNT,* 3.142. These passages are especially relevant to the interpretation of the situation described in Second Thessalonians.

³⁶For a general discussion of the messianic woes in Jewish sources, cf. Str-B 4. 977-86, as well as the index under "Wehen des Messias" and "Drangsalsperiode." See also P. Volz, *Die Eschatologie der jüdischen Gemeinde im neutestamentlichen Zeitalter* (Tübingen: Mohr, 1934) par. 31: Die letzte böse Zeit, 147-63. Billerbeck is certainly correct in asserting that by the expression "birth pang(s) of the Messiah" one understood "not the pangs or sufferings which come upon the Messiah, but according to passages such as Isa 16:17; 66:8 [sic]; Jer 22:23; Hos 13:13; Mic 4:9-10 the pains by which the messianic period is to be born" (Str-B 1.950). For a survey of the motif complex of the pregnant woman and her birth pangs in the OT and the pseudepigrapha, see also W. Harnisch, *Eschatologische Existenz. Ein Beitrag zum Sachanliegen von 1 Thess* 4_{13}-5_{11} (Göttingen: Vandenhoeck & Ruprecht, 1973) 62-72. Harnisch is not aware of a Jewish messianic interpretation of Isa 66:7, which he treats on pp. 66-67, nor does he perceive the relevance of the verb "restrain" in 66:9 for 2 Thess 2:6-7.

³⁷Cf. Strack and Stemberger, *Einleitung* 77.

³⁸Mekilta Vayassaʿ 5 on Exod 16:16-27, specifically on "And Moses Said: 'Eat that today.'" The translation is from *Mekilta de-Rabbi Ishmael,* ed. J.Z. Lauterbach (Philadelphia: The Jewish Publication Society of America, 1949) vol. II, 120. Cf. Eliezer's using the same expression in b. Sanh. 98b.

The woes at the time of the revelation of the King Messiah are also reflected in Pesikta Rabbati 36, where R. Isaac[39] taught that "in the year in which the king Messiah will reveal himself, all the kings of the nations of the earth will be at strife with one another." All the nations of the world will be agitated and frightened; "they will be seized with pangs like the pangs of a woman in labor." God will then say to a frightened Israel: "The time of your redemption is come."[40] After this final redemption there will be no more enslavement.

It should be noted that the sufferings described here as the messianic birth pangs signify that Israel's redemption "is come." This is important for the interpretation of 2 Thess 2:2, where the Day of the Lord, the Day of the Messiah, "has come."[41]

B) In the apocalypses of the pseudepigraphical writings the messianic woes are a stock theme.[42] The various woes to precede the coming of the Son of man in the synoptic apocalypse of the NT (Mark 13, Matthew 24, Luke 21) and in Revelation 8, 9 and 11, directly before chapter twelve, are also well-known. It should be emphasized that in all these passages the woes, both celestial and terrestrial, do not all occur at once, but are spread out over a certain period of time. When they become most intense, when men think that God has forgotten the earth, the King Messiah will come.[43]

C) That the idea of the birth pangs was already employed messianically between the Jewish War of 66-70 C.E. and by yet another section of Judaism, is shown in one of the hymns from Qumran, 1QH

---

[39]R. Isaac was probably a third generation Palestinian Amora (Strack and Stemberger, *Einleitung* 94).
[40]English translation by W.G. Braude, *Pesikta Rabbati* (New Haven: Yale, 1969) vol. II, 681-82. The original in M. Friedmann, *Pesikta Rabbati* (Vienna: Selbstverlag des Herausgebers, 1880) on Piska 36 (162), reads: הגיע (ימי)[זמן] גאולתכם. That "is come" and not "is near" is the correct translation here is shown in the LXX, which translates נגע of time in Ezra 3:1; Neh 7:73; and Cant 2:12 with φθάνειν, "to arrive," "to come." In Est 9:1 πάρειμι, "to be present," is found. Only in Ps 87 (88):4 does ἐγγίζειν, "to approach," "to come near," occur. Ezek 7:12 has הגיע parallel to בא: "the time has come, the day has come" (my translation). In this chapter "the end has come upon the four corners of the land" (v 12); it is the "day of the wrath of the Lord" (v 19). The tension between "coming" and "having come" is shown clearly in v 6: "the end has come ...; behold, it comes."
[41]Cf. F. Delitzsch's translation of the phrase from 2 Thess 2:2 into Hebrew in his ספרי הברית החדשה (London: British and Foreign Bible Society, 1958) 385: כְּאִלּוּ הִגִּיעַ יוֹם הַמָּשִׁיחַ (יי).
[42]Cf., for example, 2 Apoc Bar 25-30:1; 48:33-37; 70; and 4 Ezra 4:51-5:13; 6:21-24; 9:1-6.
[43]Cf., for example, Sib Or 5.106-07 and 2 Apoc Bar 25.

3:2-18.[44] After comparing himself to a ship in the depths of the sea and to a fortified city, the author of this psalm employs the imagery of a woman in her birth pangs to describe himself. The Hebrew here uses both צירים and חבלו of the pangs, as in Jer 49:24. The setting of the community is that of intense persecution: "the children have reached as far as the billows of Death" (1.8). In this context the pregnant woman shall give birth to a man-child (1.9), a "Marvellous Counsellor with his might" (1.10), which is a clear allusion to the Messiah of Isa 9:6. It is a hotly debated question whether the Messiah, an individual, is to be born by the author, whom many interpreters consider the Teacher of Righteousness,[45] or whether the Teacher as the woman gives birth to a collective child, which would be the members of the Teacher's community.[46] In view of the clear allusion to the messianic text Isa 9:6; the improbability of the members of the Teacher's congregation being described as "a Marvellous Counsellor with his might"; and the targumic interpretation of a very parallel text, Isa 66:7, the probability is that an individual, the Messiah, is meant. If so, this text offers another example of how the intense persecution felt by the Qumran community led to

---

[44]The hymns are very difficult to date. G. Vermes in *The Dead Sea Scrolls in English* (Baltimore: Penguin, 1962) 149, believes that "the collection as such probably attained its final shape during the last century of the sect's history," i.e., before the destruction of the monastery in the Jewish War of 66-70 C.E. There are indications, however, that many of the hymns are older and were probably used for liturgical purposes.

The Hebrew of 1QH3 is found in *Oṣar hammegillôt haggĕnûzôt* (Jerusalem: Bialik Institute and the Hebrew University, 1954), ed. E.L. Sukenik, plate 37 and p. 37. An English translation is offered by A. Dupont-Sommer, *The Essene Writings from Qumran* (Cleveland and New York: World, 1962; translated from the French by G. Vermes) 208.

[45]For this viewpoint, cf., for example, W.H. Brownlee, "Messianic Motifs of Qumran and the New Testament" in *NTS* 3 (1956) 12-30. Brownlee specifically buttresses his argument with references to Isa 66:7 and Rev 12:5 (pp. 24-25). The woman in 1QH 3 may also be the Qumran community, which is to give birth to the Messiah, as maintained by Dupont-Sommer, *The Essene Writings from Qumran,* 208, n. 3.

[46]Cf., for example, O. Betz, "Die Geburt der Gemeinde durch den Lehrer. Bemerkungen zum Qumranpsalm 1QH iii, iff. (1QH ii. 21-iii. 18)," in *NTS* 3 (1956/57) 314-26. Betz too considers Isa 66:7 an especially important parallel (p. 316), yet in view of the plural "sons" in v 8 also interprets the זכר of this Thanksgiving Psalm collectively. He concedes that the author of Rev 12:5 interprets the "son" of Isa 66:7 as an individual, the Messiah, yet that this is the meaning of the author's Jewish source is for him "more than doubtful" (p. 319). In light of Targum Isaiah and the Midrash Rabbah passages cited above, Betz's interpretation of the "son" of Isa 66:7 as exclusively collective seems forced.

their interpreting their own condition as the birth pangs to precede the advent of the Messiah.[47]

The above examples of the messianic birth pangs as found in various Jewish sources show that the Jewish-Christian authors of Revelation and Second Thessalonians could very naturally employ Isa 66:7, with its "son" and "birth pangs" imagery in a setting of the final coming of the Lord, in their own descriptions of the coming of the Messiah, especially in a situation of persecution.

III. *Second Thessalonians 1.* The author of Second Thessalonians, whether Paul or a member of the Pauline "school," clearly addresses a severely persecuted community.[48] Because the addressees believe their sufferings have reached their peak, they conceive of them as one of the elements in the messianic woes, themselves part of the coming of the Day of the Lord.[49] They argue as follows: "Our intense persecution shows that the End has come (that is, it has started to come). The birth pangs of the Messiah, the Lord, a part of his coming, are already here. The Messiah's Day,[50] the Lord's Day, therefore, has started to come."[51]

---

[47]If the collective interpretation of the male-child is preferred, the fact remains that a community described in the messianic terms of Isa 9:6 is born of the birth pangs of a woman, probably the Teacher of Righteousness. In a major study of Qumran messianism, A.S. van der Woude's *Die messianischen Vorstellungen der Gemeinde von Qumran* (Assen: van Gorcum, 1957), the author denies that the (or "a") Messiah is meant in 1QH 3:10, yet acknowledges that the זכר תמליט of 1.9 recalls Isa 66:7 (149, n. 17). As I do, he believes that the Teacher of Righteousness and his congregation, subject to the persecution of the godless priest, considered their tribulations as the messianic woes here in 1QH 3 (p. 155).
[48]The following verses attest this: 1:4 ("all your persecutions"; "the afflictions you *are* enduring"), 5, 6, 7, 8; 2:7 (the mystery of lawlessness, a form of persecution, is already at work), 15 (stand firm), 16-17 (comfort and hope); 3:3 (strengthen and guard), 5 (the steadfastness of Christ). The concentration of these indications in the first chapter shows that the author considers this the most important issue with which he must deal. He therefore handles it first.
[49]Isa 13:6-8 clearly shows a direct connection between the Day of the Lord and the birth pangs, later used to describe the messianic woes.
[50]For the rare singular "Day of the King Messiah," cf. Targ Jon Gen 3:15 (Aramaic text in McNamara, *The New Testament,* 218). This is in all probability modeled on the Hebrew of Hos 7:5: "on the day of our king." The motif of enthronement is certainly present here. See also 4 Ezra 13:52 for the Messiah's "Day." Note how easily the "Day of the King Messiah" could be equated with, or at least made parallel to, the Day of the Lord.
[51]The position of A.M.G. Stephenson in "On the Meaning of ἐνέστηκεν ἡμέρα τοῦ κυρίου in 2 Thessalonians 2,2," SE IV (=TU102 of 1968, 442-51), that "is just at hand" is the preferable translation, shows no appreciation of the various stages involved in the arrival of the Day of the Lord, including the intense persecution of believers. This forces him to translate as he does. For the OT

The same reasoning is followed here as in Pesikta Rabbati 36, mentioned above, where the sufferings of Israel, also described as the messianic birth pangs, signify that Israel's redemption "has come." The addressees of Second Thessalonians do not maintain that the *parousia* (2:1), the visible coming of the Lord Jesus in his glory, has occurred. They do maintain, however, that his Day has *started* to come, therefore they can also express it as "having come."

As shall now be shown, Isaiah 66 was chosen by the author of Second Thessalonians as the background for his remarks in chapter one. Two major reasons caused him to do so. First, Isa 66:9 provided him with the delaying factor he needed to convince his addressees in chapter two that the Day of the Lord had not yet arrived.[52] In the meantime, however, as a good pastor he needed to comfort them in their present tribulation. This he does by portraying in a judgment theophany in 1:7-10 how at the Lord's coming they will receive rest from their persecutions, and their persecutors will be repaid with affliction. The second impetus he had for employing Isaiah 66 in chapter one was the fact that as an OT passage describing the final coming of the Lord, it fitted his subject matter very well, especially since the birth pangs occur in 66:7, which, as has been seen, was probably already in the author's time part of a known messianic tradition.[53] Even if he independently

---

precedent of the Day of the Lord as "having come" in a setting of suffering, distress and affliction, cf. for example the Hebrew of Lam 1:21. This day is the day of the Lord's fierce anger (1:12), when fallen Zion has no one to "comfort" her (1:21). The author calls for one-to-one vengeance on his enemies (1:22), as in 2 Thess 1:6, 8, 9, another Day of the Lord passage (cf. "that day" in 1:10 and the Day of the Lord as "having come" in 2:2).

[52]In 2:6 and 7 the terms τὸ κατέχον and ὁ κατέχων derive from the Hebrew of Isa 66:9: עצר, "to withhold," "to restrain." This Hebrew verb is translated twice by *katechein* in the LXX: Judg 13:15-16 Vaticanus. In addition, *katechein* is directly associated with the birth woes in Jer 6:24 (θλῖψις κατέσχεν ἡμᾶς, ὠδῖνες ὡς τικτούσης); 13:21; 37 (30):6 (a Day of the Lord context); and Ps 47 (48):7 Symmachus (the final battle of the heathen against Jerusalem). The propinquity of the עצר of Isa 66:9 to v 7, interpreted messianically in Jewish sources, and to other verses in Isaiah 66 employed in 2 Thessalonians 1, argues strongly for its forming the background of the author's thought here. It also argues against any theory of the composition of Second Thessalonians which makes chapter one and chapter two parts of two separate letters.

I would also maintain that in 2 Thess 2:4 the phrase ὁ ἀντικείμενος occurs to the author because of its being found in Isa 66:6: τοῖς ἀντικειμένοις; ναὸν is also suggested by the same Isaianic verse.

[53]For recent research on the dating of the targums, cf. McNamara, *The New Testament*, ch. 1, VI, and ch. 2; as well as J. Bowker, *The Targums and Rabbinic Literature* (Cambridge: The University Press, 1964) ch. 1. J.F. Stenning in *The Targum of Isaiah,* ix-x, states that the present form of Targum Isaiah is not earlier than the fifth century C.E., and places the fixing of the

The Relevance of Isaiah 66:7 to Revelation 12 and 2 Thessalonians 1 139

made the same exegetical re-interpretation of v 7 as others did,⁵⁴ the fact remains that he was aware of these "woes" in v 7 and applied imagery from nearby verses to the Messiah, the Lord.⁵⁵ This is most logical if he interpreted or knew of the situation of his addressees as characterized by intense persecution, part of the messianic birth pangs.

The following passages in 2 Thessalonians 1 show the author's heavy indebtedness to Isaiah 66 here.

1) The phrase in 1:6, δίκαιον παρὰ θεῷ ἀνταποδοῦναι τοῖς θλίβουσιν...θλῖψιν, "it is just before God to repay with affliction those afflicting you," recalls the motif and phraseology of Isa 66:6: φωνὴ κυρίου ἀνταποδίδοντος ἀνταπόδοσιν τοῖς ἀντικειμένοις, "the voice of the Lord rendering recompense to his opponents."⁵⁶ At the time of the Lord's coming in the OT, of the King Messiah's coming in the targum, and of the Lord Jesus' coming here in the NT, recompense will be meted out to those opposing the final coming.⁵⁷

2) In 1:8 the phrase ἐν φλογὶ πυρός, "in a flame of fire," "in flaming fire," is to be preferred to ἐν πυρὶ φλογός (Nestle, following B. Weiss) and derives from Isa 66:15: ἐν φλογὶ πυρός. The main support for this assertion is the fact that Isa 66:15 is alluded to in the next phrase of 1:8. The MT has here "in flames of fire," the targum in contrast "in a flame of

---

traditional rendering of the prophets in the third century C.E. Nevertheless, "it was the living tradition of the Targum scholars which was the actual authority for determining the accepted interpretation" (p. ix). How far back the oral tradition behind the "king" of Isa 66:7 reaches is no longer ascertainable with certainty. In light of the messianic use of Isa 66:7 in the Jewish and Jewish-Christian sources cited above, however, the probability is that the expression "king," which is still found in the present state of the targum, was the basis for later messianic interpretations.

⁵⁴For the Greek-speaking Christian the κύριος of the LXX easily lent itself to being interpreted as the "Lord" (Jesus). Thus imagery describing the final coming of the kyrios in Isaiah 66 could understandably be applied to the Lord Jesus' final coming by the author of Second Thessalonians.

⁵⁵If Second Thessalonians is by Paul, it should be noted that in Acts 17:7 the Jews of Thessalonica accuse him and his fellow missionaries of saying "there is another king, Jesus." They cleverly interpret this as "acting against the decrees of Caesar," an action which would immediately lead to the Christians' being indicted for insurrection in Thessalonica, the capital of Macedonia and the seat of the Roman proconsul. Since the author of Acts in all probability found the term "king" in his source, the question must be raised whether Paul and his companions used the title "Christ the King" or "King Messiah" in their missionary preaching or catechesis in Thessalonica. If so, did it derive from Targ Isa 66:7?

⁵⁶For Isa 66:6 used in rabbinic sources for eschatological punishment, cf. for example Pesiq. R. 17/8; Pesiq. Rab Kah. 7; Sifre Numbers 77; Numbers Rabbah 10; and Midrash Psalms 18/11; 84/1.

⁵⁷Cf. the similar imagery in another Day of the Lord passage, Obad 14-15.

fire," agreeing with the LXX.[58] Nestle's comma after *en phlogi pyros* is correct. The phrase describes here the splendor of the Lord Jesus' revelation, not how he will render vengeance. The author of Second Thessalonians intentionally is more reticent than Third Isaiah.[59]

3) In 1:8 the two phrases διδόντος ἐκδίκησιν τοῖς μὴ εἰδόσιν θεὸν καὶ τοῖς μὴ ὑπακούουσιν, "inflicting vengeance upon those who do not know God and upon those who do not obey (the gospel of our Lord Jesus)," are a conflation of LXX Isa 66:15 (ἀποδοῦναι ... ἐκδίκησιν) and 66:4 (ἀνταποδώσω ... οὐχ ὑπήκουσαν) with LXX Ps 78:6 (S [א]: μὴ εἰδότα σε.[60] It was natural for the author to employ LXX 66:15 here, for it is the main theophanic passage in Isaiah 66, the other being v 18. It not only expresses the certainty of the Lord's coming, but also the motif of vengeance upon the opponent, both of which are intended to comfort the addressees.

4) The phrase in 1:12, ὅπως ἐνδοξασθῇ ... ἐν ὑμῖν, "so that the name of our Lord Jesus may be glorified in you," derives from LXX Isa 66:5, ἵνα τὸ ὄνομα κυρίου δοξασθῇ, "in order that the name of the Lord be glorified." The *en* of *endoxasthē* stems from the use of *endoxasthēnai* in 2 Thess 1:10, this in turn stemming from LXX Ps 88:8. Of the six occurrences of *onoma* with *doxazein* in the LXX, only Isa 66:5 uses *to onoma kyriou* and introduces the glorification of the name with *hina*.[61] This makes the identification of the allusion certain.

In addition to the above verses in 2 Thessalonians 1 which derive from the LXX of Isaiah 66, there are three other elements which may show the influence of the targum.

1) Verse seven speaks of the "revelation" (ἀποκάλυψις) of the Lord Jesus from heaven with the angels of his might. In the MT of Isa 66:15 the Lord will come in fire (יבוא; cf. LXX ἥξει). This verb, אתה and ירד are the most common Hebrew theophanic verbs. In the targum on 66:15, in contrast, the Lord "revealeth himself" (מתגלי) in fire." In addition, two

---

[58]The strength of the reading *en pyri phlogos* derives from LXX Exod 3:2 B, another theophany, the appearance of God to Moses in the bush. However, even in the LXX the dominant reading appears to be *en phlogi pyros*, agreeing with the MT, "in a flame of fire." For the reading *en pyri phlogos* in 2 Thess 1:8, see P. Katz, Ἐν πυρὶ φλογός, *ZNW* 46 (1955) 133-38, where he bases his argument on the Hebrew construct state of Exod 3:2, which he sees alluded to here. See also *BDF* § 165, p. 92.

[59]For a discussion of this fire imagery, including reference to the *phlox pyros* of God's throne in Dan 7:9, cf. *Comfort in Judgment* 80-82.

[60]The justification for the conflation with LXX Ps 78:6 is too extensive to be outlined here. Cf. *Comfort in Judgment* 83-88, and the commentators. The use of Isa 66:15 and 4, however, is clear.

[61]The author of Second Thessalonians changes the *hina* to *hopōs* in 1:12 for stylistic reasons. He does not wish to duplicate the *hina* of v 11.

other usages of "to be revealed" occur in ch. 66 which are lacking in the MT. In v 14 the might of the Lord shall be revealed (תתגלי). The strongest influence exerted here, however, is from v 7, where the King (Messiah) shall be revealed (יתגלי). The targum thus may have supplied the author of 2 Thessalonians with his term "revelation" in 1:7.[62]

2) The motif of the "might" of the Lord in 1:7 is suitable pastorally as comfort for the presently weak addressees. It may be due to the targum's accentuation of the might of the Lord. In four verses of Targum Isaiah 66 (vv 2, 14, 15, 19) the motif is added to the MT.

3) Isa 66:15, with its motif of vengeance, is alluded to in 1:8, as is Isa 66:4. Targ Isa 66:4 accentuates this motif of vengeance in regard to the misery to be inflicted by God on false worshipers. Instead of the Hebrew תעלולים, "evil deeds," or the ἐμπαίγματα ("mockeries," "tricks") of the LXX, it employs the noun תברא, which literally means "what is broken up," then "misfortune." Stenning translates "destruction." The targum thus may have aided in influencing the vengeful tone in 1:6-10.[63]

While these elements individually are not totally convincing, cumulatively they do speak for the possibility that the targum in an earlier form, in addition to the messianic interpretation of Isa 66:7, influenced the author of Second Thessalonians.

* * *

This essay has been concerned with the influence of Isa 66:7 on Revelation 12 and 2 Thessalonians 1. Jewish interpretations of this verse show that it was understood messianically precisely because of the "birth pangs" or "woes" associated with the Messiah's coming. Because the Jewish-Christian authors of Revelation and Second Thessalonians addressed severely persecuted Christian communities, they could very

---

[62]For a well-documented survey of the "revelation of the Messiah" in the targums, cf. McNamara, *The New Testament* 246-52, where the author relates the term to the *epiphaneia* of Christ in 2 Thess 2:8. He strangely omits 1:7. His references (pp. 250-51) to Targ Isa 24:23 and 31:4-5, where the targum says that the *kingdom* of the Lord of hosts shall be "revealed" on Mount Zion, should be noted. See also Targ Jon Obad 21 and Targ Jon Zech 14:9.

The revelation of the Man of Lawlessness and the Lawless One in 2 Thess 2:3, 6 and 8 is a counterpart to the revelation of Jesus in 1:7. The term "revelation" in 1:7 may, of course, simply be a standard term in apocalyptic language associated with the Day of the Lord. Cf. its use in another thanksgiving, 1 Cor 1:7, as well as its association with present sufferings, future glory, and birth pangs in Rom 8:18-22.

[63]Cf. also the "eternal destruction" of 2 Thess 1:8. The last chapter of Isaiah on the whole is very much concerned with a vindication of the righteous, which means for the author the punishment of all opponents. See vv 4-6, 14-17, 24.

appropriately employ this and neighboring verses from the final theophany of the Lord in Isaiah 66 to describe the coming of Jesus, their Messiah, who for them was soon to become King over the entire world.

7

God's Plan and God's Power: Isaiah 66 and the Restraining Factors of 2 Thess 2:6-7

One of the most puzzling problems in the NT, even before the advent of modern critical study of the bible, has been the interpretation of the phrases τὸ κατέχον and ὁ κατέχων in 2 Thess 2:6-7. Throughout the centuries the most varied suggestions as to the meaning of the expressions have been made, including the favorite view of the Roman state and the Roman emperor, as well as the binding of Satan or evil by an angel or God.[1] More recently scholars have thought of the preaching of the gospel to the heathen, and Paul;[2] God's own will and plan for both expressions;[3] a "seizing force," and an (unknown) individual

---

[1] For a good survey of recent and previous research, cf. the most recent commentary on Thessalonians, that of E. Best: *The First and Second Epistles to the Thessalonians* (Black's; London: Black, 1972) 295-301. For older research the survey found in W. Bornemann, *Die Thessalonicher* (Meyer 10; Göttingen: Vandenhoeck & Ruprecht, 1894) 400-459, is invaluable.

[2] Cf. O. Cullmann, "Der eschatologische Charakter des Missionsauftrages und des apostolischen Selbstbewusstseins bei Paulus. Untersuchung zum Begriff des κατέχον (κατέχων) in 2 Thess. 2,6-7" (German translation of French original, in *RHPR* 16 [1936] 210-45) in *Vorträge und Aufsätze. 1925-1962* (Tübingen: Mohr; Zurich: Zwingli, 1966) 305-36. Cullmann maintains (317) that the term κατέχειν is the "exact rendering of the Aramaic עכב." His basic theses were taken over and adapted by J. Munck, *Paul and the Salvation of Mankind* (Richmond: John Knox, 1959), see especially pp. 36-68.

[3] Cf. "Die theozentrische Katechon-Argumentation 2. Thess 2, 1-12," especially p. 103, in A. Strobel's *Untersuchungen zum eschatologischen Verzögerungsproblem* (NovTSup 2; Leiden/Köln: Brill, 1961). Strobel correctly sees that τὸ κατέχον is God's will or plan, and ὁ κατέχων, more narrowly defined, is God himself in 2 Thess 2:6-7 (107). He maintains that the אחר of Hab 2:3 is the background of the two κατέχειν phrases (101-2, 110; אחר in the form of מעכב, 104-5). He has the methodological difficulty that he assumes Pauline authorship of 2 Thessalonians from the outset.

incorporating this force;[4] the "mystery of lawlessness" and the "man of lawlessness";[5] and the idea of restraining and its function, in and of themselves.[6] A Hebrew verbal parallel from Qumran has also been thought to be of aid here.[7] Because of the great number of interpretation possibilities in the text of 2 Thessalonians 2, most commentators simply present the major alternative solutions and let the reader choose between them, presuming that no probable answers can be reached.[8]

The use of definite passages from the OT in the first chapter of 2 Thessalonians, however, offers the possibility that the author[9] has used one of these same passages for part of the background of his thought on the κατέχον/κατέχων complex several verses later.[10] First, it is probable that Psalm 88(89) is employed both in 2 Thess 1:10 and in 2:3.[11]

---

[4]See the monograph of C.H. Giblin, *The Threat to Faith: An Exegetical and Theological Re-examination of 2 Thessalonians 2* (AnBib 31; Rome: Pontifical Biblical Institute, 1967) 246. Like Strobel, Giblin assumes the Pauline authorship of 2 Thessalonians. He was not aware of Strobel's study, nor does he once mention the ancient church's interpretation (see below) of τὸ κατέχον as the gospel first being preached to all the nations before the end comes, and ὁ κατέχων as God. He considers אחר to be the most probable Hebrew background of κατέχειν (183).

[5]Cf. J. Coppens, "Les deux Obstacles au Retour glorieux du Sauveur (II Thess., II, 6-7)," *ETL* 46 (1970) 383-89.

[6]Cf. W. Trilling, *Untersuchungen zum zweiten Thessalonicherbrief* (Erfurter theologische Studien, 27; Leipzig: St. Benno, 1972) 85. In contrast to Giblin and in accordance with Strobel's interpretation, Trilling maintains that the function of κατέχειν in 2 Thess 2:6-7 is definitely that of "delaying"; it is positive; and it proceeds from and is produced by God (83-84).

[7]Cf. O. Betz, "Der Katechon," in *NTS* 9 (1962/63) 276-91, who points to the תומכים of the Book of Mysteries, 1Q27, 1.7.

[8]Although B. Rigaux had written a major work on the traditions of the Antichrist, he could not, for example, use his insights to clarify in a major way the interpretation of the κατέχειν problem. Cf. his statement in *Les Epîtres aux Thessaloniciens* (Etudes bibliques; Paris: Lecoffre; Gembloux: Duculot, 1956) 279: "Nous nous avouons incapable de découvrir en quoi elle [the reality which restrains the satanic activity] consiste."

[9]The question of Pauline authorship is left open here. However, the author is definitely a member of the Pauline "school" and wishes his writing to be viewed as if from Paul. It is intended as a correction and/or supplementation of 1 Thessalonians.

[10]Bornemann (*Die Thessalonicher*, 357) laid down five principles according to which one must interpret 2 Thessalonians 2. The first is most important: the OT must be understood in a Christian sense, and Jewish or Christian apocalyptic writings should be consulted as the author's source for his teaching regarding the last things.

[11]In 2 Thess 1:10, Ps LXX 88:8 is alluded to in the phrase ὅταν ἔλθη ἐνδοξασθῆναι ἐν τοῖς ἁγίοις αὐτοῦ. Of the thirteen occurrences of ἐνδοξάζω in

God's Plan and God's Power

Secondly, I have elsewhere proposed that the last chapter of Isaiah (66), describing the final theophany of the Lord, has influenced the presentation of Jesus' final appearance in 2 Thessalonians 1 in a major way.[12] This essay will now point out how other verses in Isaiah 66 help to explain what and who are "holding up"[13] the coming of the Day of the Lord, his return in glory, in 2 Thess 2:6-7. Part I discusses reflections of Isaiah 66 in 2 Thessalonians 2, excluding ὁ κατέχων in v 7. Then evidence will be presented that the author of 2 Thessalonians independently translated various Hebrew OT expressions into Greek, or was aware of them, in chapter two (Part II). This leads to the proposal that the Hebrew verb עצר found in Isa 66:9 forms the background of the phrase ὁ κατέχων in 2 Thess 2:7 (Part III). The above findings are then applied to the context of 2 Thess 2:6-7 (Part IV). A table is appended summarizing the employment of various verses from Isaiah 66 in 2 Thessalonians 1-2.

I

(1) 2 Thess 2:4 states that the man of lawlessness, the son of perdition, "opposes and exalts himself against every so-called god or object of worship, so that he takes his seat in the temple of God, proclaiming himself to be God." The Greek for "opposes" is the participle ὁ ἀντικείμενος. This is most probably borrowed from the phrase τοῖς ἀντικειμένοις of Isa 66:6, referring to the "enemies" of God,

---

the LXX, only in Psalm 88 does the verb occur with οἱ ἅγιοι, as in 2 Thess 1:10. For a detailed discussion, including the use of Ps LXX 67:36 here, see my Yale dissertation, *Comfort in Judgment: The Use of Day of the Lord and Theophany Traditions in Second Thessalonians 1* (New Haven, 1971) 97-99.

Ps LXX 88:23 speaks of God's servant David: "The enemy shall not outwit him, the wicked shall not humble him" (translation is from RSV, which is also employed elsewhere unless stated otherwise). "The wicked," singular, is υἱὸς ἀνομίας in the Greek. This phrase forms part of the background of the expressions ὁ ἄνθρωπος τῆς ἀνομίας, ὁ υἱὸς τῆς ἀπωλείας in 2 Thess 2:3, who are the same figure. In *Pesiq. R.* 36/1 (W.G. Braude, *Pesikta Rabbati* [Yale Judaica Series, 18; New Haven/London: Yale University, 1968] 678) the "him" of Ps 89:23 is also God's "true Messiah." To my knowledge it was Bornemann (*Die Thessalonicher, 356*) who first called attention to the allusion to Psalm 88(89) in 2:3.

[12]Cf. "The Relevance of Isaiah 66:7 to Revelation 12 and 2 Thessalonians 1" in *ZNW* 67 (1976) 252-68, and earlier in *Comfort in Judgment.* Space does not allow a repetition of those arguments here. See, however, the Table appended to this essay.

[13]Since the first meaning of κατέχειν given in LSJ 926, is "hold back," "restrain," I assume this basic meaning from the outset. It is accepted by the great majority of the commentators and is corroborated by the results of this essay.

those "opposed" to him. As in 2 Thess 2:4, in Isaiah the opponents are also associated with the (Jerusalem) temple.[14]

(2) The "Temple" in 2 Thess 2:4, ναὸν, in all probability derives from the ναὸν of Isa 66:6. As will be proposed below, ναός has been inserted into an allusion to Ezek 28:2 in 2 Thess 2:4 to fit the author's needs here. The Ezekiel text speaks of the seat of the gods as being in the heart of the seas, not in the Jerusalem *temple*. It would be logical for the author to continue his borrowing from the same Isaianic verse, 66:6, and to employ its ναός, not a different Greek expression such as ἅγιον or ἱερόν. Also, he derived the motif and some of the phraseology of δίκαιον ... θλῖψιν in 1:6 from Isa 66:6.[15] He thus easily could have the same Isaiah verse in mind several verses later in the expressions ὁ ἀντικείμενος and ναὸν. Finally, if the "son" of Isa 66:7, interpreted in the targum as the "king," is for the author of 2 Thessalonians the messianic King, as is the case in several Jewish and Jewish-Christian sources,[16] the author may have employed phrases from the adjacent verse (66:6) partially because of their propinquity to this term.[17]

(3) After the eschatological judgment theophany of Isa 66:15-16, which is employed in the judgment theophany of 2 Thess 1:7-10, and which emphasizes the fact that the Lord will execute judgment upon "all flesh" (cf. 66:23), the author of the latter chapters of Isaiah describes in 66:18-21 how the Lord will come to gather all nations and tongues. The latter will come to Jerusalem and see his glory. From the nations which have come to Jerusalem, and which apparently have participated in the judgment of v 16, the Lord will send survivors to the nations (Tarshish, Put, Lud, Tubal, Javan and the coastlands) "that have not heard my fame or seen my glory" (v 19). After declaring God's glory among the nations, these survivors will bring all the Jewish people from all the nations to Jerusalem as an offering to the Lord (v 20). Some of these pagans the Lord will even take as priests and Levites. In fact (v 23), "all flesh shall come to worship before me, says the Lord."

---

[14]Strobel (*Untersuchungen*, 104) maintains that the closest parallel to ὁ ἀντικείμενος in 2 Thess 2:4 is the ἀντικεῖσθαι phrase of Zech 3:1 LXX, connected with Satan. Yet the man of lawlessness, described as ὁ ἀντικείμενος, cannot be Satan, as 2 Thess 2:9 shows.

[15]See "The Relevance," 266 (here, p. 139), which also suggests that in 2 Thess 1:8 (τοῖς μὴ ὑπακούουσιν) the author had borrowed from Isa 66:4, and in 1:12 (ὅπως ἐνδοξασθῇ τὸ ὄνομα ... ἐν ὑμῖν) from Isa 66:5. This borrowing from neighboring verses makes the use of expressions from Isa 66:6 in 2:4 all the more probable.

[16]See "The Relevance," 253-60, here pp. 127-133.

[17]This whole argument deals in probabilities and is cumulative.

God's Plan and God's Power   147

The LXX reads in Isa 66:19: ἐξαποστελῶ ἐξ αὐτῶν σεσῳσμένους εἰς τὰ ἔθνη ("From them I will send [those who are] saved to the nations"). For the Christian reading this Isaiah text, the "saved" would be those who believed in the redemption found in Jesus the Messiah. This is shown, for example, in Paul's use of this same expression in 1 Cor 1:18 and 2 Cor 2:15. The "saved" or "redeemed" would then be Christian missionaries whom God sends to the nations.[18] As the Gentile survivors were to bring the Jews of the diaspora back to Jerusalem, so it will be the Christian missionaries sent out to the coastlands, to the islands afar off, who will bring representatives from all the nations to Jerusalem as an offering to the Lord.[19]

Isaiah 66, an OT text employed extensively in 2 Thessalonians 1, thus may offer a solution to the meaning of the puzzling phrase τὸ κατέχον ("that which is restraining") in 2 Thess 2:6. It is the mission to the Gentiles, to the coastlands and islands afar off, which could be the (neuter) restraining factor of the author of 2 Thessalonians. It is *God's will or plan* that the gospel first be carried to all men before the Day of the Lord arrives. Passages from Paul, other parts of the NT, and the church fathers strengthen the probability of this view and have been dealt with extensively elsewhere.[20]

(4) The phrase ὁ ἄνομος, "the lawless one," in 2 Thess 2:8 may derive from the same Greek phrase in Isa 66:3, ὁ δὲ ἄνομος, used to

---

[18]Cf. the statement of C. Westermann on the survivors of the nations going to the far isles as missionaries in Isa 66:19 in *Das Buch Jesaja, Kapitel 40-66* (ATD 19; Göttingen: Vandenhoeck & Ruprecht, 1966) 377: "Hier ist zum erstenmal ganz eindeutig von Mission in unserem Sinne die Rede: Sendung einzelner Menschen zu den fernen Völkern, um dort die Herrlichkeit Gottes zu verkündigen. Es entspricht genau der apostolischen Mission am Anfang der christlichen Kirche." G. Fohrer in *Das Buch Jesaja* (Züricher Bibelkommentare; Zurich/Stuttgart: Zwingli, 1964) 3.284 also emphasizes the missionary aspect of the survivors of the nations here.

[19]In another article I shall elaborate how this motif is related to Paul's basic understanding of his mission, particularly the collection enterprise, which in part consisted of bringing representatives from each missionized area as an "offering" to Jerusalem. [See the essay in this collection: "Paul's Travel Plans to Spain and the 'Full Number of the Gentiles' of Rom 11:25," pp. 163-191.]

[20]Cf. especially Rom 15:22; Mark 13:10; Matt 24:14; 28:19; Luke 24:47; Acts 1:8; 3:21; 1 Cor 15:24-25; 2 Pet 3:9; Justin Martyr, *First Apology* 45 (with κατέχειν); Theodore of Mopsuestia in Migne's *PG* 66.936; and Theodoret of Cyrus in *PG* 82.665. The latter church father directly identifies the τὸ κατέχον of 2 Thess 2:6 with the mission to the Gentiles, necessary before the end comes. Many of these passages are discussed by O. Cullmann, "Der eschatologische Charakter," 311; "Wann kommt das Reich Gottes? Zur Enderwartung der christlichen Schriftsteller des zweiten Jahrhunderts" (German translation of French original in *RHPR* 18 [1938] 174-86) in *Vorträge und Aufsätze*, 541; and by J. Munck, *Paul*, 39-40.

describe him "who slaughters an ox," in the LXX but not in the MT compared to "him who kills a man." This is all the more probable since such people are among those who will be put to shame (v 5); they are the "opponents" of the Lord unto whom he will render recompense (v 6). The Greek for "opponents," as noted above, is most probably used to describe the "man of lawlessness" in 2 Thess 2:4 (ὁ ἀντικείμενος), who in turn is the same figure as ὁ ἄνομος in 2:8.[21]

These four reflections of Isaiah 66 in 2 Thessalonians 2 individually cannot be made certain. Cumulatively, however, they strengthen the proposal to be made below that another verse from Isaiah 66 provides the background of the κατέχειν factors in 2 Thess 2:6-7.

II

There are a number of expressions in 2 Thessalonians 2 which indicate that the author was not only aware of the Greek text of the OT, but also of the Hebrew. At several points he made independent translations of the Hebrew into Greek or was dependent on the Hebrew text.[22]

(1) 2 Thess 2:4 speaks of the man of lawlessness, who "opposes and *exalts himself against every so-called god* or object of worship." The commentators correctly call attention to the allusion to Dan 11:36 here: "And the king shall do according to his will; he shall exalt himself and *magnify himself above every god,* and shall speak astonishing things against the God of gods." The phrase ἐπὶ πάντα (λεγόμενον) θεόν in 2 Thess 2:4 is taken directly from the Greek of Dan 11:36: ἐπὶ πάντα θεόν. J. Frame correctly notes that the author of 2 Thessalonians "inserts λεγόμενον to prevent the possibility of putting the would-be gods on a level with the true God."[23] Thinking of the Hebrew text here, he translates the ויתגדל of Dan 11:36, directly before the phrase "above every god," not with the ὑψωθήσεται of the LXX or the μεγαλυνθήσεται of Theodotion, but with ὑπεραιρόμενος, meaning "to lift oneself above," "to exalt oneself above," a good Greek translation of the Hebrew in this context.

---

[21]There is no reason for Nestle to italicize ὁ ἄνομος in his edition of the Greek NT since the phrase is found in neither of the passages noted by him in the margin, Job 4:9 and Isa 11:4.

[22]Cf. also "The Liturgical Background of the Necessity and Propriety of Giving Thanks According to 2 Thes 1:3," *JBL* 92 (1973) 436-37 for the Hebrew background of εὐχαριστεῖν ὀφείλομεν ... καθὼς ἄξιόν ἐστιν in 2 Thess 1:3 (here pp. 193-97).

[23]Cf. *The Epistles of St. Paul to the Thessalonians* (ICC; New York: Scribner's, 1912) 255.

God's Plan and God's Power

(2) In the same verse, 2 Thess 2:4, another independent translation of the Hebrew OT into Greek occurs. Virtually the same nations as mentioned in Isa 66:19, a text emphasized above as important in regard to τὸ κατέχον in 2 Thess 2:6, are found in Ezek 27:10-25, upon which Isa 66:19 is probably dependent, as the commentators state. This Ezekiel passage is a lamentation concerning Tyre, "merchant of the peoples on many coastlands" (27:3). It is this Tyre to whom the Lord shortly thereafter says (28:23): "because your heart is proud, and you have said, 'I am a god, I sit in the seat of the gods,' and yet you are a man, and no god, though you consider yourself as wise as a god – you are indeed wiser than Daniel ...." Tyre's heart has become proud because of its wealth; it considers itself as wise as a god; it states that it is a god; it is proud of its beauty (28:5, 6, 9, 17).

Because of the mention of the same nations as in Isa 66:19, the motif of hybris, the *Stichwort* "Daniel" in the adjacent verse, and the fact that the rabbis employed Ezek 28:2 as a proof text for Hiram of Tyre's calling himself "god,"[24] Ezek 28:2 forms the background of most of the author's phrases in 2 Thess 2:4: "he takes his seat in the temple of God, proclaiming himself to be God," as almost all the commentators agree. The author of 2 Thessalonians translates the יָשַׁבְתִּי of Ezek 28:2 not with the κατῴκηκα of the LXX, meaning "dwelt," but with the simpler καθίσαι, "to sit," "to take a seat," which is closer to the Hebrew. In the modification of the Ezek 28:2 allusion to fit the author's needs, the apocalyptic motif of the final enemy's establishing himself in the "temple" (ναός) is inserted, the word borrowed from Isa 66:6, as suggested above, since the Ezekiel text speaks of the seat of the gods as being in the heart of the seas, not in the Jerusalem temple.

(3) One of the most puzzling expressions in 2 Thessalonians 2 is found in v 7: ἕως ἐκ μέσου γένηται. As has often been noted, the term ἐκ μέσου corresponds to the Hebrew מִתּוֹךְ. Secondly, since the account in Daniel of the desecration of the temple by Antiochus IV Epiphanes forms the background of much of the author's thought in 2 Thessalonians 2, as will be indicated below, it was only natural for him to employ a Hebraism deriving from this account. In Dan 11:31,[25] forces from Antiochus "appear and profane the temple and fortress, and shall take away the continual burnt offering." The Hebrew for "take away" is the Hiph. form וְהֵסִירוּ, from סוּר, "to turn aside," "to depart (from the

---

[24]Cf. *Gen. Rab.* 96/5; *Exod. Rab.* 8/2; *Mek. R. Ish. Shirata* 2 on Exod 15:1, and 8 on 15:11; *Tanḥuma B* וארא § 7ff. (translated in Str-B, 2.463), as well as Schatzhöhle, 35:27.
[25]Cf. the allusion to the nearby verse, Dan 11:36, in 2 Thess 2:4 surveyed above in section II/1.

way)," "to come to an end"; Hiph. "to remove"; Hoph. "to be taken away," "to be removed."[26] The same verb occurs in Dan 12:11 in connection with the same object: "And from the time that the continual burnt offering is taken away, and the abomination that makes desolate is set up, there shall be a thousand two hundred and ninety days." The Hoph. of the above verb occurs here: הוּסַר.[27] It is an attempt to render this latter expression, connected with the desecration of the temple, and found in a favorite OT text used by the rabbis to calculate the coming of the "end" or the second coming of the Messiah,[28] which results in the ungreek Greek phrase: ἕως ἐκ μέσου γένηται, for which no convincing Greek parallel relevant to 2 Thess 2:7 has yet been found.[29] Thinking of the Hebrew text of Dan 12:11, the author has given an *ad hoc* Greek rendering of the Hebrew expression הוּסַר. The fact that סוּר is connected with מתוך twice in 1 Sam 15:6 also may have influenced the author's choice of words here. Both of the latter occurrences are translated in the LXX by ἐκ μέσου.

The general meaning of ἕως ἐκ μέσου γένηται as "being removed" or "disappearing" is probable because of the origin of the phrase in הוּסַר. The exact meaning is nevertheless unclear and can only be determined from the context, to be discussed below.

(4) 2 Thess 2:8, directly following the Hebraism discussed above, states: "And then the lawless one will be revealed, and the Lord [Jesus] *will slay him with the breath of his mouth* and destroy him by his appearing and coming." The italicized passage, as noted in the Nestle

---

[26]Cf. BDB, 693.
[27]For "is taken away," the LXX reads ἀποσταθῇ; Theodotion has the noun παραλλάξεως, "change of position." E. von Dobschütz notes that if one considers the book of Daniel as providing part of the background for 2 Thessalonians 2, it would be tempting to derive the ἀποστασία of 2 Thess 2:3 from Dan 9:26 or 12:11. The noun would then mean the cessation of the legitimate temple worship. See *Die Thessalonicher-Briefe* (Meyer 10; Göttingen: Vandenhoeck & Ruprecht, 1909) 270 n. 3.
[28]For the importance of Dan 12:11-12 in calculating the end, cf. the explanation of these verses in Str-B, 4.999-1000. According to rabbinic tradition, between the first and second appearances of the Messiah there were to be forty-five days, based on Dan 12:11-12. See, for example, *Pesiq. R.* 15/10 on Cant 2:9 (Braude, *Pesikta Rabbati*, 319-20) as well as the parallels cited in Str-B, 1.87.
[29]Cf. the commentators as well as the three non-biblical examples noted in BAG, 159 on γίνομαι, I.4.C.β. To these should be added the following from LSJ, 349: "γ. ἐξ ὀφθαλμῶν τινι *to be* out of sight, Hdt. 5.24; ἐξ ἀνθρώπων γ. *disappear* from ..., Paus. 4.26.6." Bauer also cites a Latin expression, *e medio tolli*, hardly relevant in this context. For my proposal concerning this Greek expression, see also the translation of ἐκ μέσου γένηται as שֶׁיּוּסַר מִתּוֹךְ in F. Delitzsch, ספרי הברית החדשה (London: The British and Foreign Bible Society, 1958) 385.

God's Plan and God's Power 151

Greek text and many of the commentaries, is an allusion to Isa 11:4.[30] The author of 2 Thessalonians chose this verse from Isaiah for his description of the destruction of the "lawless one" for two reasons. First, it was frequently employed in connection with the Messiah in Jewish writings and was thus suitable to describe the activity of the Messiah, the Lord, in 2 Thess 2:8.[31] Secondly, the author of 2 Thessalonians was still modelling his description of the final battle between the Lord Jesus and the lawless one on the figure of Antiochus IV Epiphanes in the book of Daniel, which states that a king of bold countenance will arise at the end of the rule of the four kingdoms, and his "destruction" will be great (8:23-24).[32] By his cunning he shall make deceit prosper (8:25),[33] and in his own mind he shall magnify himself, even rising up against God (8:25).[34] Nevertheless, states the Hebrew, "by no human hand, he shall be broken" (8:25).[35] Since the LXX and Theodotion offer no direct translation of the latter phrase, the author of 2 Thessalonians thought of an OT verse, Isa 11:4, which employs the same motif of the enemy of the Lord being supernaturally destroyed, here in Isa 11:4 by the messianic King.[36]

III

If it is correct that Isaiah 66 is employed not only as part of the background of 2 Thessalonians 1, but also of chapter two, and that the author of 2 Thessalonians shows knowledge of the Hebrew OT in 2:4 (twice), 7 and 8, it should not be surprising that he employed another expression from the Hebrew text of Isaiah 66 to describe the masculine restraining factor ὁ κατέχων in 2 Thess 2:7.

---

[30]The Greek text of 2 Thess 2:8 reads ὁ ἄνομος, ὃν ὁ κύριος ['Ιησοῦς] ἀνελεῖ τῷ πνεύματι τοῦ στόματος αὐτοῦ, and should be compared with the LXX of Isa 11:4: καὶ πατάξει γῆν τῷ λόγῳ τοῦ στόματος αὐτοῦ καὶ ἐν πνεύματι διὰ χειλέων ἀνελεῖ ἀσεβῆ. The allusion is most probably from memory.
[31]Cf., for example, the Jewish references to Isa 11:4 in the scripture index of Str-B, 4.1297.
[32]Cf. the ἀπώλεια of the LXX and Theodotion here with the title ὁ υἱὸς ἀπωλείας in 2 Thess 2:3.
[33]Cf. the ψεῦδος of the LXX here with the τέρασιν ψεύδους of the coming of the lawless one in 2 Thess 2:9, as well as τῷ ψεύδει in 2:11.
[34]Cf. 2 Thess 2:4.
[35]Cf. also Dan 2:34, 45.
[36]It should also be noted that Isaiah 10, directly before 11:4, deals with the Lord's punishing the arrogant boasting of the king of Assyria and his haughty pride (10:12). The Assyrians *smite* with the *rod* and lift their staff against Israel (10:24), yet the Lord will lift his own *rod* against the Assyrians (10:26). Cf. the arrogant pride of the man of lawlessness in 2 Thess 2:4, as well as the Messiah's *smiting* with the *rod* of his mouth in Isa 11:4.

(1) *The* עצר *of Isa 66:9.* Isa 66:7-9 reads in the *RSV:*

7 Before she was in labor she gave birth;
      before her pain came upon her she was delivered of a son.
8 Who has heard such a thing?
      Who has seen such things?
    Shall a land be born in one day?
      Shall a nation be brought forth in one moment?
    For as soon as Zion was in labor she brought forth her sons.
9 Shall I bring to the birth and not cause to bring forth? says the Lord;
      shall I, who cause to bring forth, shut the womb? says your God.

The Hebrew for "shut" in "shut the womb" of v 9 is עָצַרְתִּי, "to restrain," "to retain," "to hinder," "to stop," "to shut up," "to keep away," "to detain," "to rule over."[37] In the context it means "to shut up" Zion's womb so that it will not bear the "son" of v 7, who in the MT is equated with the "sons" of v 8. In the MT they are the Jewish "land" or "nation" (v 8). The Hebrew says that just as ineluctably as a woman in her birth pangs[38] must bear her child, so certain[39] is it that God will restore Jerusalem, who will then suckle and console her people.[40]

---

[37]Cf. BDB, 783. For a detailed study of this Hebrew verb, see E. Kutsch, "Die Wurzel עצר im Hebräischen," *VT* 2 (1952) 57-69. My attention was called to this article by W. Harnisch, *Eschatologische Existenz. Ein exegetischer Beitrag zum Sachanliegen von 1. Thessalonicher 4,13-5,11* (FRLANT 110; Göttingen: Vandenhoeck & Ruprecht, 1973) 67. For עצר in the sense of "restrain" or "hinder" in a translation of the NT into Hebrew, cf. for example Rom 15:22; 1 Cor 9:12; 1 Thess 2:18; and Acts 14:18 in F. Delitzsch, ספרי הברית החדשה. For a good example of rabbinic usage of this verb in the same sense of "restrain," cf. for example *Sipre Num.* § 151 on Num 29:35 in *Sipre zu Numeri,* tr. K.G. Kuhn (Stuttgart: Kohlhammer, 1959) 606-7.

[38]For the pregnant woman as one of the four scriptural/rabbinic metaphors for redemption (besides grape-gathering, harvest and spices), see *Midr. Ps* 8/1, tr. W.G. Braude, *The Midrash on Psalms* (Yale Judaica Series 13; New Haven: Yale University, 1959) 1.119.

[39]J. Muilenburg ("The Book of Isaiah," *IDB,* 5.766) describes this certainty well: "The solemnity of [the Lord's] assurance is marked by the repetition of vs. 9b, 9d, the twofold emphatic *I,* and the direct questions." Cf. also J. Smart, *History and Theology in Second Isaiah. A Commentary on Isaiah 35, 40-66* (Philadelphia: Westminster, 1965) on Isa 66:7-9, who says (290) that the believer's "faith does not depend on the new nation being born tomorrow, but rather, is so rooted and grounded in the promise of God that it remains unshaken no matter how long the day of redemption is delayed."

[40]It should be noted that making Jerusalem fertile, i.e., placing her in a status whereby she will bear a son = sons (her exiles will return to her), is the fulfillment of the Lord's promise to barren Jerusalem in Isa 54:1: "the children of the desolate one will be more than the children of her that is married, says

God's Plan and God's Power

It is important to note here, first, that it is *God* who is the subject of the verb "restrain" (v 9). Secondly, he will definitely not restrain the birth of the son (the restoration of Jerusalem) by shutting up the womb.[41] The ineluctability of the event is emphasized; it cannot be held back.[42] Thirdly, since it is probable that the interpretation of the "son" of v 7 as the King (Messiah) was already current at the time of the writing of 2 Thessalonians, the restraining factor of the adjacent v 9 could easily have been appropriated by a Jewish-Christian author to describe why, in a situation of intense persecution interpreted as the messianic birth pangs (part of the coming of the Day of the Lord), the messianic King's coming had not yet occurred. Since the author of 2 Thessalonians knew that the Day of the Lord had not yet (started to) come, he quenched the aroused messianic fervor of his addressees by saying that first certain things must happen. These are enumerated in 2 Thess 2:3-12. Nevertheless, he says, the Lord Jesus definitely will come, granting consolation to the persecuted addressees and vengeance to their persecutors (1:7-10). To portray this judgment theophany, the author makes abundant use of Isaiah 66, as I have indicated elsewhere.[43]

It has often been maintained that there is no traceable OT or Jewish background to the κατέχειν motif in 2 Thess 2:6-7.[44] Scholars have been led to this conclusion by an inability to find the appropriate Hebrew or Aramaic verb.[45] No one has thought of the Hebrew verb עצר in Isa 66:9

---

the Lord." Paul employs the latter Isaianic verse in Gal 4:27 for the Jerusalem "above."

[41] A later writer, of course, is free to select those motifs from a biblical passage which are of most importance to his own situation. If the author of 2 Thessalonians says that God is he who *does* restrain in 2:7, he has intentionally modified the meaning of Isa 66:9 to emphasize the delay needed for the spread of the gospel (τὸ κατέχον). For him, while God now delays the end, he definitely will later cause the son of v 7 to be born.

[42] In 1 Thess 5:3 the metaphor of the woman in travail is also associated with the Day of the Lord. While the Day's sudden arrival is primarily emphasized, the following phrase, "and they will not escape," brings out the *ineluctability* of the destruction spoken of, compared to a woman in travail. Cf., for example, the commentaries on Thessalonians of Morris, Rigaux and Best on this passage for a similar interpretation. It should also be noted that *Tg. Isa* 60:8 (cf. the text in J. F. Stenning, *The Targum of Isaiah* [Oxford: Clarendon, 1949] 200-201) adds to the Hebrew text that the exiles of Israel gather together and come to their land; they "cannot be held back" (עכב). This is exactly the same motif as in Isa 66:9, where God will not "hold back" the birth of the nation, the return of the exiles.

[43] Cf. "The Relevance," 266-68 (here, pp. 139-40).

[44] Cf., for example, E. von Dobschütz, *Die Thessalonicher-Briefe*, 283.

[45] As in Greek, there are a number of Hebrew verbs which, in various forms, can convey the meaning "restrain." The following, with the exception of עכב found in the MT, are listed alphabetically: אחר; ארך; בוש; חסם; חשך; כלא; מנע; משך; עכב; עצר; שמר; שוב.

as the background of κατέχειν before, for example, because the LXX does not employ κατέχειν here but rather paraphrases the Hebrew expression for shutting the womb. It reads: ἐγὼ δὲ ἔδωκα τὴν προσδοκίαν ταύτην, καὶ οὐκ ἐμνήσθης μου, εἶπεν κύριος. οὐκ ἰδοὺ ἐγὼ γεννῶσαν καὶ στεῖραν ἐποίησα; εἶπεν ὁ θεός. The Hebrew עצרתי, "Have I restrained?" (meant here as "Shall I restrain?"), is translated in the LXX by the paraphrase στεῖραν ἐποίησα; "Have I made barren?" (also probably meant here as "Shall I make barren?").

There are indications in the OT that עצר and κατέχειν are closely related and in places identical. Of the various Greek verbs used to translated עצר in the LXX, κατέχειν appears in Judg 13:15 and 16 Vaticanus. It is also connected with the birth woes in Jer 6:24 (θλῖψις κατέσχεν ἡμᾶς, ὠδῖνες ὡς τικτούσης); 13:21; 37 (30):6 (a Day of the Lord context); and Ps 47 (48):7 Symmachus (the final battle of the heathen against Jerusalem).

The author of 2 Thessalonians used Isaiah 66 as the main background for his portrayal of Jesus' final coming in 2 Thessalonians 1, and also in 2:4. He then employed the term κατέχειν in 2:6-7 because it was a direct translation, not a paraphrase (the LXX's "to make barren"), of the verb עצר, meaning "to restrain," a term he knew from Isa 66:9 and needed for his explanation of the delay of Jesus' return.[46] It also fit the setting of his letter eminently, for it too was associated in the Greek bible with birth pangs, tribulation and the Day of the Lord. Finally, there even was LXX precedent for God as ὁ κατέχων.[47]

(2) *Other OT Usage.* In other passages of the OT it is always God who closes a woman's womb. Gen 20:18 may serve as an example: "For the Lord had closed [עצר] all the wombs of the house of Abimelech because of Sarah, Abraham's wife."[48] As it is only the Lord who closes wombs, so also it is only he who can open them again.[49] Everything lies in his power. This is also true for Isa 66:9. "Shall I, who cause to bring

---

[46]Cf. again the other examples in Part II of the author's practice of independently translating expressions from the Hebrew OT into Greek in 2:4 and 6.
[47]Cf. Isa 40:22, where it is God who "*covers* the circle of the earth."
[48]Cf. also Gen 16:2 and 1 Sam 1:5-6 (סגר).
[49]Cf., for example, Gen 29:31 and 30:22, where God opens (פתח) the wombs of Leah and Rachel, respectively. A widely attested rabbinic tradition maintains that there are three (later four) keys which God retains for himself alone. One of these is to the womb, for which Gen 29:31 and 30:22 are cited as scriptural proofs. Cf. the many sources noted in Str-B, 1.437, 523. See also Pseudo-Philo, *Book of Biblical Antiquities,* 23:7; 42:3; and 50:4 for God alone who opens the womb of a woman.

God's Plan and God's Power 155

forth, shut the womb? says your God." God alone determines the course of events.⁵⁰

(3) *Isa 66:9 in Rabbinic Literature.* The only occurrence of Isa 66:9 in rabbinic literature to my knowledge is in Aggadat Bereshit 29.⁵¹ Here, in a discussion of barrenness in which various relevant OT texts are cited, Isa 66:9 also occurs. Again, it is the Lord who controls the fruit of the womb here. Since the passage contains no mention of the Messiah, it seems fair to assume that Isa 66:9 was probably not interpreted messianically by the rabbis, nor was it given any special significance by them as a delaying factor.⁵² This fact supports the view that the author of 2 Thessalonians is working independently here, modifying the context of what was probably a known Jewish messianic passage, Isa 66:7, for his own purposes.⁵³

(4) *The Woman in Travail in 2 Esdras.* A passage from Jewish apocalyptic literature also describes the delay of the end in terms of a woman in travail, as does Isa 66:9. In 2 Esdras the angel Uriel relates to the seer Ezra how the age is hastening swiftly to its end, the time of threshing or judgment is coming. Ezra asks him whether the time of threshing is perhaps "delayed" for the sake of the righteous (4:39), to which the angel replies:

> 40 "Go and ask a woman who is with child if, when her nine months have been completed, her womb can keep the child within her any longer."
> 41 And I said, "No, Lord, it cannot."
> And he said to me, "In Hades the chambers of the souls are like the womb. 42 For just as a woman who is in travail makes haste to escape the pangs of birth, so also do these places hasten to give back those things that were committed to them from the beginning. 43 Then the things that you desire to see will be disclosed to you."⁵⁴

---

⁵⁰It was a major tenet of the rabbis that *God alone* will determine the time of the redemption, the "day of comfort." They often buttressed this by citing Isa 60:22 in the translation, "I the Lord will hasten it in its time." Cf. *Cant. Rab.* 8:14 § 1 (in the edition of *Midrash Rabbah* [London: Soncino, 1961] 9.327); the early tradition recorded in *Pal. Ta'anith* 1/1 (Str-B, 1.163); *Gen. Rab. Toledoth* 65/12 (Soncino 1.588); and *Eccl. Rab.* 11/5 (Soncino 8.293-94), as well as Matt 24:36 and Acts 1:7.
⁵¹Cf. the text in אגדת בראשית, ed. S. Buber (New York: Menora, 1959; reprint of the 1903 Cracow edition) 50.
⁵²A favorite OT text used as a delaying factor by the rabbis was, for example, Hab 2:3 (אחר). Cf. Strobel, *Untersuchungen,* 23-27.
⁵³His spontaneity is attested not only by his independent translations of expressions from the Hebrew into the Greek, but also by the anacolutha between 1:5-6 and 2:4-5.
⁵⁴It is impossible to reconstruct the Hebrew original or the Greek translation(s) of the Hebrew on the basis of the extant Latin, Syriac, Ethiopic, Arabic and Armenian translations. The Latin term for "delay" in v 39 is *prohibeatur,* for

Here comfort is given to the troubled seer by the author's emphasizing that the "Highest," God, "hastens on behalf of many" (v 34).⁵⁵ He is in control of the scheme of things and is steering the course of history. No definite sign of the approaching end is given to Ezra. The angel does not tell him when the number of souls will be "completed" or "fulfilled" (4:36-37), or how many souls there are.⁵⁶ What is imparted to him, however, is that God is in control of the course of events, and the world is irresistibly hastening towards its completion, just as a pregnant woman about to bear cannot retain her child in the womb.⁵⁷

These are exactly the same motifs stressed in Isa 66:9, that God, associated with the verb "restrain," is in charge of the scheme of things, and that a redemptive event (for Isaiah the restoration of Jerusalem), associated with birth pangs, will ineluctably take place. 2 Esdras 4 shows that a later Jewish or Jewish-Christian writer, such as the author of 2 Thessalonians, could well employ the imagery of Isa 66:9 in a description of the delay of the end.⁵⁸

While other passages from the pseudepigrapha, the NT, patristic and rabbinic writings also point to *God* as he who "restrains" or "keeps" the primeval monsters or the Messiah until the end time, the latter a motif quite similar to that found in 2 Thess 2:7, they have for the most part

---

"keep" in v 40 *retinere*. Cf. B. Violet, *Die Esra-Apocalypse* (Leipzig: Hinrichs, 1910) 44. That עצר is ultimately behind what is found in the extant translations is probable since the imagery of the passage seems directly dependent on Isa 66:7-9, the only OT passage dealing with both birth and delay, and because עצר is the most frequent Hebrew verb used for restraining or shutting the womb. For the certainty of a Hebrew original to 2 Esdras, see Violet, XIII.

A passage very similar in content to 2 Esdras 4:33-43 is 16:37-39, which compares the non-delay of the "calamities," when they draw near, to the birth of a child by a woman in her ninth month. For the Latin, cf. R. Bensly, *The Fourth Book of Ezra* (Cambridge: Cambridge University, 1895) 80 and 91.

⁵⁵That God hastens "on behalf of many" here probably means that more people be given the possibility of repenting. This motif is parallel to that ascertained above in the Christian understanding of Isa 66:18-21, that the gospel first be offered to all mankind before the end comes.

⁵⁶Cf. the similar expression in Rom 11:25: "until the full number of the Gentiles come in."

⁵⁷Womb and travail imagery occur frequently in 2 Esdras. Cf. also 5:37, 46-55; 8:8-11 (v 9 reads: "But that which keeps and that which is kept shall both be kept by thy [God's] keeping"); 10:12; 16:37-39.

⁵⁸In his analysis of the pregnant woman in the OT and intertestamental literature, Harnisch also surveys 2 Esdras 4:40-42 in connection with Isa 66:7-9, as had C.M. Edsman before him (*Eschatologische Existenz*, 69-70). Harnisch also emphasizes the motif of "Unaufhaltsamkeit" or "Zwangsläufigkeit" in the passage. However, he uses this passage to illuminate 1 Thess 5:3, and does not perceive its relevance to 2 Thess 2:6-7.

God's Plan and God's Power

been dealt with in detail elsewhere and need not be surveyed here.⁵⁹ It should also be noted that the patristic writers Theodore of Mopsuestia and Theodoret of Cyrus expressly state or assume that God is "he who restrains" in 2 Thess 2:7.⁶⁰ These passages, especially those which speak of God's "keeping" the Messiah until the appointed time, supplement the probability given in the above interpretation of Isa 66:9 that the ὁ κατέχων phrase in 2 Thess 2:7 should be interpreted theocentrically.

IV

There is an anacoluthon at the end of 2 Thess 2:4. The writer, ostensibly dictating (cf. 3:13), has not completed the thought he began in v 3b.⁶¹ Before he continues his description of the destruction of the man of lawlessness in v 8, he parenthetically inserts remarks in vv 5-7 on why the latter has not yet been destroyed.⁶² He writes in v 5: "Do you not remember that when I was still with you I told you this?"⁶³ V 6: "Now you know⁶⁴ what is restraining [it], so that he may be revealed in his time."⁶⁵ According to the proposal made above, τὸ κατέχον, "what is restraining," derives from the motif found in Isa 66:18-21, and signifies here God's will or plan that the gospel first be preached to all nations before the end, the Day of the Lord, comes.

If this is correct, the question must be raised whether τὸ κατέχον in 2 Thess 2:6 has an implied object, as most of the modern translations suggest. The *RSV*, for example, supplies "him," meaning the man of lawlessness, described in the preceding verses, 3-4. It is he who shall be revealed "in his time" in v 6b. Nevertheless, if "that which restrains" is the will or plan of God that salvation first be preached to all the nations, it is more logical to consider the coming or Day of the Lord in vv 1-3, in other words salvation or the end, as that which is being held up, as in the synoptic apocalypse (Mark 13:10; Matt 24:14) and 2 Pet 3:9, since

---

⁵⁹Cf. *2 Apoc. Bar.* 29:3-4; 2 Esdras 12:32; 13:26; *1 Enoch* 62:7; *Pesiq. R.* 34/2 and 36/1; Revelation 20; and Justin Martyr, *First Apology*, 45, a discussion of which is for the most part found under the relevant subject headings in Strobel, *Untersuchungen*.
⁶⁰Cf. Migne's *PG* 66.933-36 and 82.663-66, respectively.
⁶¹Cf., again, the anacoluthon between 1:5-6.
⁶²The "revelation" of the lawless one in v 8 takes up again the "revelation" of the man of lawlessness in v 3.
⁶³The imperfect of the verb "told" (ἔλεγον) implies that the writer had done this repeatedly.
⁶⁴This knowledge (οἴδατε) is not experiential (against Giblin, *Threat to Faith*, 166), but conceptual. Cf. 1 Thess 5:2.
⁶⁵My translation.

the Day of the Lord will only come when the gospel has been preached everywhere.[66]

2 Thess 2:7 continues: "For the mystery of lawlessness is already at work; only he who now restrains [it will do so/let him do so][67] until it [the mystery] is removed/disappears." Also according to the proposal made above, ὁ κατέχων, "he who restrains," derives from Isa 66:9 and is God here. This means that τὸ κατέχον and ὁ κατέχων are integrally related: "that which restrains" is the will or plan of God that the gospel be proclaimed to all men, and "he who restrains" is God himself.

The author of 2 Thessalonians, whether Paul or a member of his "school," writes in 2:5 that the addressees *know* what is restraining Jesus' return, his Day. Even if they had not been instructed as to the exact identity of ὁ κατέχων, they could have understood it in the Greek text by reasoning that if they are already acquainted with the neuter τὸ κατέχον, God's plan that all men be saved, the masculine form ὁ κατέχων would be directly related to this, that is, the restrainer is God.[68]

A final reason from the context for interpreting ὁ κατέχων in 2 Thess 2:7 as God is the further development of the author's argument in this section of the chapter.[69] The text states that "those who are to perish"[70] will be deceived at and/or through the *parousia* of the lawless one (2:10). Because of this, their refusal to love the truth and thus be

---

[66]This does not prevent one's taking the αὐτὸν of v 6b as referring to the man of lawlessness. If one prefers to consider the man of lawlessness as the supplied object of τὸ κατέχον, the meaning of the phrase τὸ κατέχον can nevertheless be: "that which is restraining" is the will or plan of God.

[67]Here lat, Tert, Aug and Ambrst have correctly interpreted the text by adding *teneat*, which in Greek would be κατεχέτω (third person singular, present imperative), as noted by Nestle. For these MS witnesses the activity of ὁ κατέχων may be thought of as beneficial: "let him continue restraining." See also the translation of the *RSV*, "will do so," as well as Rigaux's statement (*Les Epîtres aux Thessaloniciens*, 275) that ὁ κατέχων is "une force bienfaisante. Elle s'exerce contre le mystère d'iniquité." Cf. the critical apparatus of Nestle and other texts cited by von Dobschütz, *Die Thessalonicher-Briefe*, 281.

[68]If Paul is the author, it is probable that he explained the content of both τὸ κατέχον and ὁ κατέχων to the Thessalonians while he was with them. This would explain the author's assuming their identity as known in 2:6-7, he not having to elaborate on them there. It is difficult to understand why a pseudonymous writer, composing carefully, would deliberately choose expressions which his addressees could not immediately comprehend. He would also pay more attention to his grammar so that anacolutha would not arise, and the subjects of his verbs would also be clear to the normal Greek reader, even today.

[69]For the following remarks, cf. also the discussion in Strobel, *Untersuchungen*, 107-9.

[70]The phrase (τοῖς ἀπολλυμένοις) is typical of apocalyptic thinking, where everything is a part of God's plan.

God's Plan and God's Power

saved, "God sends upon them a strong delusion, to make them believe what is false, so that all may be condemned who did not believe the truth but had pleasure in unrighteousness" (2:11-12). Here, too, God is the subject; he does the deluding, although it is based on the individual's rejection of the gospel. The theocentric significance of this summary statement should not be overlooked because of the more interesting details of the whole paragraph, 2:1-13. The next verses also testify to God's being in control of things. In contrast to those who are to perish, the addressees have been chosen by God as the first fruits[71] to be saved "through sanctification by the Spirit and belief in the truth" (2:13). God ("he") has called them to this through the writer's gospel (2:14).[72]

The main exegetical problem in 2 Thessalonians 2, beyond the meaning of the two κατέχειν phrases, now appears. What does ἕως ἐκ μέσου γένηται mean, and how is it to be understood in the context? As 2 Thess 2:7b now stands, the present reader of the Greek text would most naturally assume that ὁ κατέχων is the subject of γένηται. Many commentators translate ἐκ μέσου γένηται as "to be removed," which was also ascertained above as the basic meaning of the phrase. This would rule out God as the subject of γένηται since God is not "removed," he does not "disappear from the scene" *(NEB)* or become "out of the way" *(RSV)*. According to the suggestion made above, ἐκ μέσου γένηται is an *ad hoc* translation into Greek of the Hebrew Hoph. הוּסַר of Dan 12:11. There it is the continual burnt offering of the temple which is spatially "removed" or "taken away" by the forces of Antiochus IV Epiphanes, after whom the figure of the "lawless one" in 2 Thessalonians 2 is in part modelled, as also proposed above. The expression ἕως ἐκ μέσου γένηται in 2 Thess 2:7 would then most probably mean "until it/he is removed." Yet what is the subject of γένηται? God as ὁ κατέχων is one possibility; the second is the man of lawlessness of v 3, described

---

[71] While "from the beginning" would emphasize the aspect of being called, the better attested reading here is ἀπαρχὴν (cf. the Nestle text). It reflects eschatological terminology: God has chosen the addressees of 2 Thessalonians as the "first fruits" (converts) to be saved in that region. See Rom 16:5 and 1 Cor 16:15 for a similar use of the term. Other reasons for preferring the reading ἀπαρχὴν in 2 Thess 2:13 are given in B. Metzger, *A Textual Commentary on the Greek New Testament* (London/New York: United Bible Societies, 1971) 636-37.

[72] The expression "to be revealed in his time," used of the man of lawlessness in 2:6, also shows that it is God who determines the time of the lawless one's revelation. Although evil is already present and active (2:7), it is clear that God is in control of everything.

with participles in v 4 and meant again by the αὐτὸν of v 6; and the third is the mystery of lawlessness in v 7a.[73]

If the identity of ὁ κατέχων is God, he cannot be the subject of γένηται since God, as stated above, cannot be "removed," he does not "disappear." Nor can the man of lawlessness be the subject of γένηται because if he is "removed" or "disappears" in v 7b, the following remarks in the text, v 8, concerning his appearance and destruction would be out of place: "And then the lawless one will be revealed, and the Lord [Jesus] will slay him ...."

The third possibility is thus to be preferred, that the mystery of lawlessness in v 7a is the subject of γένηται in v 7b. The writer admittedly should have been more careful with his grammar, yet his excited mood causes him to make this slip,[74] as he is careless elsewhere in this section.[75] The mystery of lawlessness is to be active until its mysterious aspect is removed or disappears. That is, evil or lawlessness has not yet reached its peak. Only then, when it is most intense and apparent to all, will God cease his restraining, the Messiah will come, and the decisive battle between the lawless one and the Lord Jesus will take place.[76] This accords with the suggestion that the addressees of 2 Thessalonians conceive of their intense sufferings as the messianic woes, part of the coming of the Day of the Lord. The author, however, states that first certain things must happen before the Day of the Lord

---

[73] Cullmann maintains that Paul himself is the subject of γένηται, Paul's death enabling the final events to begin (cf. "Der eschatologische Charakter," 314, 333-34). Yet this is improbable because the phrase in its origin does not mean "to die," but "to be removed," "to disappear." Secondly, Paul himself expected to participate in the final events during his own lifetime (see 1 Thess 4:15, 17). Cullmann's thesis has not been generally accepted.

[74] Bilingual myself, I am well aware of the psychological phenomenon of expressing oneself somewhat indistinctly while in an excited mood because of one's having thought in another language of something of relevance to a topic of discussion.

[75] Cf. again the anacoluthon between 2:4-5; the long interval between the αὐτὸν of v 6 and its antecedent in vv 3-4; and the indistinct antecedent of οὗ in v 9, only intelligible by the reader's own logic as referring back to ὁ ἄνομος in v 8. For a somewhat similar analysis, see Strobel, *Untersuchungen*, 108, who, however, conceives μόνον ὁ κατέχων ἄρτι as parenthetical. Yet ἕως ἐκ μέσου γένηται clearly limits the participle κατέχων temporally, not the verb ἐνεργεῖται. Trilling (*Untersuchungen,* 85) correctly criticizes Strobel on this point. M. Dibelius (*An die Thessalonicher, an die Philipper* [HNT; 3rd ed.; Tübingen: Mohr, 1937] 49) also considered the mystery of lawlessness as the subject of γένηται, understanding it as the "hardening of the Jews," their unwillingness to believe in Jesus as the Messiah.

[76] Cf. the references to Jewish writings in "The Relevance," 262 n. 43 (here p. 135), as well as the rabbinic material cited in Str-B, 4.983, o.

will arrive (2:2). Evil and suffering will become even more intense (2:3-7). Only then will the final time have come.

Another apocalyptic writing, Revelation, aids in determining the meaning of the mystery of lawlessness as being removed or disappearing in 2 Thess 2:7. "Babylon the great, mother of harlots and of earth's abominations," is the name, a "mystery," written on the head of Rome, which now persecutes the addressees of Revelation (17:5, 7). The latters' comfort is not that their persecutions will cease, but that an angel discloses to the seer that all evil forces, including Rome, are to be delivered to perdition (17:8); the Lamb Jesus will definitely conquer them (17:14). Assurance of final victory is thus given, enabling the addressees to bear their present afflictions. In chapter twenty the author tells them that even though evil in the final period will be restrained for a length of time by an angel, it again will be loosed "for a little while" to deceive the entire world and wage the eschatological battle. The evil forces will then be consumed supernaturally.[77] There are close parallels to 2 Thessalonians here. At present it is an angel of God who restrains evil.[78] Only when this evil reaches worldwide proportions, i.e., its peak, will it be destroyed by God supernaturally. Only then, so to speak, will the mystery of evil be lifted; the latter will become most intense, and a full-scale battle will be waged against the forces of good.

TABLE
(showing the employment of various verses from Isaiah 66 in 2 Thessalonians 1-2)

(1)	Isa 66:3	in 2 Thess 2:8	:	ὁ ἄνομος
(2)	66:4	1:8	:	τοῖς μὴ ὑπακούουσιν
(3)	66:5	1:12	:	ὅπως ἐνδοξασθῇ τὸ ὄνομα...ἐν ὑμῖν
(4)	66:6	1:6	:	The motif and some of the phraseology of δίκαιον...θλῖψιν
(5)	66:6	2:4	:	ἀντικείμενος and ναὸν

---

[77]Cf. Rev 20:2-3, 7-10. On the remarks made here, see also the comments of G. Bornkamm in *TDNT*, 4.823-24.
[78]It should be noted that R.H. Charles (*The Revelation of St. John* [ICC; Edinburgh: Clark, 1920] 2.143) on Rev 20:3 emphasizes that when the beast and the false prophet are cast into the lake of fire and Satan is bound in the abyss, "the time for the Millenial reign has arrived and for the evangelization of the surviving heathen nations ...." This motif of evangelization is very similar to the explanation of τὸ κατέχον in 2 Thess 2:6 given above.

(6)	66:7	1-2	:	The "son" is assumed to be the Messiah, whom God definitely will not "hold back"
(7)	66:9	2:7	:	ὁ κατέχων (and thus also the Greek term for "that which is restraining," τὸ κατέχον, in 2:6)
(8)	66:15	1:8	:	ἐν πυρὶ φλογός and διδόντος ἐκδίκησιν
(9)	66:18-21	2:6	:	The motif background of τὸ κατέχον

For a detailed exposition of the employment of Isa 66:4, 5, 6 and 15, cf. "The Relevance," 266-67, cited in n. 12 (here pp. 139-40).

The above interpretation of the κατέχειν motif in 2 Thess 2:6-7 does not solve all the difficulties inherent in the text. There are too many variables in these verses to attain any absolute certainty. Nevertheless, the solution offered above has two major arguments in its favor. First, it means that τὸ κατέχον and ὁ κατέχων are intimately related. God, he who now restrains the Day of the Messiah, does so because of his plan or will that the gospel first be brought to all men. Secondly, it is based on an OT text, Isaiah 66, which is extensively employed elsewhere in 2 Thessalonians. The author then employed imagery from the same OT chapter for his description of the restraining factors in 2:6-7.

8

Paul's Travel Plans to Spain and the "Full Number of the Gentiles" of Rom 11:25

The majority of scholars specializing in Pauline studies maintain that the Apostle to the Gentiles conceived of his own call and ministry at least partially in the light of OT prophecy. Gal 1:15-16, for example, is thought to recall Isa 49:1 and Jer 1:5.[1] Throughout his letters Paul quotes or alludes to the OT to show that the acceptable time, the day of salvation, is now,[2] the period between Jesus' resurrection and his return, the parousia. This interim period, which Paul expects to be completed within his own lifetime,[3] provides him who was "called to be an apostle" and "set apart for the gospel of God which [God] promised beforehand through his prophets in the holy scriptures" (Rom 1:1-2)[4] with the opportunity of converting Gentiles from "among all the nations" (Rom 1:5) to belief in the Lord Jesus as the Christ. Nowhere else in his letters does Paul base his argumentation more heavily on the OT than in Romans 9-11, where he deals with the question of unbelieving Israel's

---

[1] Cf. a summary of the discussion in B. Rigaux, *Letters of St. Paul. Modern Studies* (Chicago: Franciscan Herald, 1968) 55-58.
[2] 2 Cor 6:2, quoting Isa 49:8. Cf. 1 Cor 10:11, where Paul states that evil events recorded in the Pentateuch "were written down for our instruction, upon whom the end of the ages has come." For the Apostle, all the promises of God (in the OT) find their Yes in Jesus Christ (2 Cor 1:20), who is the end of the Law (Rom 10:4). See also the statement of R. Joḥanan (bar Nappaḥa), a second generation Palestinian Amora according to H. Strack and G. Stemberger, *Einleitung in Talmud und Midrasch* (Munich: Beck, 1982[7]) 91, in b. Sanh. 99a: "All the prophets prophesied only in respect to the Messianic era" (translation by H. Freedman in the *Hebrew-English Edition of the Talmud*. Sanhedrin [London: Soncino, 1969]). A parallel is found in b. Ber. 34b (Soncino 215).
[3] Cf. 1 Thess 1:10; 4:15, 17; 1 Cor 7:26, 29, 31; 15:51; 16:22; Rom 13:11 ("salvation is nearer to us now than when we first believed"); Phil 4:5.
[4] The translation is that of the Revised Standard Version of the Bible, also employed elsewhere unless stated otherwise.

salvation.⁵ For this reason it is probable from the outset that there is also an OT background to, and perhaps an exegetical tradition behind, the Apostle's thinking about the "full number of the Gentiles" (πλήρωμα τῶν ἐθνῶν) in Rom 11:25, as a number of authors in the past and more recently have maintained.⁶ Here Paul imparts to his readers a

---

⁵In addition to the Romans commentaries, cf. O. Michel, *Paulus und seine Bibel* (Gütersloh: Bertelsmann, 1929), chart p. 74, where the exceptionally large number of OT quotations in Romans 9-11 can be noted. See also pp. 125-26 on Paul's use of Deutero-Isaiah in Romans to justify scripturally the mission to the Gentiles. L. Goppelt in his *Theologie des Neuen Testamentes* (Göttingen: Vandenhoeck & Ruprecht, 1976) II.379 points out that while First Corinthians contains only 16 citations from the OT, Romans has 52, and 28 of these are in chapters 9-11.

⁶O. Cullmann in his 1936 essay "Der eschatologische Charakter des Missionsauftrages und des apostolischen Selbstbewusstseins bei Paulus," now in *Vorträge und Aufsätze. 1925-62* (Tübingen: Mohr; Zurich: Zwingli, 1966) 305-36, had already connected Mark 13:10 (before the parousia of Jesus "the gospel must first be preached to all nations"), the restraining force (κατέχειν) of 2 Thess 2:6, and Rom 11:25. Only the preaching of the gospel to *all* the nations would achieve the "fulness of the Gentiles," of which Paul speaks in Romans (328-30). Cullmann is followed here by J. Munck in *Paul and the Salvation of Mankind* (Richmond, Virginia: John Knox, 1959) 47-49, who also connects the "fulness" with Paul's collection for Jerusalem and the OT motif of a pilgrimage of the Gentiles to Jerusalem in the final time ("Völkerwallfahrt") (303-04). C. Plag in *Israels Wege zum Heil. Eine Untersuchung zu Römer 9-11* (Arbeiten zur Theologie. 1. Reihe, 40; Stuttgart: Calwer, 1969) 41-47, 65 attempts to show that Rom 11:25-27 is a secondary insertion into the text; for him it is the remains of an additional Pauline letter. According to Plag, one reason for this is that the verb εἰσέρχεσθαι in v 25 is connected with the motif of the pilgrimage of the Gentiles to Jerusalem, for which he cites several Jewish references on p. 57. Since Paul does not refer to this pilgrimage elsewhere in this section of Romans, 11:25-27 are foreign to their context. In his essay "Zur Interpretation von Römer 11, 25-32" in *Probleme biblischer Theologie.* Festschrift von Rad (Munich: Kaiser, 1971), P. Stuhlmacher disagrees with Plag's insertion hypothesis, yet also advocates a Christian interpretation of the motif of a Gentile pilgrimage to Zion as the background of Rom 11:25 (560). He believes that the motif behind the "fulness of the Gentiles" is older than that found in Mark 13:10 (565-66). In his study *Juden und Heiden in der Mission des Paulus. Studien zum Römerbrief* (Forschung zur Bibel; Stuttgart: Katholisches Bibelwerk, 1973), D. Zeller deals extensively with Rom 11:25 ff. (245-58) and categorically denies a connection between the "fulness of the Gentiles," Paul's collection enterprise, and the eschatological pilgrimage of the Gentiles to Zion (282-84). For him the origin of 11:25 may lie in the thoughts of 9:2 and 10:1 on Paul's sorrow over the fate of Israel (253).

In his essay "Das Volk Gottes. Juden und Christen in der Botschaft des Paulus" in *Paulus – Apostat oder Apostel?* Jüdische und christliche Antworten (ed. F. Henrich; Regensburg: Pustet, 1977) 45-134, M. Barth maintains that the content of the "mystery" of Rom 11:25b-26a derives from a citation from a "mystery"[7]: "a hardening has now come upon part of Israel, until the full number of the Gentiles come in, and so all Israel will be saved" (vv 25, 26). When the full number[8] comes in, the Deliverer (Jesus) will come (again) from Zion (v 26).[9]

In this essay I would like to suggest that the "full number of the Gentiles" in Rom 11:25 will only "come in" when Paul has brought Christian representatives from *Spain* to Jerusalem as a part of his collection enterprise. For him this is the fulfillment both of OT prophecy and Jewish tradition concerning Gentiles from *all* the nations coming in the end time to Jerusalem with their gifts.[10] This thought, in turn, is intimately connected with the "offering of the Gentiles" of Rom 15:16.[11]

I. The "Offering of the Gentiles" of Rom 15:16

When Paul wrote Romans he was somewhere in Greece, probably in Corinth, and had completed – at least in Macedonia and Achaia – his

---

prophetic-apocalyptic book, or it is the saying of a NT prophet (79, n. 66; cf. also p. 94).

[7]O. Michel in *Der Brief an die Römer* (Meyer 13; Göttingen: Vandenhoeck & Ruprecht, 1966[4]) 280 correctly points out that Paul speaks as an apocalyptist here. As in 1 Cor 15:51, he reveals now, at the end of days, that which up to this point has been hidden.

[8]Close parallels to this expression are to be found in 2 Apoc. Bar. 23:4 (Charles, *APOT* 495, with parallels); 2 Esdr 2:38, 40, 41; and Rev 6:11; 7:4; and 14:1, as the Romans commentators note. Elsewhere I have called attention to the connection of the restraining factor of the mission to the Gentiles in 2 Thess 2:6 and 2 Esdr 4:36 ("When the number of those like yourselves is fulfilled"). See "God's Plan and God's Power: Isaiah 66 and the Restraining Factors of 2 Thess 2:6-7," in *JBL* 96 (1977) 537-53. N. Dahl in *Das Volk Gottes. Eine Untersuchung zum Kirchenbewusstsein des Urchristentums* (Oslo: Dybwad, 1941) also relates Rom 11:25 to the rabbinic view that the Messiah will not come until all the pre-existent souls are born (245; cf. n. 152 and the sources cited on p. 227). See also the expression "until the times of the Gentiles are fulfilled" in Luke 21:24, and Tob 14:5. For my own suggestion of Isa 60:5 as the background of the "full number of the Gentiles" in Rom 11:25, see the discussion of Isaiah 60 below in IV B.

[9]This is a free citation of Isa 59:20-21 and 27:9, the first passage also interpreted messianically by R. Joḥanan (bar Nappaḥa) in b. Sanh. 98a.

[10]The "representative universalism" of Jer 3:14, to be examined below in connection with the collection, helps to explain the meaning of the "full number" of the Gentiles, made parallel in Rom 11:25-26 to "all Israel."

[11]As observed in n. 6, other authors have also connected the "fulness of the Gentiles" with the eschatological pilgrimage of the Gentiles to Jerusalem. However, none has connected this before with OT and rabbinic traditions concerning *Spain,* nor with a thorough analysis of the rabbinic parallels to the pilgrimage of the Gentiles with their gifts for the King Messiah, nor with Jer 3:14.

task of collecting contributions for the poor among the saints in Jerusalem (15:25-26). This enterprise, to which the Apostle had devoted a large number of his final years as a missionary to the Gentiles, entailed not only a sum of money but also an unusually large number of accompanying representatives or delegates from the contributing churches founded by Paul.[12] So many representatives were neither necessary to guard the collected money, nor to insure Paul that he would not be suspected of misusing funds;[13] nor did the Apostle intend to give the new converts a tour of Palestine. Rather, these representatives were to demonstrate to the Jewish mother church in Jerusalem that Paul's mission to the Gentiles, agreed upon with the leaders of the Jewish-Christian church in Jerusalem in Gal 2:9-10, had borne fruit. Paul's missionary efforts from Jerusalem to Illyricum (Rom 15:19), though entailing many disappointments and hindrances, had been successful, and the Jerusalem mother church should now in a concrete way perceive that the good news of salvation in the Lord Jesus was for all men, not just for Jews. Connected with this aspect of the collection was Paul's hope that his fellow Jews would thus become jealous enough of the Gentiles' acceptance of Jesus as the Messiah to accept him also.[14] After delivering this collection of money and representatives of the Gentile churches to Jerusalem, the Apostle plans to missionize new land up to now barren of the Christian gospel. For many years he has longed to visit the Christians in Rome, a church he himself had not founded. Yet he will only "pass through" (διαπορευόμενος) the capital of the Roman Empire and use it as a stopping-off point. His real goal is in fact Spain (Rom 15:24, 28).

In the meantime Paul hopes that his service (διακονία; 15:31)[15] for Jerusalem may be acceptable to the Christians there; he wishes to seal to them the fruit (χαρπόν; 15:28)[16] he has gathered together from the

---

[12]Cf. the discussion of the participating churches in J. Munck, *Paul* 292-97; D. Georgi, *Die Geschichte der Kollekte des Paulus für Jerusalem* (TF 38; Hamburg-Bergstedt: Reich, 1965) 87; and K. Nickle, *The Collection. A Study in the Strategy of Paul* (1963 Basle dissertation) 68-69. Nickle (92) estimates that it took Paul eight years to complete the collection he brought to Jerusalem.
[13]Cf. 2 Cor 8:20 and 12:15-16.
[14]Rom 10:19; 11:11, 14. This motif will be considered in more detail below.
[15]Other important MS witnesses (B D *G) here read δωροφορία, which more closely resembles the δῶρον of Isa 66:20, to be examined below, and the προσφορά τῶν ἐθνῶν of Rom 15:16. Nickle (*The Collection* 134, n. 259) argues for it as the original reading here.
[16]For "fruit" in Paul as meaning "converts," cf. also Rom 1:13, as well as the "first-fruits" (ἀπαρχαί) of 16:5; 1 Cor 16:15; 2 Thess 2:13. In 1 Cor 9:2 the Apostle calls the converts in Corinth the "seal of my apostleship in the Lord." For a connection of the "sealing" of Rom 15:28 to the pilgrimage of the Gentiles

various Gentile-Christian churches founded by him.[17] The same wish is expressed in 15:16: Paul, a minister (λειτουργόν) of Christ Jesus to the Gentiles in the priestly service (ἱερουργοῦντα) of the gospel of God, hopes that the "offering of the Gentiles" (προσφορὰ τῶν ἐθνῶν) which he has gathered may be acceptable (in Jerusalem), sanctified by the Holy Spirit.[18] Is the latter Greek expression to be understood as the money which the Gentile Christians bring as financial aid for the Jerusalem Christian church, or epexegetically (as a genitive of apposition): The offering of the Gentiles is the Gentiles themselves? Along with major commentators,[19] I would maintain that the latter is the proper interpretation of this phrase. The reason for this is that Paul is thinking here in terms of OT eschatology, according to which the Gentiles in the end time are to bring the Jews from all the nations of the Jewish diaspora as an offering to the Lord in Jerusalem. Paul's modification of this motif, according to which he himself will bring not Jews but Gentile Christians from the congregations founded by him to Jerusalem as an

---

to Zion, see H.-W. Bartsch, "... wenn ich ihnen diese Frucht versiegelt habe. Röm xv 28. Ein Beitrag zum Verständnis der paulinischen Mission," in *ZNW* 63 (1972) 95-107, especially 107.

[17]Paul did not think that his collection enterprise would be complete when representatives from the churches up to now founded by him reached Jerusalem. In 1 Cor 16:4 he is not even sure that he will accompany them. Although something happened which caused him to change his mind by the time he wrote Romans (15:25), he still plans to missionize in Spain and, presumably, also bring "fruit" from there to Jerusalem.

[18]Cf. the sacrificial offering (θυσία καὶ λειτουργία) of the Philippian Gentile Christians' faith in Phil 2:17. For the above discussion, see also J. Munck, *Paul* 49-51. I do not believe that Paul saw himself as Elijah, one of whose tasks was to prepare for the coming of the Messiah (against E. Käsemann, *An die Römer* [HNT 8a; Tübingen: Mohr, 1974³] 291). Paul's explicit mention of Elijah in Rom 11:2 precludes in my opinion his identifying himself with this OT figure.

[19]For this interpretation, cf. the Romans commentaries of H. Lietzmann, *An die Römer* (HNT 8; Tübingen: Mohr, 1933⁴) 120; F. Leenhardt, *The Epistle to the Romans* (London: Lutterworth, 1961) 368; J. Murray, *The Epistle to the Romans* (NICNT; Grand Rapids, Michigan: Eerdmans, 1965) 210; O. Michel, *Der Brief an die Römer* 365; and E. Käsemann, *An die Römer* 379, probably all following Billerbeck in Str-B 3.315.

offering to the Lord Jesus,[20] is due to his reading through Christian eyes one of the basic OT texts concerned with this motif, Isaiah 66.[21]

II. Paul's Christian Interpretation of Isaiah 66

Elsewhere I have proposed that Isaiah 66 forms the background for much of the imagery and vocabulary of 2 Thessalonians 1-2, primarily due to the messianic interpretation of the "son" of 66:7 as the Messiah.[22] If Second Thessalonians is by Paul (scholarly opinion seems equally divided on this question), the Apostle not only knew of Isaiah 66 but employed it extensively as part of the background of his letter. If Second Thessalonians is by a pupil of Paul, it may not be used to assert something about the genuinely Pauline letters. Regardless of the question of the authenticity of Second Thessalonians, I would maintain that Isaiah 66 played a major role in Paul's entire collection enterprise, as it provided him with the urgency of missionizing in Spain.[23]

---

[20]In 2 Cor 11:2 Paul writes that he wishes to present (παραστῆσαι) the Corinthian congregation to the Lord Jesus (at his parousia) as a pure bride to her one husband. The sacrificial overtone of παραστῆσαι (BAG 633, 1d) should not be overlooked here. Paul plans to "offer" his congregations to Christ at the latter's return. (See also Col 1:28 for the same usage of παραστῆσαι, if this epistle is by Paul). For Paul as the parent of his congregations, see also 1 Thess 2:11; 1 Cor 4:15; 2 Cor 12:14; and Gal 4:19.

[21]O. Michel (*Der Brief an die Römer* 365); F. Leenhardt (*The Epistle to the Romans* 368); J. Murray (*The Epistle to the Romans* 210); and E. Schweizer, "The Church as the Missionary Body of Christ," 317-28 in *Neotestamentica. Deutsche und englische Aufsätze 1951-1963* (Zurich/Stuttgart: Zwingli, 1963) 320, all point to the relevance of Isa 66:20 here. As noted above, they probably have adopted the interpretation of P. Billerbeck on this verse. U. Luz in *Das Geschichtsverständnis des Paulus* (BEvT 49; Munich: Kaiser, 1968) 391, and D. Zeller, *Juden und Heiden* 283, emphatically deny the relevance of Isa 66:20 here.

[22]Cf. "The Relevance of Isaiah 66:7 to Revelation 12 and 2 Thessalonians 1" in *ZNW* 67 (1976) 252-68, as well as the relevant article cited in n. 8. In addition to Second Thessalonians, it is also noteworthy that Pesikta Rabbati 1, one of the few chapters of this work which deal with the coming of the Messiah, is based on Isaiah 66. See the English translation of W.G. Braude, *Pesikta Rabbati* (New Haven and London: Yale, 1968) 1.35-48, especially 36, n. 1. Finally, 2 Clem 17:4, certainly not dependent on Paul, has Jesus speak through Isa 66:18, "I come to gather together all the nations, tribes, and languages," meaning the "day of his appearing," when unbelievers "will see his [Jesus'] glory." Isa 66:24 is then quoted. For the Greek and an English translation, cf. K. Lake, *The Apostolic Fathers* (LCL; Cambridge, Mass.: Harvard, 1959) 1.156-59.

[23]In his essay "Die Ursprünge der christlichen Mission" in *NTS* 18 (1971-72) 15-38, M. Hengel also connects Rom 11:25 with Paul's planned trip to Spain in 15:24, 29, maintaining that the Gentiles are Paul's "offering" in 15:16 (pp. 19, 20). However, Hengel is not aware of the OT/rabbinic background of the Spain

In the grand eschatological vision of Isaiah 66 the certainty of Jerusalem's restoration is stressed. Her sons, the exiles, will definitely return to her and be comforted by her consoling breasts. The Lord will "extend prosperity to her like a river, and the wealth of the nations like an overflowing stream" (v 12). He will come in fire to execute judgment upon all flesh (vv 15-16).[24] He will come to gather all nations and tongues, who shall come and see his glory. From the latter he shall send survivors to the nations, to Tarshish, Put, Lud, Tubal and Javan, to the coastlands afar off, that have not heard his fame or seen his glory. They will then declare his glory among the nations, who in turn will bring all Israel's brethren from all the nations as an offering to the Lord, to Jerusalem. Indeed, some of the latter bearers the Lord will even take as priests and Levites (vv 18-21). All flesh will come to Jerusalem to worship before the Lord (v 23).

As one who believed that the messianic prophecies of the OT had been fulfilled in Jesus, who would return in the Apostle's lifetime,[25] it was natural for Paul also to interpret this chapter of the OT through Christian eyes. V 7 states that the birth of Jerusalem's "son" will not be held up by the Lord (v 9). As other Jewish and Jewish-Christian sources interpreted this "son" as the messianic King,[26] so Paul most probably also did. The Lord definitely will not delay the return of the Messiah (v 9). The wealth of the nations (v 12), to flow to Jerusalem, could have been thought of by Paul as the gifts to be brought to the messianic King by all the nations in the end time, an important motif in Judaism to be discussed below.[27] The content of the "sign" whom the Lord sets among the nations in v 19[28] could have been for him the same as that promised in the messianic passage of Isa 7:14: "The Lord himself will give you a sign (אות; σημεῖον). Behold, a young woman will conceive and bear a son, and shall call his name Immanuel." The same type of imagery is employed in Isa 11:10-12 of the messianic King: "in that day the root of

---

motif, nor does he accept a connection between Rom 15:16, Paul's collection and the Gentile pilgrimage to Jerusalem (20, 21).
[24]According to G. Fohrer, *Das Buch Jesaja* (Zürcher Bibelkommentare; Zurich/ Stuttgart: Zwingli, 1964) 3.282, the judgment spoken of here is one of purgation; it removes the evil-doers.
[25]Cf. the references in note three.
[26]See the sources cited in "The Relevance of Isaiah 66:7," 255-60 (here pp. 127-33).
[27]For the association of the messianic King, the world to come, and the "peace" ("prosperity"; שלום) of Isa 66:12, cf. Lev. Rab. 9/9 in the English translation of *Midrash Rabbah* (London: Soncino, 1939) 4.120.
[28]The LXX MSS are divided as to the plural σημεῖα and the singular, σημεῖον. Both Codex Sinaiticus in the original reading and Codex Vaticanus as well as the MT (אות) have the singular here, which argues strongly for σημεῖον.

Jesse shall stand as an ensign[29] to the peoples; him shall the nations seek, and his dwellings shall be glorious." In that day the Lord will extend his hand yet a second time to recover the remnant which is left of his people, from the various nations and from the "coastlands of the sea." "He will raise an ensign (נס; σημεῖον) for the nations, and will assemble the outcasts of Israel, and gather the dispersed of Judah from the four corners of the earth."[30]

From those who have come and seen the Lord's glory, God will send in Isa 66:19 survivors[31] to the nations, the first nation mentioned being Tarshish, then Put, Lud, Tubal and Javan. The survivors will also go to the coastlands afar off, to all those regions which have not heard the Lord's fame or seen his glory; there they will declare his glory among the nations (v 19). The LXX reads here: ἐξαποστελῶ ἐξ αὐτῶν σεσῳσμένους εἰς τὰ ἔθνη ("From them I will send [those who are] saved to the nations"). For Paul as a Christian reading this text, the "saved" would be those who believed in the redemption found in Jesus the Messiah.[32] They would be Christian missionaries, primarily Paul and his helpers, whom God sends to the Gentiles.[33] In Rom 15:20-21 Paul, quoting Isa 52:15, part of a Servant of the Lord passage, relates that he is now going on to Spain, for he lays great emphasis on not preaching the gospel where Christ has already been named, but where "they shall see who have never been told of him, and they shall understand who have never heard of him." One possible support for the

---

[29]The Hebrew is נס; the targum, which interprets messianically, has את; the LXX reads ὁ ἀνιστάμενος ἄρχειν ἐθνῶν.

[30]For the same motif of a signal or sign to the nations connected with the nations' returning the diaspora Israelites to Jerusalem, cf. Isa 49:22-23. It should also be noted that Paul quotes Isa 11:10 in Rom 15:12. Isa 11:12 is interpreted of the coming of the Star of Jacob (= Messiah) of Num 24:17 in connection with the gathering of the exiles in the late Jewish midrash Leḳaḥ Ṭob on Num 24:17 (Str-B 1.960).

[31]For the motif of the survivors coming to Jerusalem, cf. Zech 14:16, in a Day of the Lord context (see vv 1, 4, 6, 8, 9, 13, 20, 21), when the Lord will become king over all the earth (v 9; see also v 17). The motif of the wealth of the nations being collected should also be noted in v 14.

[32]This is shown, for example, in Paul's use of this same expression in 1 Cor 1:18 and 2 Cor 2:15.

[33]Cf. the statement of C. Westermann on the survivors of the nations going to the far isles as missionaries in Isa 66:19 in *Das Buch Jesaja. Kapitel 40-66* (ATD 19; Göttingen: Vandenhoeck & Ruprecht, 1966) 377: "Hier ist zum erstenmal ganz eindeutig von Mission in unserem Sinne die Rede: Sendung einzelner Menschen zu den fernen Völkern, um dort die Herrlichkeit Gottes zu verkündigen. Es entspricht genau der apostolischen Mission am Anfang der christlichen Kirche." G. Fohrer in *Das Buch Jesaja* 3.284 also emphasizes the missionary aspect of the survivors of the nations here.

view that Paul perceived his own call partly in terms of imagery from the Servant of the Lord passages in Second Isaiah, indeed, that he thought of himself in a way as the Servant of the Lord to the Gentiles, could be found in v 19 of Isaiah 66.[34]

It is important to note that Tarshish is the first of the nations mentioned to whom the "saved" are to declare the Lord's fame and glory. This is probably because it is most distant. The same motif of Tarshish as first appears in Isa 60:9, to be analyzed below. Of the other nations mentioned, Lud and Tubal are probably in Asia Minor. For Javan the LXX reads Ἑλλάς, Greece, parallel here to the "coastlands afar off." Only Put refers to a country on the southern border of the Mediterranean, probably Libya, yet it may be Cyrene.[35] The parallel to Paul's "missionary career" should not be overlooked. The general direction of Paul's missionizing was Arabia, probably the area east and south of Damascus,[36] west and north to Damascus; from there to Antioch on the Orontes (Syria and Cilicia); from there to Asia Minor (the so-called "first journey"); from there a retracing of the Asia Minor route via Antioch in Pisidia to Troas, then Macedonia and the Peloponnesus in Europe (the so-called "second journey"). During his "third journey," which embraced western Asia Minor and Greece again, Paul wrote to the Romans, saying that he hoped to visit them in passing as he went to Spain (15:24, 28), the extremity of the west. The general direction, east to west, thus corresponds to a combination of those nations found in Isa 66:19, Tarshish being equated with Spain, as will be shown below.[37]

After the Lord's fame and glory have been proclaimed to all the nations in Isa 66:19, the Gentiles are to bring all the Israelites' brethren

---

[34] Cf. note one on this issue.
[35] For the identification of these various place names, cf. the respective articles in the *IDB*. Virtually the same nations as mentioned in Isa 66:19 are found in Ezek 27:10-25, upon which Isa 66:19 is probably dependent, as the Isaiah commentators state.
[36] Cf. the article "Arabia" in the *IDB* 1.179-81, and the commentaries on Gal 1:17.
[37] I do not maintain that Paul directly after his conversion had this missionary plan in mind. He first remained relatively close to Jerusalem, from which he expected the Messiah to return. Only after apparently unsuccessful missionizing in Arabia (Gal 1:17) did he undertake his collection enterprise, partly inspired by the promise he made to aid the poorer saints of the Jerusalem church (Gal 2:10 and Rom 15:26). See also Hengel, "Die Ursprünge" 18, who sees Paul's world-wide concept of mission as stemming from the time of the Apostolic Council. Georgi (*Die Geschichte* 85) thinks it possible that it was only on his second stay in Macedonia that Paul connected the collection with the goal of his entire mission.

from all the nations to Jerusalem as an offering or gift (מנחה; δῶρον) to the Lord, "just as the Israelites bring their cereal offering (מנחה; θυσίας) in a clean vessel to the house of the Lord" (v 20).[38] Some of these Gentile "bearers" the Lord will even accept as priests and Levites (Isa 66:20-21).[39] Then all flesh will come to worship before him (v 23). I propose that Paul read this Isaiah text to mean that Christian missionaries, primarily he himself with his helpers, were, in a complete reversal of the normal Jewish thought regarding the end time, to gather representatives[40] from all the *Gentile* nations and to bring them, the Gentiles, and not the diaspora Jews, to Jerusalem as an "offering" or "gift" to the Lord Jesus, the Messiah. This would be the "offering of the Gentiles" of which Paul speaks in Rom 15:16.

This reverse of a major Jewish motif formed a large part of the inspiration for Paul's collection enterprise, to which he devoted the decisive latter years of his life. It was the Apostle's hope that when this collection was complete, when representatives from *all* the nations mentioned in OT eschatological prophecy had been brought to Jerusalem, the Messiah would return, at which time *both* Gentiles and Jews would become worshippers of the Lord. Indeed, "all flesh" is to worship before him (Isa 66:23). This parallels the Apostle's hopes in Romans 9-11, where Paul says that through his successful missionizing of the Gentiles he hopes to make Israel jealous and thus save some of them (11:14). A hardening has now come upon part of Israel until the "full number of the Gentiles" come in. When the latter happens, however (and Paul expects it to happen during his lifetime), all Israel will be saved and the Lord Jesus, the Deliverer, will come from Zion (11:25-26).[41] Although not openly stated by Paul in Romans 11,[42] his

---

[38]It should be noted that frankincense (along with oil and salt) was employed with the minḥa, cereal offering (Lev 2:1). For frankincense as a gift to the King Messiah, cf. the rabbinic interpretation of Isa 60:6 below, as well as Matt 2:11.

[39]Beyond Midr. Ps. 87/6, to be discussed below, the closest rabbinic parallel to this motif of Gentiles becoming priests is, to my knowledge, Exod. Rab. Bo 19/4 (Soncino 3.232-35), where Isa 14:1 is used as a proof-text. The context clearly shows, however, that Gentile *proselytes* are meant. For the offerings of the foreigners who join themselves to the Lord in the end time as being "acceptable," see also Isa 56:6-8, for the temple will be called a house of prayer "for all peoples" (v 7). Cf. Mark 11:17.

[40]The rabbinic interpretation of Jer 3:14 helps to explain this idea of a limited number of "representatives"; see below.

[41]Paul changes the ἕνεκεν of the LXX Isa 59:20 to ἐκ Σιών, "from Zion." In this respect cf. Gen. Rab. Vayesheb 85/9 (Soncino 2.795) for the King Messiah as the staff of Ps 110:2 whom the Lord will send *from Zion.*

[42]For a discussion of why the Apostle does not do so, cf. the concluding section of this essay.

Paul's Travel Plans to Spain

thinking here is intimately tied to the collection enterprise he mentions some chapters later (15). Only when the most distant of all the nations mentioned in Isa 66:19, Tarshish (= Spain; see below), also sends its representatives to Jerusalem, will Paul's collection enterprise or gift to the Messiah be truly complete. Only then will the "full number of the Gentiles" have come in (Rom 11:25). This is the reason for Paul's travel plans to Spain and not to Alexandria in Egypt, or to Ethiopia or Libya, or to the east – Babylonia. Before pointing out Jewish parallels to this messianic interpretation of Isaiah 66, including the bringing of gifts to the messianic King in the end time, it is necessary to ascertain whether the Tarshish of Isa 66:19 would have been logically interpreted by Paul as Spain.

III. Tarshish as Spain

In Isa 66:19 Tarshish is mentioned as the first site to which the "saved" should go to proclaim the Lord's glory among the nations. Typical of the OT commentators' identification of this city is that of J. Muilenberg: "*Tarshish* or Tartessus is a Phoenicien mercantile city in Spain (cf. 2:16; 60:9; Ezek. 27:12)."[43] Many of the classical dictionaries and lexica confirm this statement.[44] Located in southern Spain at the mouth of the Guadalquivir River, somewhat northwest and thus on the Atlantic side of the present Straits of Gibraltar, Tarshish (Hebrew תרשיש; Greek Θάρσις or Τάρσις) was known in non-biblical Greek as Ταρτησσός and was already known in the eleventh century B.C.E. The earliest non-biblical attestation of Tarshish reaches back to the early seventh century B.C.E., when an Assyrian inscription calls Tartessos *tarsisi*.[45] The area around Tartessos was so rich in silver that the city became especially known for this metal. Jer 10:9 relates, for example, that beaten silver is brought from Tarshish to be made into idols.[46] In the

---

[43] Cf. "The Book of Isaiah, Chapters 40-66," in *The Interpreter's Bible*, 5 (New York and Nashville: Abingdon, 1956) 381-773, quotation p. 771. See also C. Westermann, *Das Buch Jesaja* 338.

[44] Cf. A. Schulten's monograph *Tartessos* (Abhandlungen aus dem Gebiet der Auslandskunde, 8; Hamburg: L. Friedrichsen, 1922) and his article "Tartessos" in PW, 2. Reihe, 8. Halbband, cols. 2246-51; the entry Ταρτησσός in LSJ 1759; the *IDB* article by J. Finegan on "Spain" (4.429-30); and Str-B 2.691. It should also be noted that the targum to Ps 48:8 ("the ships of Tarshish") and 72:10 ("the kings of Tarshish") also has טרסוס at both places, which spelling corresponds more to the Greek Τάρσις. See M. Jastrow, *A Dictionary of the Targumim, the Talmud Babli and Yerushalmi, and the Midrashic Literature* (New York: Pardes, 1950) 1.555 on טרסוס.

[45] Cf. the translation of the inscription in Schulten, *Tartessos* 6.

[46] Cf. also Isa 60:9, Ezek 27:12, and 38:13. 1 Macc 8:3 relates how the Romans exerted themselves to gain control of the silver and gold mines of Spain. The

OT the "ships of Tarshish" are mentioned in connection with the mercantile enterprises of Solomon and of Hiram of Tyre (Phoenicia).[47] Since Tartessos was thoroughly destroyed ca. 500 B.C.E. by the Carthaginians, a rival trading nation which for trade reasons closed the Straits of Gibraltar to others for three centuries,[48] its exact position gradually became forgotten by the Greeks and the city was confused with Gades, a town only about 30-35 kilometers (20 miles) to the south, founded by the Tyrians and presently known as Cadiz.[49] Later under Augustus three Roman provinces existed in Spain, one of them being in the south and called Baetica because of the Baetis or Guadalquivir River.[50]

Although it was known in NT times that peoples existed to the north of Spain, this country was nevertheless still regarded as the "end(s) of the earth." The Pillars of Hercules (Straits of Gibraltar) between Spain and Africa were for centuries thought of as the non-plus-ultra for ships.[51] Only under Roman dominion, i.e., after ca. 200 B.C.E., did seafaring proceed again into the Atlantic. Before the Roman general Pompey

---

latter reference shows that the silver of Spain was also known in Jewish sources ca. 120-100 B.C.E., when First Maccabees was probably composed. For this dating, cf. O. Eissfeldt, *The Old Testament. An Introduction* (Oxford: Blackwell, 1966) 579. It also shows that the OT references to the silver of Tarshish could be linked with the silver of Spain.

[47]Cf., for example, 1 Kgs 10:22. The connection of Solomon and Tarshish should be noted for, as will be seen, the messianic King is compared in rabbinic sources to Solomon, and gifts are also brought to him from Tarshish.

[48]The LXX's translation of Tarshish as Καρχηδών in Isa 23:6, and in several other OT passages, rests on the fact that the Carthaginians controlled southern Spain in the third century B.C.E., establishing their own capital in what is now Cartagena. See Finegan, "Spain" 430.

[49]For evidence of this confusion, perhaps since Aristotle, certainly since Plato, cf. Schulten, *Tartessos* 52, 56, 59-60. He shows that it was especially common in the Roman period (59).

[50]It is interesting to note that the Roman philosopher and advisor to Nero, Seneca, who lived from 4 B.C.E. to 65 C.E. and was thus almost an exact contemporary of Paul, came from Cordoba, Spain. Because of this contemporaneity Seneca, whose brother was the Gallio of Corinth in Acts 18:12, was later thought to have exchanged letters with Paul. See the apocryphal "Correspondence Between Seneca and Paul," as well as the article on Seneca in the *RGG*³ 5.1698-99. According to Josephus (*Bell.* 2.183) Herod Antipas was banished by Gaius (Caligula) to Spain ca. 39 C.E. If this tradition is correct (*Ant.* 18.252 says it was to Lyons in Gaul), Paul would have known of this event.

[51]Cf. Schulten, *Tartessos* 48. For the Pillars called the "Strait of Tartessos" (Ταρτησοῦ πύλη) in the third century B.C.E., see p. 28. In *Bell.* 2.363 Josephus has Agrippa give a speech to the inhabitants of Jerusalem in order to convince them not to wage what became the war of 66-70 C.E. Agrippa relates how many truly mighty nations have become subservient to Rome, whose empire's eastern border is the Euphrates, and western border Gadeira, Gades (Cadiz in Spain).

Paul's Travel Plans to Spain

came to Palestine to conquer Jerusalem in 63 B.C.E., he had been active fighting in Spain from 77-72 B.C.E. W.C. van Unnik has pointed out that Sallustius describes him then as waging war *in extremis terris*. He also calls attention to Pss Sol 8:16 (15)-17, which states that "He [God] brought him that is from the end of the earth, that smitith mightily; he decreed war against Jerusalem and against her land." Pompey is undoubtedly meant here and is described as coming to Palestine ἀπ' ἐσχάτου τῆς γῆς, "from the end of the earth," that is, from Spain.[52]

Biblical references also indicate that Tarshish is thought of as the end of the earth. Jonah 1:3 relates that Jonah went to Joppa and boarded a ship going to Tarshish in his attempt to flee from the presence of the Lord. He wanted to get away as far as possible from God, thus the selection of a ship of *Tarshish*. The same is true for Ps 72:8-11. The psalmist wishes for the Hebrew king:

8) May he have dominion from sea to sea,
and from the River to the ends of the earth!

9) May his foes bow down before him,
and his enemies lick the dust!

10) May the kings of Tarshish and of the isles
render him tribute,
may the kings of Sheba and Seba bring gifts!

11) May all kings fall down before him,
all nations serve him!

---

[52]Cf. *Sparsa collecta*. The Collected Essays of W.C. van Unnik. Part One: Evangelia-Paulina-Acta (NovTSup 29; Leiden: Brill, 1973) 399, part of the article "Der Ausdruck ἕως ἐσχάτου τῆς γῆς (Apostelgeschichte 1 8) und sein alttestamentlicher Hintergrund." The English translation is that of Gray in Charles' *APOT* 641. I would suggest that the description of Zion's children, the Jews, in Pss Sol 1:3 ("Their wealth spread to the whole earth, and their glory unto the end of the earth [ἕως ἐσχάτου τῆς γῆς])" stands as a direct contrast to the world-wide fame of Pompey, the subject of psalm two in the collection. For all the historical allusions to this Roman general in the Psalms of Solomon, cf. Gray's evidence assembled in *APOT* 629. The psalms are to be dated in the middle of the first century B.C.E. See *APOT* 630, as well as A.-M. Denis, *Introduction aux Pseudepigraphes Grecs d'Ancien Testament* (Leiden: Brill, 1970) 64.

The notice in 1 Clem 5:7 of Paul having taught righteousness to "all the world" and having reached the "end of the West" (τὸ τέρμα τῆς δύσεως), then giving his testimony before the rulers and dying, seems to rest more on a knowledge of his travel plans to Spain in Romans 15 than on historical knowledge, for Rome in other sources can be described as the west (see, for example, Pss Sol 17:14 [12] and Gray's note here in *APOT* 648), but not as the "end" of the west.

The "River" here in v 8 is the Euphrates in the east. The kings of Tarshish are mentioned because they are the farthest point in the west, the "ends of the earth."[53]

It is thus most probable that the "Tarshish" of Isa 66:19, the first site to which the "saved" are to go to missionize, would have been understood by Paul of Tarsus in Cilicia,[54] a Jew of the eastern Mediterranean, as Spain, the country still then thought of as the "end of the earth."

IV. OT Passages Later Interpreted of the Gentiles Bringing Gifts to the Messiah

There are a number of OT passages which were interpreted by Jews and/or Jewish Christians as indicating the world-wide dominion of the King Messiah and of the submission of the Gentiles to him. In Psalm 2, for example, the Lord says to his Anointed: "You are my son, today I have begotten you. Ask of me, and I will make the nations your heritage, and the ends of the earth your possession" (vv 7-8).[55] Later rabbinic traditions also spoke of the messianic King's world-wide dominion, but in addition of the wealth of the Gentiles being presented to him in Jerusalem. Just as each of the nations of the earth brought its present to King Solomon, and the ships of Tarshish were used to bring the wealth of the nations to him,[56] rabbinic sources relate that so too each of the nations in the messianic era is to present its gift to the King

---

[53] For the expression "to the ends of the earth" the Hebrew reads עד-אפסי-ארץ, translated in LXX Ps 71:8 as ἕως περάτων τῆς οἰκουμένης, which emphasizes that Tarshish for the user of the LXX is the end of the *inhabited* world. In Ps 48:10 (Heb 11) God's praise is to reach to the "ends of the earth." This most likely is to be associated with the "ships of Tarshish" in v 7 (Heb 8).

It should also be noted that as late as the second half of the third century C.E., a Palestinian Jewish rabbi could equate Spain (אספמיא) with the end of the world. See the saying of R. Simlai, a second generation Amora (Strack and Stemberger, *Einleitung* 92), in b. Nid. 30b. Other rabbinic references to Spain as the most distant land in Jewish thinking are m. B. Bat. 3:2 (also b. B. Bat. 39a), and b. Ber. 62a, which is a saying by Ben Azzai, a second generation Tanna (*Einleitung* 81).

[54] Paul, a Roman citizen from Tarsus in Cilicia, would certainly not have identified his paternal home with the Tarshish of the OT, as Josephus did (*Ant.* 1.127; 8.181; 9.208). He knew that his own Tarsus was not located at the "ends of the earth."

[55] Cf. also Ps 22:28 (Eng. 27), a psalm employed by the synoptic gospels as part of the background of the crucifixion of Jesus; Mic 5:3 (Eng. 4); Zech 9:10 (see also Ps 72:8); and Dan 7:13-14.

[56] Cf. 1 Kgs 10:22-25 and 2 Chr 9:21-24.

Paul's Travel Plans to Spain

Messiah in Jerusalem. OT passages mentioning Tarshish are often used by the rabbis to buttress this assertion.[57]

Isaiah 66, the importance of which was pointed out above, as well as Isaiah 60 and Psalms 72 and 68, will now be examined in this respect.

A) Isaiah 66

a) The earliest probable use of Isa 66:20 in connection with gifts to the messianic King is found in the statement of Pss Sol 17:34 (31) regarding the "king, the anointed of the Lord": "nations shall come from the ends of the earth to see his [the Messiah's] glory, bringing as gifts her sons who had fainted, and to see the glory of the Lord, wherewith God hath glorified her [Jerusalem]".[58] Since there are a number of clear allusions to Pompey in this psalm,[59] it is possible that the author is contrasting the glory of the Messiah, to whom nations shall come with their gifts from the end of the earth (ἀπ' ἄκρου τῆς γῆς), that is, in Jewish eschatological thought, from Tarshish or Spain, with the false earthly glory of the "lawless one," the "enemy who acted proudly" (vv 13 [11] and 15 [13], that is, the conqueror of Palestine, Pompey, who in fact came "from the end of the earth," Spain, to wage war against Jerusalem and her land (Pss Sol 8:15 [14]), as noted above.

b) Isa 66:20 also occurs as the background of the thought in 4 Ezra 13:13, which describes the nations' bringing back the ten tribes (v 40) as an offering to the "man who comes up out of the heart of the sea," the Messiah (13:26, 32, 37, 52).[60] The final redaction of this work, which incorporates many earlier traditions, probably occurred ca. 100-120 C.E.[61]

---

[57]For five different aspects of the eschatological pilgrimage of the Gentiles to Zion, including the gifts they are to bring, cf. J. Jeremias, *Jesu Verheissung für die Völker* (Stuttgart: Kohlhammer, 1959²) 48-52. Many of the rabbinic parallels are noted by Billerbeck in Str-B 1.84.

[58]Translation Gray, *APOT* 650. For Jerusalem's sons who "had fainted" the Syriac reads, according to Gray, "been scattered from her," which makes more sense in the context since it points to the eschatological motif of the gathering of the diaspora Jews. For the motif of the nations coming to Jerusalem to see the glory of the Lord, cf. Isa 66:18-19. P. Volz in *Die Eschatologie der jüdischen Gemeinde im neutestamentlichen Zeitalter* (Tübingen: Mohr, 1934²) 345 also sees Isa 66:20 as the background of Pss Sol 17:34 [31], as of 4 Ezra 13:13 (see below). For the dating of the Psalms of Solomon in the middle of the first century B.C.E., see n. 52, above.

[59]Cf. the notes by Gray, *APOT* 646-51.

[60]Cf. the note by G.H. Box on this verse in *APOT* 617, which also calls attention to Pss Sol 17:34. See also Str-B 4.903.

[61]Cf. *APOT* 552-53, as well as Denis, *Introduction* 200 (ca. 100 C.E.).

c) In Midr. Ps. 87/6 on Ps 87:4 ("I will make mention of Rahab and Babylon as among them that acknowledge Me"), R. Judah bar Simon[62] taught: "And the nations will bring gifts to the King Messiah, as it is said 'Gifts *(tašuri)* from the head of Amana (Song 4:8).'" [63] The English translator of this midrash, W. Braude, acknowledges that he has emended the phrase "themselves" of the first half of this sentence, which reads in Hebrew: והן עצמן למלך המשיח דורונות, "And they themselves for/to the King Messiah gifts," to "they will bring."[64] Instead, the Hebrew should be read as "And they themselves [the nations, not the diaspora Jews, brought by the nations] shall be gifts to the King Messiah," as A. Wünsche expressly noted in his German translation of this midrash.[65] Later in this same section of Midr. Ps. 87 R. Eleazar (ben Pedath),[66] basing his comments on Isa 66:21, states that God will take from the *heathen* who bring the diaspora Israelites to the King Messiah some to become priests and Levites. This is also the way the medieval Jewish commentator Rashi understood Isa 66:21 since in his interpretation of this verse he only cites the opinion of R. Eleazar, and not others which attempt to make those who bring the diaspora Jews to Jerusalem Israelites who in times of duress had become pagan.[67]

These were very liberal thoughts contrary to the spirit of most post 70 C.E. Jewish thinking in regard to Gentile participation in final salvation,[68] as well as a close parallel to Paul's interpretation of the very

---

[62] According to Strack and Stemberger, *Einleitung* 98, this rabbi was a fourth generation Palestinian Amora.

[63] English translation by W.G. Braude, *The Midrash on Psalms* (Yale Judaica Series, 13; New Haven: Yale, 1959) 2.77.

[64] Cf. *The Midrash on Psalms* 2.493, n. 14. For the Hebrew, see the edition of S. Buber, מדרש תהלים (Vilna: Romm, 1892) 378.

[65] Cf. his *Midrasch Tehillim* (Hildesheim: Olms, 1967 [original Trier, 1892]) 2.51, where his note on "they themselves" as gifts reads: "Nämlich die Völker der Welt." Wünsche also employed the Buber edition. It should be noted that shortly after this statement Isa 66:20 is cited as a proof-text. A tradition parallel to that of Midr. Ps. 87/6 is found in Cant. Rab. 4/8.2, which also employs Isa 66:20 as a proof-text. It reads in the Hebrew: "Moreover, they themselves [the nations] in the future will bring gifts to the King Messiah." This is a later toning down of an earlier, more generous spirit. The Soncino English translation (9.208) incorrectly expands the Hebrew.

[66] A third generation Palestinian Amora (Strack and Stemberger, *Einleitung* 94).

[67] Cf. מקראות גדולות (Tel Aviv: Schocken, 1959) 96b-97a. For this reference from Rashi I am grateful to Dr. M. Krupp of Jerusalem, who also notes that the saying by R. Eleazar in Midr. Ps. 87/6 is a new paragraph in Buber's edition. Braude's addition of "accordingly" in his English translation (2.78) is misleading because it implies that Eleazar's opinion accords with the preceding, which is definitely not the case.

[68] A semi-liberal position, whereby the Messiah will receive only those nations which have not enslaved Israel, is found in Pesiq. R. 1/3 (Braude, *Pesikta*

Paul's Travel Plans to Spain

same verses, Isa 66:20-21, sketched above. In Isaiah the nations will bring the diaspora Jews to Jerusalem as an offering (LXX δῶρον; cf. the Hebrew loan word דורון used above), some of the Gentile bearers of the Jews being taken by the Lord as priests and Levites in the temple, which is modified by Paul to mean the nations or *Gentiles themselves* as the offering he brings to Jerusalem (for the Messiah) (Rom 15:16).

d) Finally Isa 66:20 is also found in the ninth sign of the late Jewish midrash "Signs of the Messiah," the ninth sign being concerned with the gathering of the Israelites in the diaspora by the Messiah.[69]

B) Isaiah 60

In Isa 66:18, when the Lord gathers all nations and tongues, the latter come to Jerusalem and see his glory. In chapter 60 the glory of the Lord is to rise upon fallen Jerusalem, nations will come to its light, kings to the brightness of its rising (vv 1-3). Jerusalem's children, the diaspora Jews, will be brought from afar (v 4); and the wealth of the nations, including gold and frankincense from the east, will flow to Jerusalem (vv 5-6). The heathens' animal sacrifices for the Jerusalem temple will meet with God's "acceptance" (v 7).[70] The nations of the west, the ships of Tarshish *first,* will bring Jerusalem's sons home, with silver and gold (v 9). The city's gates shall then never be closed, always ready to receive the "wealth of the nations, with their kings led in procession" (v 11).

Precisely these verses form the background of Matthew's account of the wise men from the east who present their gifts of gold, frankincense and myrrh[71] to the King of the Jews, the Messiah (Matt 2:1-12). It should be noted that they first go to Jerusalem, seeking the King

---

Rabbati 1.41), based on Isa 66:23. See also 2 Apoc Bar 72:4 for this view. For a general discussion of universalism versus particularism in Jewish sources, cf. the material gathered in Str-B 3. 144-55, as well as Volz, *Die Eschatologie,* 356-59.

[69]Cf. the German translation in A. Wünsche, *Aus Israel's Lehrhallen.* III. Kleine Midraschim zur jüdischen Eschatologie und Apokalyptik (Hildesheim: Olms, 1967; reprint of Leipzig: Pfeiffer, 1909) 115. The original of the midrash is found in A. Jellinek, *Bet ha-Midrasch* (Jerusalem: Wahrmann Books, 1967³) 2.58-63.

[70]This Isaianic verse was already interpreted in the first century C.E. of the nations of the world coming to Jerusalem in the messianic period. Cf. the saying by R. Eliezer ben Hyrcanus, a second generation older Tanna (see Strack and Stemberger, *Einleitung* 77), cited in Str-B 2.538. For Isa 60:7 in connection with the gifts brought to God in the time to come, see also n.97.

[71]Cf., for example, Cant 3:6 and 1 Enoch 29:2 for myrrh and frankincense together. Leḳaḥ Ṭob on Num 24:17 also has the treasures of Isa 60:5-6 in connection with the revelation of the King Messiah. For a German translation, see Str-B 1.960.

Messiah, for it was here according to Jewish tradition that he would appear. Indeed, they must be told to go to Bethlehem instead. Secondly, only here and in chapter 27 is Jesus called "King of the Jews" in Matthew. In 2:2 this again is due to Jewish tradition regarding the bringing of gifts from distant lands to the *King* Messiah, in Jerusalem. Matthew, the only evangelist with this motif of gifts from afar to the messianic King,[72] either himself is acquainted with this rabbinic tradition or has taken it from his source.[73] What is important to note, however, is that the motif of gifts from distant lands to the messianic King in Jerusalem was definitely a Jewish tradition before the writing of Matthew's gospel, which most critics put somewhere between 80-100 C.E.[74]

Isa 60:5 says that "the abundance of the sea" and the "wealth of the nations" shall come to Jerusalem. For the first phrase the targum reads "the wealth of the west,"[75] which is taken up again in v 9, where the ships of Tarshish in the west are the *first* of the swarms of people (v 8) to bring the diaspora Jews and wealth to Jerusalem. Here again, the primary role of Tarshish, later interpreted as Spain, among the coastland or Mediterranean peoples is emphasized in the eschatological drama.

The nations will bring their wealth to Jerusalem "with their kings led in procession" (v 11). Although the latter expression originally derived from war imagery,[76] its significance for Paul's collection should not be overlooked. The king in the Near East always represented his entire people. Thus individuals representing their respective nations are thought of here as being led in procession to Jerusalem. Later rabbinic tradition interpreted this procession as bringing gifts to the King Messiah, as will be indicated below.

It is important to note that the diaspora Jews return to Jerusalem, but only when her King Messiah comes to her, triumphant and victorious, humble and riding on an ass (Zech 9:9), will she have real joy, as one rabbinic tradition relates in respect to Isaiah 60.[77] It is then

---

[72] The shepherds of Luke 2 are from the region of Bethlehem and bring no gifts.
[73] If the first is true, it would be another indication that "Matthew" may have been a converted scribe. See also here, p. 96, n. 7.
[74] Cf. W.G. Kümmel, *Introduction to the New Testament* (Nashville/New York: Abingdon, 1966[14]) 84.
[75] Literally "sunset," "evening." See J.F. Stenning, *The Targum of Isaiah* (Oxford: Clarendon, 1949) 200-201.
[76] Cf. Westermann, *Das Buch Jesaja, Kapitel 40-66* 228, n. 35, as well as the targum's "their kings in chains" (Stenning 200-201).
[77] Cf. Cant. Rab. 1/5.1 (Soncino 9.49-50) in regard to the return of Jerusalem's children (Isa 60:4) in the time to come.

Paul's Travel Plans to Spain

that all the nations will walk by the light of the Messiah and of Israel,[78] when Jerusalem's lamp is the Lamb and the kings of the nations of the earth bring their glory and honor (or better, "possessions") to the city.[79]

The above discussion of Isaiah 60 also points to the origin of the phrase τὸ πλήρωμα τῶν ἐθνῶν εἰσέλθῃ in Rom 11:25. As pointed out above, in the very next verse (26) Paul quotes LXX Isa 59:20-21, modifying this passage to mean that Jesus the Deliverer will come *from* Zion. Only five verses later in the Isaiah text (60:5) the irregular Hebrew phrase occurs, also regarding Zion: "the wealth [sing.] of the nations, they shall come to you." The verb יָבֹאוּ, 3. m. pl. impf., is Qal here. It has the connotation of "to come *in*," "to go *in*."[80] It is the nations or Gentiles here in the Hebrew who shall "come in" to Zion. The LXX understandably had trouble with the Hebrew pl. impf. Qal, which literally would be εἰσελεύσονται, and instead paraphrased the entire sentence: ὅτι μεταβαλεῖ εἰς σὲ πλοῦτος [Sinaiticus in the original has πλῆθος] θαλάσσης καὶ ἐθνῶν καὶ λαῶν. Paul, already with the modified citation of Isa 59:20-21 in his mind, intentionally changed the πλοῦτος/πλῆθος [τῶν] ἐθνῶν of the nearby verse Isa 60:5 to the similar sounding τὸ πλήρωμα τῶν ἐθνῶν and ad hoc correctly translated the Hebrew Qal יָבֹאוּ as εἰσέλθῃ. If the Apostle was acquainted with the textual tradition now found in the original of Sinaiticus, it would have been only a small step from πλῆθος, "a large number," to τὸ πλήρωμα, "the full number" (of the Gentiles).

This means that εἰσέλθῃ in Rom 11:25 should not be connected with entering the "kingdom of God," as in the gospels, but rather with the eschatological motif of the wealth (or a "large number") of the nations/Gentiles, who are to enter or "come into" the city Jerusalem.[81] It is possible that the exalted Lord Jesus at his parousia may be thought to come from heavenly Zion in 11:26, yet the full number of the Gentiles

---

[78]Cf. Pesiq. R. 36/2 (Braude, *Pesikta Rabbati* 2.682) regarding the year in which the King Messiah will appear, when the time or day of the Jews' redemption "is come." Here Isa 60:1, 2 and 3 are cited as proof-texts in a discussion of the Messiah's light.
[79]Cf. the vision of the new Jerusalem which descends from heaven in Rev 21:23-27, based on Isa 60:1-3, 5, 11, 19-20. Τιμή in Rev 21:26 probably refers to the kings' possessions, in other words their wealth. See BAG 825.
[80]Cf. BDB 97. The antonym is יָצָא, "to go *out*." See also the Hiph'il of the same verb, לְהָבִיא, with the same expression "wealth of the nations" in Isa 60:11, translated in the LXX as εἰσαγάγειν. The latter verse is quoted almost literally in connection with the glorification of Jerusalem at the time of the eschatological war in 1 QM 12:13-14.
[81]To this extent Plag (*Israels Wege* 43-45) and Stuhlmacher ("Zur Interpretation" 560) are correct regarding the general motif to which εἰσέρχεσθαι belongs.

for Paul are in fact to enter earthly Zion at the time the Apostle accompanies the Gentile-Christian representatives of the churches founded by him, and the gifts they bring, to Jerusalem. This later is also to include representatives from Spain/Tarshish (Isa 60:9). It also means that the verb εἰσέλθῃ in 11:25 does not in itself point to a pre-Pauline tradition, as most recently proposed by Käsemann (*An die Römer* 303), but rather to an intelligent, ad hoc interpretation by Paul of a verse from Isaiah very close to the Isaianic verses the Apostle cites in 11:26.

C) *Psalm 72*, which the MT says was written "by" Solomon, the LXX on the other hand "for" Solomon, is interpreted in the targum messianically,[82] as is the case in many rabbinic references to this psalm concerning the "royal son" (v 1). It is the Messiah who is to judge the people with righteousness, defend the poor and deliver the needy (vv 2, 4). It is also he who shall rule as κύριος or lord (LXX) from sea to sea, from the Euphrates in the east to the "ends of the earth" in the west (v 8).[83] The latter phrase, as pointed out above, should be interpreted as Spain since v 10 proceeds by naming the ends of the earth for the Hebrew-Jewish mind. The kings of Tarshish and of the isles are to render the Messiah tribute, the kings of Sheba and Seba to bring him gifts.[84] In fact, *all* kings and nations are to be subservient to him (v 11)[85] to whom the gold of Sheba/Arabia is to be given (v 15). His name will endure forever, and *all* the tribes and nations of the earth shall be blessed through him (v 17 LXX).

In rabbinic sources this psalm is often interpreted of the nations' bringing their gifts to the King Messiah in the time to come. Gen. Rab. Vayyishlach 78/12 on Gen 30:11, for example, relates how

---

[82]For an English translation, cf. S.H. Levey, *The Messiah: An Aramaic Interpretation.* The Messianic Exegesis of the Targum (Monographs of the Hebrew Union College, 2; Cincinnati: Hebrew Union College – Jewish Institute of Religion, 1974) 115-18.

[83]The targum reads here (Levey, *The Messiah* 116): "He shall have dominion from one side of the Mediterranean to the other, and from the Euphrates to the ends of the earth." Here the "ends of the earth" clearly are the west side of the "Great Sea," Spain.

[84]Tribute here is מנחה, as in Isa 66:20. Both it and the "gifts" of v 10b are δῶρα in the LXX, as LXX Isa 66:20 has δῶρον.

[85]An intensification of this motif is found in Tg. Ps 72:9, where instead of the Hebrew "May those who dwell in the wilderness bow down before him," the targum reads (Levey, *The Messiah* 116): "Governors of provinces shall bow down before him ...." The importance of Paul's thinking in terms of provinces is pointed out in "V" below.

Paul's Travel Plans to Spain 183

One of the common people said to R. Hoshaya:[86] "If I tell you a good thing, will you repeat it in my name?" "What is it?" asked he. "All the gifts which the Patriarch Jacob made to Esau," replied he, "the heathens will return them to the Messiah in the Messianic era." "What is the proof?" "The kings of Tarshish and of the isles shall return tribute" (Ps. LXXII, 10) ....[87]

Num. Rab. Naso 13/14, on Nashon's offering in Num 7:13 for the service at the altar of the tabernacle set up by Moses, compares the universal reign of Solomon to that of the King Messiah in the future. Just as Solomon reigned over the ends of the earth and the sea, and every nation brought its present to him,[88] so the King Messiah will reign from sea to sea and over all the earth, for which Ps 72:8 and 11 are cited. Indeed, *all* the nations are to serve him who is like a son of man (Dan 7:13-14). Both Solomon and the Messiah are to hold sway over the seventy nations which live "from one end of the world to the other." As the latter brought gifts to Solomon, so in the time to come they will do the same to the King Messiah, for which Ps 72:10 is cited.[89]

The world-wide dominion of Ps 72:8 is referred to the Messiah in other sources as well,[90] and Psalm 72 is also related to the nations' bringing gifts to the King Messiah in the following example.

D) *Psalm 68,* a "partial score" to the liturgy of the festival worship service in the Jerusalem temple,[91] mentions the processions which enter the sanctuary there (v 24). It is not only the tribes of Israel and the

---

[86]Probably a first generation Palestinian Amora (Strack and Stemberger, *Einleitung* 89).
[87]English translation in Soncino 2.724.
[88]The proof-text 1 Kgs 10:22 with Tarshish is given here.
[89]English translation in Soncino 6.526-28. The "Q" tradition found in Matt 12:42 and Luke 11:31 should also be noted here. The queen of Sheba, who came from the ends of the earth to hear Solomon's wisdom, will damn Jesus' generation at the (last) judgment, for it does not acknowledge that "something greater than Solomon is here" in the person of Jesus. Does Jesus indirectly maintain his messiahship here, and was Paul aware of this tradition? If at least the latter is true, it would have made Paul's association of gifts to the Messiah Jesus dependent not only on rabbinic traditions regarding Solomon and the Messiah, but also on a tradition found in the early church.
[90]Cf. Pesiq. R. 13/2 on Num. 24:19 (Braude 1.246); Pirqe R. El. 11 (Of the ten kings who rule from one end of the world to the other, the Messiah is the ninth. Ps 72:8 is cited as a proof-text for this in the edition of G. Friedlander, *Pirkê de Rabbi Eliezer* [New York: Bloch, 1916] 83); Midr. Ps. 72/5 (Braude 1.562); and Midr. Ps. 2/10 on the heathen and the ends of the earth of Ps 2:8 as the Messiah's inheritance and possession, for which the printed edition of Warsaw cites Ps 72:8 as the proof-text, which is accepted by Billerbeck (Str-B 3.676) but not translated by Braude (1.41-42; cf. 2.405, n. 18).
[91]Cf. A. Weiser, *The Psalms* (OT Library; Philadelphia: Westminster, 1962) 483.

temple personnel who take part, however. Foreigners from the various nations also participate. "Because of the temple at Jerusalem kings bear gifts to thee" (v 29). Egypt is to bring bronze (to the temple as a gift), Ethiopia shall hasten to stretch out her hands to God (v 31). The kingdoms of the earth are to sing to, and praise, the Lord (v 32).

Esth. Rab. 1/4 on Esth 1:1, which relates that Ahasuerus reigned from Hodu to Cush (India to Ethiopia), states that even though this may appear to be a short distance, it in fact means over the whole world. The same was true of Solomon, who ruled from Tiphsah to Gaza, which means he reigned over the "whole world."[92]

> Similarly we find, "From the Temple up to Jerusalem, kings shall bring presents to Thee" (Ps LXVIII, 30). Is it not only a short distance from the Temple to Jerusalem? What it means, however, is that just as the offerings extend from the Temple to Jerusalem, so there will be a procession of messengers with gifts for the Messiah, as it is written, "Yea, all the kings shall prostrate themselves before him" (*ib.* LXXII, 11). R. Cohen the brother of R. Ḥiyya b. Abba said: As the Divine Presence stretches from the Temple to Jerusalem, so will the Divine Presence one day fill the world from end to end, as it is written, "And let the whole earth be filled with His glory. Amen and Amen" (*ib.* 19).[93]

Here the kings of Ps 72:11 are interpreted as the same kings who will bring presents to the Messiah in Ps 68:30. They are to be a "procession of messengers with gifts for the Messiah," showing his dominion over the entire world. The "kings led in procession," associated with the nations' bringing their wealth to Jerusalem in Isa 60:11, also belong to this thought complex, as indicated above on Isaiah 60. These two scriptural references, along with Jer 3:14 to be analyzed below, most probably provided Paul with the background for his own idea of a collection or procession of Gentile converts bearing gifts to Jerusalem.[94]

Another rabbinic passage regarding the Gentiles' bringing gifts to the King Messiah and mentioning Psalm 68 provides a good parallel to Paul's making his fellow Jews jealous through the Apostle's bringing converted

---

[92] 1 Kgs 5:4 (Eng 4:24) is so interpreted here.
[93] English translation in Soncino 9.21. R. Ḥiyya bar Abba was a fifth generation Tanna according to Strack and Stemberger, *Einleitung* 87-88.
[94] Related to this complex is Paul's use of θριαμβεύω in 2 Cor 2:14. Here God in Christ "leads in triumph" Paul and his co-workers, spreading the knowledge of the gospel everywhere. Paul is pictured as a victorious general leading his army in a triumphal procession, those led being his converts, some of whom will partake in the "procession" to Jerusalem. Cf. BAG 364, LSJ 806 (2b), and J. Héring, *The Second Epistle of Saint Paul to the Corinthians* (London: Epworth, 1967) 18.

Gentiles to Jerusalem, in the hope that the Jews would then also believe in the Messiah and be saved (Rom 10:19; 11:11, 14).

B. Pesaḥ. 118b relates that one of the things R. Ishmael ben R. Jose told in his father's name to Rabba[95] and others when he became sick was that all the nations of the world are to praise the Lord. Another is that Egypt is destined to bring a gift to the Messiah. If the Messiah does not want to accept it, God will encourage him to do so since the Egyptians provided hospitality to the Israelites in Egypt. "Immediately, 'Nobles shall come out of Egypt [bearing gifts]' [Ps. 68:32]." Then Ethiopia will reason that if the Egyptians who enslaved the Israelites are treated so well, all the more will they who did not enslave Israel be treated well. God then will bid the Messiah to accept the Ethiopians' gift too. "Straightway, 'Ethiopia shall hasten to stretch out her hands unto God' *(ibid.).*" Then the Roman State will argue: If the Messiah accepts gifts from those who are not his brothers, how much more so will he accept my gifts, since I am his brother.[96] Ps 68:31 is then cited as a proof-text.[97]

Just as the Romans/Edomites, kinsmen of Israel, become jealous of the Messiah's acceptance of gifts from heathen nations and argue that if the pagans' gifts to the Messiah in Jerusalem are acceptable, theirs also should be because of their blood relationship to Israel, so according to Paul in Romans 10-11 the Jews, through the acceptance of the "offering of the Gentiles" in Jerusalem, hopefully will become jealous of the Gentiles, "those who are not a nation" (10:19), who did not seek the Lord (10:20), and also believe in Jesus as the Messiah, who will then come.[98] This becomes in fact the main purpose of Paul's collection

---

[95]The first is a fourth generation Tanna. Cf. Strack and Stemberger, *Einleitung* 85.

[96]Rome here, as in rabbinic writings in general, is Edom, the state built by Esau's descendants (Gen 36:1), Esau being the brother of Jacob/Israel.

[97]For Ps 68:32 employed regarding the gifts of the nations to the King Messiah, who shall reign from "sea to sea" (Zech 9:10), see also Tanḥuma שופטים 19a, translated in Str-B 3.148 under "h." For Ps 68:30, 32 and Isa 60:7 interpreted as gifts to God in the time to come, cf. Midr. Ps. 68/15 (Braude 1.548-49). Ps 68:30, Isa 66:23 and Zech 14:9 appear in the same connection in Midr. Ps. 96/2 (Braude 2.139-40).

[98]A somewhat parallel thought may be found in T. Benj. 10:10: "And he shall convict [ἐλέγξει] Israel through the chosen Gentiles, as He convicted [ἤλεγξε] Esau through the Midianities who loved their brethren." The English is found in APOT 359, the Greek in R.H. Charles, *The Greek Versions of the Testaments of the Twelve Patriarchs* (Oxford: University Press, 1908; reprint Darmstadt: Wissenschaftliche Buchgesellschaft, 1966) 230. Some MSS of 11:2 refer the passage to Paul, thus caution must be observed here. Yet the inclusion of the Gentiles in God's salvation is too strong a motif in the Testaments merely to

enterprise, which was thus designed not merely to alleviate poverty in the Jerusalem Christian congregation.[99]

Although other rabbinic and pseudepigraphic sources also mention the gifts to be brought to the messianic King in the end time,[100] the examples cited above suffice to show that this motif played a major role in Jewish thought concerning the events of the last days before the "End."

It should not be assumed that all or even the majority of the Jewish/rabbinic traditions cited above were known to Paul. The earliest reference to the nations' bringing gifts to the messianic King from the ends of the earth, however, does go back to the middle of the first century B.C.E., the Psalms of Solomon. Matthew's employment of this motif also shows that it was well enough known before 100 C.E. for him to have incorporated it in his account of Jesus' birth, and 4 Ezra 13 demonstrates that the motif was known in another circle of Judaism at least shortly thereafter. A number of the rabbinic traditions cited above stem from Tannaim. That is, they belong to the earliest rabbinic traditions recorded. They thus may even transmit material from earlier rabbis. What is most important to note, however, is that the various rabbinic developments of OT texts capable of being related to the gifts or offering to be made to the messianic King, offer astonishingly close thought parallels to how Paul, a Pharisee who advanced in Judaism beyond many of his own age since he was so extremely zealous of the traditions of his fathers (Gal 1:14), also interpreted these same OT texts, especially Isaiah 66, according to the proposal made above. The procession of Gentile messengers from the churches founded by the Apostle, later to include Spain/Tarshish, was to bring the Gentiles' gifts or offering to Jerusalem in the expectation of the coming of the messianic King. This offering, the Gentiles themselves, when it was "completed" by also winning representatives from *Spain,* was to make

---

ascribe it to later Christian hands. Cf., for example, T. Sim. 7:2; T. Levi 2:11; T. Dan. 6:9; T. Naph. 8:3.

[99]The "provocative character" of Paul's collection is also emphasized by Georgi (*Die Geschichte* 84-86), who agrees on this point with Munck. Neither, however, notes the above rabbinic and pseudepigraphical traditions.

[100]Cf. Tg. Isa 16:1 (Stenning 52-53); Gen. Rab. Vayyishlach 83/4 (Soncino 2.768); Vayechi (New Version) 97 (Soncino 2.906-07); 1 Enoch 53:1 (probably referring to the Elect One of 52:9) in *APOT* 220; Sib. Or. 3.772-73, regarding the converted heathen at the time of the messianic kingdom, in *APOT* 392; and the late Messiah Haggada translated in Wünsche, *Aus Israel's Lehrhallen* 3.104, the original being found in Jellinek, *Bet ha-Midrasch* 3.141-43.

Paul's fellow Jews jealous enough also to believe in Jesus as the Messiah.[101]

V. Jer 3:14 and Paul's "Representative Universalism"

The Apostle to the Gentiles made it his practice to gather representatives or delegates from each of the areas he missionized for the task of bringing the collected gifts to Jerusalem. In addition to the relevance of Isa 60:11 and Ps 68:29 pointed out above, including rabbinic interpretation of the latter; and the fact that the diaspora Jews in every major city made an annual contribution of first-fruits (ἀπαρχαί)[102] to the temple in Jerusalem, employing "sacred envoys" (ἱεροπομποί), men of highest repute, to bear them;[103] the messianic interpretation of another OT passage, Jer 3:14, probably provided Paul with his inspiration for bringing representative Gentile Christians to Jerusalem. According to this verse, at the time of the exiles' return the Lord will take one from a city and two from a family or nation, and will bring them to Zion.[104] At that time all nations shall gather to Jerusalem, Israel and Judah will be one (3:17-18).

---

[101]At this time Paul hoped that the "hardening" of Israel would be removed (Rom 11:25). This is (as in the Apostle's reversal of the motif of the Gentiles in the end time coming to Jerusalem and converting to Judaism) the opposite of Isa 25:6-7, where on the mountain of the Lord, Jerusalem, God in the final days will make a feast for *all* peoples and destroy the "covering that is cast over all peoples, the veil that is spread over all nations." It is Paul's fervid hope that when all his Gentile Christian representatives have come to Jerusalem, *Israel's* "veil" or "hardening" will be cast off and the Jews will accept Jesus as their Messiah. For Isa 25:6 as the background of the Jewish motif of the eschatological "messianic banquet," cf. Volz, *Die Eschatologie* 367. See also the many sources on the banquet cited by Billerbeck (Str-B 4.1146-47, 1154-59), which show that, contrary to Paul, rabbinic exegesis did not espouse the lifting of the veil spread over all the nations. The Apostle quotes the nearby verse Isa 25:8 in 1 Cor 15:54.

[102]For Paul's use of ἀπαρχαί/ἀπαρχή and καρπός for the first-fruits of his ministry, cf. n. 16.

[103]Cf. Philo, *De spec. leg.* 1.78 and *De leg. ad Gaium* 216 and 312, where the hopes of the pious rest on these first-fruits. References from Nickle, *The Collection* 83, n. 66. For the importance of the annual gathering of the first-fruits in the smaller towns of Palestine, their first being brought to the "Maamad," the local central collection point, then being carried to Jerusalem, where the rulers, prefects and treasurers of the temple went forth to meet the bearers (in procession), see the Mishnah tractate Bikkurim 1-3, especially 3:2-4. For the "Maamad" as a "group of representatives from outlying districts," see H. Danby, *The Mishnah* (Oxford: University Press, 1933) 794, n. 21.

[104]Munck (*Paul* 278) called this principle "representative universalism" and labeled it Semitic. He was not aware of its OT background in Jer 3:14.

The Hebrew for "family" in Jer 3:14 is משפחה (LXX here has πατριά): "clan," "tribe," "people," "nation."[105] It is the same term as that employed in Gen 12:3 regarding Abram: "by you all the families of the earth shall bless themselves." When Paul quotes this Genesis verse in Gal 3:8, he employs τὰ ἔθνη, not the αἱ φυλαί of the LXX, to buttress scripturally God's justifying the Gentiles by faith, not by works of the law. It is also the same Hebrew term as used in the eschatological passage Zech 14:16-17, a text comparable to Isa 66:18-21 in its motifs, when on the Day of the Lord "every one that survives of all the nations (הגוים; τὰ ἔθνη) that have come against Jerusalem shall go up year by year to worship the King, the Lord of hosts, and to keep the feast of booths. And if any of the families (משפחות; αἱ φυλαί) of the earth do not go up to Jerusalem to worship the King, the Lord of hosts, there will be no rain upon them."[106]

Jewish sources interpreted Jer 3:14 as regarding the gathering of the Jewish exiles in the days of the Messiah.[107] In a discussion of when the end (= the days of the Messiah here) would come, Rab in b. Sanh. 97b says that all the predestined dates given for redemption have passed. Redemption now depends on repentance and good deeds. R. Eliezer and R. Joshua, earlier rabbis,[108] are then cited as debating whether repentance is necessary for redemption. R. Joshua eventually wins the debate by saying no repentance is needed, the end will come anyway (at the time God has appointed for it).[109] He rejoins Eliezer: "But is it not written, 'For I am master over you; and I will take you one of a city, and two of a family, and I will bring you to Zion [Jer 3:14].'"[110] In this late first century rabbinic passage God will gather representatives from Israel at the time of the consummation, and Jer 3:14 is used as a scriptural text to buttress this assertion.

---

[105] Cf. BDB 1046-47.
[106] For this term in the combination "families of the nations" (משפחות גוים), cf. Ps 22:27.
[107] Cf. the similar statement of Rabban Simeon ben Gamaliel, a first generation Tanna (Strack and Stemberger, *Einleitung* 75), based on Jer 3:17 in 'Abot R. Nat. 35 (translated in J. Goldin, *The Fathers According to Rabbi Nathan* [New Haven: Yale, 1955] 147): "In the future Jerusalem will be the gathering place of all the nations and all the kingdoms ...." See also the discussion of R. Azariah and R. Eleazar of Modiim (both of the older group of second generation Tannaim; cf. Strack and Stemberger, *Einleitung* 78)) on Jer 3:17 in Pesikta 143a, translated in Str-B 3.849.
[108] Second generation older Tannaim frequently in debate with each other (Strack and Stemberger, *Einleitung* 77).
[109] The parallel text is found in p. Ta'an. 1/1 (63d) and cites Isa 60:22. Billerbeck considers this the better text here (Str-B 1.162-64).
[110] Translation from the *Hebrew-English Edition of the Talmud*. Sanhedrin.

In b. Sanh. 111a Resh Laqish says Jer 3:14 is meant literally. R. Joḥanan then tells him: "Their master is not pleased that you say so of them. But [say thus]: 'one of a city' [means that his virtues] shall benefit an entire city; and 'two of a family' will benefit the entire family." Rab then concurs with him.[111] This example shows how Paul could consider a few representatives from each area in which he missionized as bringing salvation to the entire area. It was not necessary that he thoroughly evangelize one district before going on to the next.[112]

While other rabbinic texts also employ Jer 3:14 in regard to the final gathering of the exiles to Jerusalem, in the days of the King Messiah,[113] the above passages, some of which are quite early, suffice to show that these traditions in all probability formed part of the background of Paul's gathering representatives from each area he missionized for the task of bearing the gifts of the various peoples to Jerusalem.

Jer 3:14, then, probably is part of the explanation for Paul's statement in Rom 15:23 that he no longer has room to evangelize in the eastern Mediterranean. He has already won representatives there from the major Gentile cities and nations to present them and their gifts to the Messiah in Jerusalem. He wishes to complete his eschatological task by also evangelizing in the area so often mentioned in the eschatological visions of the OT as the extremity of the world, Spain (Tarshish).

---

[111]Resh Laqish and Joḥanan were brothers-in-law and were second generation Palestinian Amoraim, Rab a first generation Palestinian Amora (Strack and Stemberger, *Einleitung* 91 and 90).
[112]Corroboration of this theory of only a small number of representatives as sufficient in the days of the Messiah is found in the continuation of the argument in b. Sanh. 111a. As there were only two of 600,000 remaining at the exodus from Egypt, and as there were only two of 600,000 remaining at the taking of the land, so it will be in the days of the Messiah according to Raba, probably a fourth generation Babylonian Amora (see Strack and Stemberger, *Einleitung* 99). A similar thought is found in Pesiq. R. 50/6 (Braude 2.849), where "if even only one of the congregation of Israel resolves repentance, his repentance is accepted as though it were the repentance of an entire congregation." For a parallel thought pattern in Paul, see 1 Cor 7:14, where the unbelieving partner in a "mixed marriage" is made holy through the Christian partner, and Rom 11:16a, in the context of Paul's making his fellow Jews jealous, where the Apostle states that if the dough offered as first-fruits (Jews converted to Christianity) is holy, so is the whole lump.
[113]Cf. also Tanḥuma B ויֵרא 5 (43b), cited in Str-B 5.830, where R. Simai (according to Strack and Stemberger, *Einleitung* 88, he was a fifth generation Tanna) associates Jer 3:14 and Exod 6:7: as God redeemed his people in this world, so he will do in the world to come. Parallels, with other biblical verses substituted for Jer 3:14, are found in Num. Rab. 14/2 and b. Sanh. 111a. Jer 3:14 is also cited in the sixth of the Signs of the Messiah. After the Messiah ben Joseph reveals himself, the Israelites hear of him, and several from each province and city gather to him. See Wünsche, *Aus Israel's Lehrhallen* 3.110.

VI. The "Full Number of Gentiles" of Rom 11:25

In his letter to the Romans Paul wants his Christian addressees to understand a "mystery," that a "hardening has come upon part of Israel, until the full number of the Gentiles come in, and so all Israel will be saved" (Rom 11:25-26). According to the thesis presented above, this πλήρωμα τῶν ἐθνῶν will only be complete when Paul has also brought Christian representatives from *Spain,* the most distant site in the OT vision of the end events, with their gifts to Jerusalem. This is then the completion of the "offering of the Gentiles" of which the Apostle speaks in Rom 15:16, which in turn is based on Paul's Christian understanding of Isa 66:20. Paul firmly believed when he wrote Romans that his collection enterprise would be completed during his own lifetime[114] and primarily through his own efforts. Then the Messiah would come (again). Like the whole creation, the Apostle has until now been waiting "with eager longing for the revealing of the sons of God" (Rom 8:19; cf. v 23). He knows that salvation is now nearer to him and the Christians of Rome than when he and they first believed (13:11).

Two major objections may be raised to the above proposal. First, some rabbinic sources maintain that it is precisely the task of the messianic King to gather the exiles of Israel in the end time.[115] If Paul brings Christian representatives from the Gentile nations to Jerusalem as a gift to the Messiah, is he not in fact robbing the Messiah of his prerogative of "gathering"? In addition to the possibility that Paul was unaware of this tradition, one can say that the Apostle indeed "gathered," yet he collected representatives not from the Jewish communities in the diaspora, but from the *Gentile* "nations" or "provinces." The Messiah was then free at his coming to gather the Jewish exiles in the diaspora, which in turn could be thought of as one part of Paul's hope that "all Israel be saved" (Rom 11:26).

---

[114]This is correctly seen by Käsemann, *An die Römer* 306. See also note three.
[115]Cf., for example, the saying of R. Ḥelbo, a fourth generation Palestinian Amora (Strack and Stemberger, *Einleitung* 98), in Cant. Rab. 2/7.1 (Soncino 9.114-15): Israel "should not attempt to go up from the diaspora by force. For if they do, why should the King Messiah come to gather the exiles of Israel?" For the Messiah as gathering the exiles, see also the other Jewish sources cited in Str-B 4.907-08, as well as Frg. Tg. Num 24:7 (English translation in Levey, *The Messiah* 20, and in J.W. Etheridge, *The Targums of Onkelos and Jonathan ben Uzziel on the Pentateuch with the Fragments of the Jerusalem Targum* [New York: KTAV, 1968] 429); Tg. Ps.-J. Deut 30:4 (Levey 29; Etheridge 653); Tg. Isa 53:8 (Stenning 180-81); and Tg. Cant 1:8 (Levey 125).

The second and more serious objection centers on the fact that the proposal made above is heavily based on a messianic interpretation of Isaiah 66 found both in pseudepigraphical and rabbinic writings. However, in none of the letters generally accepted as genuinely Pauline does a quotation from, or allusion to, this OT text occur, not even in connection with the collection, where one would most expect it.[116] The probable answer to the above objection lies in the fact that Isaiah 66 would have been helpful to Paul only if he had wished to emphasize the collection's eschatological aspect by buttressing it scripturally.[117] Yet he did not want openly to accentuate the eschatological motif whatsoever. If Paul had done so, he would have had to fear that the recipients of his letters would think he was primarily interested in using them in connection with the coming of the Messiah, the Lord Jesus, and was only in a minor way interested in them as individuals. Pastorally, this would have been very poor practice. It also would have subjected the Apostle to the possible accusation of organizing the entire collection for his own glory. This possibility he would have been most anxious to avoid.[118] Also, if the Jerusalem Christians were sensitive about the relative ineffectiveness of their mission to the Jews, they may have considered Paul's group of Gentiles coming to Jerusalem as an attempt to force the "End." Paul had succeeded in bringing Gentiles to Jerusalem as a gift to the Messiah. What had the Jerusalem church's ministry to the Jews to show in this respect? Bad feelings certainly would have developed. Finally, at the Jerusalem meeting (Gal 2:9) Paul had agreed to go to the Gentiles and to leave the mission to the circumcised to James, Peter and John. Yet it was in fact his inner hope that through his *own* work of bringing Gentile Christians to Jerusalem, the Jews would become jealous and also believe in Jesus as the Messiah (Rom 10:19; 11:11, 14). Paul did not want to break openly the agreement made at the Jerusalem meeting.[119]

---

[116]Cf., however, the references in notes 8 and 22 to the extensive use of Isaiah 66 in Second Thessalonians, which may be Pauline.
[117]In the collection passages within his letters, Paul quotes the OT only to encourage the Corinthians' generosity. See 2 Cor 8:15 (Exod 16:18) and 9:9 (Ps 112:9). The allusion in 2 Cor 8:21 to Prov 3:4 (cf. its use also in Rom 12:17) is designed to remove suspicions about the intentions of Paul. Georgi's assertion (*Die Geschichte* 72-73) that the Apostle in 2 Cor 9:10 has the entire context of Isa 55:10 and Hos 10:12 in mind is reading his own proposal into the text.
[118]Faced with various charges concerning his ministry and person, Paul tactfully preferred to boast of his weaknesses. Cf. 2 Cor 12:9-10.
[119]The above arguments are a modification and elaboration of the remarks on this question made by Nickle, *The Collection* 140-41.

9

The Liturgical Background of the Necessity and Propriety of Giving Thanks According to 2 Thess 1:3

Almost all commentators have had difficulty in interpreting the phrases εὐχαριστεῖν ὀφείλομεν ... καθὼς ἄξιόν ἐστιν in 2 Thess 1:3: *"We ought to give thanks* to God always for you, brethren, *as is proper,* because your faith is growing abundantly, and the love of each of you for one another is increasing."[1] A favorite interpretation of *opheilomen* is that it is in response to an (epistolary?) declaration by the Thessalonians that they are not worthy of the praise given them by Paul in 1 Thessalonians, and Paul refutes them in return.[2] A variant of this theory is that Paul has received information from the congregation to

---

[1] Cf. the *opheilomen eucharistein* of 2:13. Since this phrase is repeated here as part of the formal style of the letter and occurs nowhere else in the Pauline corpus, it is not distinctively Pauline, but an appropriated phrase. For a discussion of the extent of the thanksgiving begun in 1:3, see my 1971 Yale dissertation, *Comfort in Judgment: The Use of Day of the Lord and Theophany Traditions in Second Thessalonians 1,* 22-31. Paul does, however, frequently make use of the root *opheilō* with the infinitive. See Rom 8:12; 13:8; 15:1, 27 (twice); 1 Cor 11:7, 10; 2 Cor 12:11, 14; Gal 5:3. For the use of *opheilō* in a sacrificial context, to be seen later in several parallels adduced from Philo, see also Heb 5:3. The closest terminological parallel to *kathōs axion estin* in the Pauline corpus is Phil 1:7: καθὼς ἐστιν δίκαιον. Other related phrases are to be found in Rom 8:26; 16:2; 1 Cor 11:13; Eph 5:3-4; 6:1; Col 3:18 and 1 Tim 2:1-3.

[2] Cf. J.E. Frame, *A Critical and Exegetical Commentary on the Epistles of St. Paul to the Thessalonians* (ICC; New York: Scribner, 1912) 221, followed by E.J. Bicknell, *The First and Second Epistles to the Thessalonians* (Westminster; London: Methuen, 1932) 68; W. Neil, *The Epistle* [sic] *of Paul to the Thessalonians* (Moffatt; London: Hodder and Stoughton, 1950) 141; and L. Morris, *The First and Second Epistles to the Thessalonians* (NICNT; Grand Rapids, Mich.: Eerdmans, 1959) 194. However, there is no reason to make 1:3-2:17 directed to the "fainthearted," the writers of such a response to 1 Thessalonians, as Frame does (219-20). There is no evidence that those addressed in 1:3-2:17 are a special group within the congregation (the idlers of 3:6-15 are a special group, but still thought of as part of the congregation).

the effect that the Thessalonians wondered at Paul's interests expressed in 1 Thessalonians. He seemed to be concerned about their faith and spiritual condition (1 Thess 1:2-10; 2:13; 3:10), but not about their physical health. The passage 2 Thess 1:3-12 then would be Paul's proof that he definitely was interested in the present persecution of the congregation.[3] This theory, however, seriously underrates the Thessalonians' faith by asserting that they believed Paul was interested only in spiritual matters. The fact that he had already dealt in 1 Thessalonians with the idlers would have been enough to disprove this for them. Bornemann sought to distinguish between the obligation of giving thanks in *opheilomen* and its appropriateness in *kathōs axion estin*. He thought that the two expressions were pleonastic, and that one could easily be left out.[4] Both Lightfoot and Findlay believed that the *opheilomen* pointed to the divine side of the obligation to give thanks (a debt to God), the *kathōs axion estin* to the human (the thanksgiving merited by the Thessalonians' conduct).[5] Finally, both von Dobschütz and Dibelius pointed out the apparently liturgical character of the two phrases.[6] Rejecting von Harnack's suggestion that 2 Thessalonians was addressed to a Jewish-Christian minority within the Thessalonian church, Dibelius proposed that

> one could also imagine that II [Thessalonians] was intended to be read aloud solemnly at a worship service. The style of the proemium [introduction] would then be explainable less because of its closeness to Jewish Christianity than because of this occasion of Christian worship ....[7]

Unfortunately for Dibelius it appears that all of the Pauline letters were intended to be read aloud at worship services, so 2 Thessalonians cannot have a special imprint from that occasion. Nevertheless, both von Dobschütz and Dibelius are correct in adducing the liturgical parallels.

That the foregoing assertion about a liturgical/prayer background to *eucharistein* etc. is correct was shown over thirty years ago by Günther Harder in his book on prayer in Paul, a work not considered by the

---

[3] G. Wohlenberg, *Der erste und zweite Thessalonicherbrief* (Leipzig: Deichert, 1903) 124.
[4] W. Bornemann, *Die Thessalonicherbriefe* (Meyer 10; Göttingen: Vandenhoeck & Ruprecht, 1894) 331.
[5] J.B. Lightfoot, *Notes on Epistles of Paul from Unpublished Commentaries* (London: Macmillan, 1895) 97; G.G. Findlay, *The Epistles of Paul the Apostle to the Thessalonians* (Cambridge Greek Testament for Schools and Colleges; Cambridge: Cambridge University, 1904) 140.
[6] E. von Dobschütz, *Die Thessalonicher-Briefe* (Meyer; Göttingen: Vandenhoeck & Ruprecht, 1909) 235; M. Dibelius, *An die Thessalonicher I, II* (HNT; Tübingen: Mohr, 1937) 40.
[7] Dibelius, *An die Thessalonicher*, 40.

commentators on Thessalonians. He had indicated briefly that these introductory formulae were part of the Jewish prayer style, as seen in Philo, Josephus, and the Apostolic Constitutions.[8]

The purpose of this article is first to show with a number of concrete examples, some taken from additional sources, that Harder was indeed correct in his assertion, and secondly to demonstrate that the phrases the author has used fit their context in 2 Thessalonians 1 very well.[9]

There are four passages in Philo which are especially close in phraseology to *eucharistein opheilomen ... kathōs axion estin*. In *Spec. Leg.* 1. 224 he who has enjoyed a prosperous life "has as his bounden duty (ἀναγκαίως ὀφείλει) to requite God his pilot ... with hymns and benedictions and prayers and sacrifices and the other expressions of gratitude (εὐχαριστίαις) as religion demands."[10] In *Mut.* 186 the phrase ἄξιον εὐχαριστεῖν occurs. In *Spec. Leg.* 2. 173 and 185 similar formulae are found: ἄξιον ἐπαινεῖσθαι τε καὶ θαυμάζεσθαι τὸν θεόν; ἐφ' οἷς ἄξιον γεγηθότας εὐχαριστεῖν.[11] Two other parallels with *axios*, found in *Leg. All.* 3. 10, are important: ἀξίως γὰρ οὐδεὶς τὸν θεὸν τιμᾷ, ἀλλὰ δικαίως μόνον, and πῶς οὐκ ἀδύνατον τὸν θεὸν ἀμείψασθαι ἢ ἐπαίνεσθαι κατὰ τὴν ἀξίαν τὸν τὰ ὅλα συστησάμενον ἐκ μὴ ὄντων;[12]

A host of other passages state the same motifs of the necessity and propriety of giving thanks. The following list is arranged alphabetically.

1) ἁρμόττει: *Sob.* 58; *Agr.* 79; *Spec. Leg.* 2. 199, 203.
2) δεῖ: *Quis Her.* 199; *Q.G.* 4. 130.
3) δίκαιον, δικαίως: *Leg. All.* 3. 10; *Sac.* 72, 74; *Agr.* 80 (noted by Harder); *Spec. Leg.* 2. 171, 180 (with ὅσιον).
4) εἰκότως: *Mos.* 2. 256.
5) ἐμπρεπής: *Quis Her.* 200.
6) εὐχαριστητέον: *Quod Deus* 7; *Congr.* 96.
7) καλόν: *Som.* 2. 268.
8) οἰκειότατον: *Plant.* 130. Cf. *Praem.* 55-56.
9) ὀρθῶς: *Q. G.* 1. 64.
10) προσήκει: *Sob.* 58; *Mig.* 142; *Mos.* 2. 256; *Abr.* 203; *Spec. Leg.* 2. 204; 3.6.[13]

---

[8]*Paulus und das Gebet* (Gütersloh: Bertelsmann, 1936) 62-63.
[9]The question of the authorship of 2 Thessalonians is left open.
[10]The Loeb Classical Library edition of Philo's works, as well as of the Apostolic Fathers, is used here.
[11]Harder had noted the latter phrase (*Das Gebet*, 62).
[12]Worthiness and the praise of God are also connected in *Sob.* 58; *Mos.* 1. 291; *Mos.* 2. 239; and *Spec. Leg.* 1.211 (the latter noted by Harder).
[13]For other passages on the propriety of giving thanks, where no Greek fragments are extant, cf. *Q.G.* 2. 50, 52; 4. 109, 115; and *Q.E.* 1. 7.

It can be seen from their contexts that the large majority of these references belong to the sphere of Jewish prayer language.

That Josephus also knew of the propriety of blessing God is shown in a fictitious letter of Hiram to Solomon, *Ant.* 8.2, 7 § 53, in which the following phrase occurs: τὸν μὲν θεὸν εὐλογεῖν ἄξιον ὅτι ....[14]

In Book 7.33-38 of the Apostolic Constitutions,[15] an ancient collection of Jewish prayers in Greek is found, at points quite naively reworked by an early Christian who usually simply interpolates.[16] The most striking parallel to 2 Thess 1:3 is 7.35:10, noted by Harder, where a list of God's benevolent functions is made, ending with ἀΐδιος ἡ εὐχαριστία. Then follows: [δι' οὗ][17] σοι καὶ ἡ ἐπάξιος προσκύνησις ὀφείλεται παρὰ πάσης λογικῆς καὶ ἁγίας φύσεως. Two other passages are of interest, the first being 35:6: Διὸ καὶ ὀφείλει πᾶς ἄνθρωπος ἐξ αὐτῶν στέρνων σοι [διὰ Χριστοῦ][18] τὸν ὑπὲρ πάντων ὕμνον ἀναπέμπειν, διὰ σὲ τῶν ἁπάντων κρατῶν. The second is 39:1, where the Christian redactor himself is apparently composing, using the Jewish prayer phraseology found elsewhere in the collection to make a transition to 39:2, where baptismal catechesis begins: Ὅπως μὲν οὖν ὀφείλουσι ζῆν οἱ κατὰ Χριστὸν μεμυημένοι καὶ οἵας εὐχαριστίας ἀναπέμπειν τῷ θεῷ διὰ Χριστοῦ, εἴρηται διὰ τῶν προλαβόντων· δίκαιον δὲ μηδὲ τοὺς ἀμυήτους καταλιπεῖν ἀβοηθήτους.[19] Thus an early collection of Hellenistic Jewish prayers contains terminology very similar to that found in 2 Thess 1:3, on which it certainly is not dependent.

Further corroboration of the liturgical/prayer background of the phrases in 1:3 is found in the Apostolic Fathers. The following are the closest phraseological parallels.

1 Clem 38:4: ὀφείλομεν κατὰ πάντα εὐχαριστεῖν αὐτῷ.

Barn 5:3: οὐκοῦν ὑπερευχαριστεῖν ὀφείλομεν τῷ κυρίῳ, ὅτι ....

7:1: ἵνα γνῶμεν, ᾧ κατὰ πάντα εὐχαριστοῦντες ὀφείλομεν αἰνεῖν.

All three passages appear in parenetic contexts. What is important to note, however, is that 1 Clem 38:4 is at the end of a parenetic section

---

[14]Cited by Harder, *Das Gebet*, 62. Cf. also *Ant.* 1.156 and 11.294.
[15]*Didascalia et constitutiones apostolorum* (ed. F.X. Funk; Paderborn: Ferdinand Schoeningh, 1905).
[16]For a description of this collection as well as a probable dating, see W. Bousset, *Eine jüdische Gebetssammlung im siebenten Buch der apostolischen Constitutionen* (Nachrichten der k. Gesellschaft der Wissenschaften zu Göttingen; Philologische-historische Klasse, 1915) 433-89.
[17]My brackets. The sentence reads much better without this Christian interpolation.
[18]My brackets.
[19]The necessity of praising God the Creator is also expressed in 35:2, where a quotation of Ps (LXX) 103:24 is preceded by πάντας ἀναγκάζει βοᾶν.

Liturgical Background

and is part of a larger doxological sentence ending in "Amen," and both Barnabas references occur in discussions of sacrifice. The same contexts for such phrases are observable in Philo. While other phrases express basically the same thought of the propriety of rendering thanks to God,[20] one stands out in particular. Herm Sim IX 28:5 reads: ὑμεῖς δὲ οἱ πάσχοντες ἕνεκεν τοῦ ὀνόματος δοξάζειν ὀφείλετε τὸν θεόν, ὅτι ἀξίους ὑμᾶς ἡγήσατο ὁ θεός, ἵνα τοῦτο τὸ ὄνομα βαστάζητε καὶ πᾶσαι ὑμῶν αἱ ἁμαρτίαι ἰαθῶσιν. The whole paragraph deals with the eleventh, the next to the last, mountain on which dwell those who did not deny under persecution, including the martyrs (v 2). V 5 encourages Christians not to deny their Lord under persecution, but *to be thankful* that God has *deemed them worthy* of bearing the Lord's name. The same connection between the propriety of glorifying/thanking God and suffering is found here as in 2 Thessalonians 1.

The foregoing discussion has been concerned with the Greek parallels to *eucharistein opheilomen ... kathōs axion estin*. Do Hebrew/Aramaic equivalents exist? The references from Philo and the Jewish collection of prayers in the Apostolic Constitutions would lead us to expect them. The obligation of giving thanks or praising God is found, for example, in the Mishnah, *Pesaḥim* 10:5, where during the Passover Jews are reminded of how the Lord redeemed them from Egypt. "Therefore are we bound to give thanks (אנחנו חייבים להודות), to praise, to glorify, to honour, to exalt, to extol, and to bless him who wrought all these wonders for our fathers and for us."[21] The phrases "bitter herbs," "bondage," and "servitude" found here point to the strong motif of oppression in the passage. The obligation to bless God is

---

[20]Cf. the following, which include some wider parallels.

(1) 1 Clem 34:2: δέον οὖν ἐστὶν προθύμους ἡμᾶς εἶναι εἰς ἀγαθοποιίαν, for (v 3) "the Lord cometh, and his word is before his face, to pay to each according to his work."

(2) 1 Clem 62:2: δεῖν ὑμᾶς ἐν δικαιοσύνῃ καὶ ἀληθείᾳ καὶ μακροθυμίᾳ τῷ παντοκράτορι θεῷ ὁσίως εὐχαριστεῖν.

(3) Ign Pol 7:3: ὅτι ἕτοιμοί ἐστε εἰς εὐποιίαν θεῷ ἀνήκουσαν.

(4) Mart Pol 10:2: δεδιδάγμεθα γὰρ ἀρχαῖς καὶ ἐξουσίαις ὑπὸ τοῦ θεοῦ τεταγμέναις τιμὴν κατὰ τὸ προσῆκον.

(5) 1 Clem 38:2: ὁ δὲ πτωχὸς εὐχαριστείτω τῷ θεῷ.

(6) Ign Eph 2:2: πρέπον οὖν ἐστὶν κατὰ πάντα τρόπον δοξάζειν Ἰησοῦν Χριστόν.

(7) Ign Mag 3:1: πρέπει...κατὰ δύναμιν θεοῦ πατρὸς πᾶσαν ἐντροπὴν αὐτῷ ἀπομένειν.

(8) 1 Clem 40:1: πάντα τάξει ποιεῖν ὀφείλομεν, ὅσα ὁ δεσπότης ἐπιτελεῖν ἐκέλευσεν κατὰ καιροὺς τεταγμένους (regarding religious services).

[21]Translation H. Danby, *The Mishnah* (London: Oxford, 1933) 151 [used for other citations as well].

also found in *Berakoth* 9:5: "Man is bound to bless [God] for the evil even as he blesses [God] for the good, for it is written, 'And thou shalt love the Lord thy God with all thy heart and with all thy soul and with all thy might [Deut 6:5].'" The Hebrew for "is bound" is חַיָּיב, which is repeated in the Gemara of the passage. A חַיָּיב is a debtor in the legal sense. This then can be taken figuratively to mean "one who is bound" to do something. Other examples are *Berakoth* 1:1 and 3:1, which have the same formula in regard to the reading of the Shema'. It is thus clear, especially from *Pesaḥim* 10:5, that *opheilomen eucharistein* is a direct translation of the Hebrew and, along with similar phrases with "ought," is a standard phrase in liturgical language.[22]

My efforts to find a Hebrew/Aramaic equivalent for the phrase *kathōs axion estin* were first to no avail.[23] Then I thought of F. Delitzsch's translation of the NT into Hebrew, which suggests כָּרָאוּי, from the Qal pass. part. of ראי, ראה.[24] That this is the Hebrew antecedent of *kathōs axion estin* is shown, for example, in the Jewish *mussaph* prayer on the Sabbath: "And thou hast commanded us, O Lord, our God, to present the Sabbath mussaph offering, *as is proper* (כראוי)."[25] Soon after this the word חובותינו appears. The sacrificial/liturgical context parallels that ascertained in many of the Philo references cited above.[26] In b. *Ḥullin* 83b, חייב and ראוי are also close together in a context of

---

[22]A further possible reason for the selection of *opheilomen* here in 2 Thess 1:3-12 is its connection in some pagan contexts with the terminology found there. In the pagan Greek examples cited by F. Hauck in his *TDNT* article on *opheilō* (5. 560, 565), there occur, for example, χάρις, χάριτας, ἀποδίδωμι, ἀποτίνω, ἐκτείσω and δίκη, all of which, at least in their roots, are reflected in 1:3-12. Since the author of 2 Thessalonians knows that in 1:8 and 12 he will allude to Isaiah 66, with its ἀποδίδωμι in vv 4 and 15, the frequent connection of *opheilō* and *apodidōmi* in profane usage may in part lead him to employ *opheilō* in 1:3. For *opheilō* with *apodidōmi*, see also Rom 13:7 and 1 Cor 7:3. That Isaiah 40-66 were often used by the Jews as passages of comfort can be seen in these chapters being read on the so-called "Consolation Sabbaths" of the Jewish liturgy (*Comfort in Judgment*, 264-66).
[23]Cf. the similar negative statement of R. Deichgräber, *Gotteshymnus und Christushymnus in der frühen Christenheit* (Göttingen: Vandenhoeck & Ruprecht, 1967) 50.
[24]ספרי הברית החדשה (Berlin: Trowitzsch and Son, 1885) 385. My suggestion that *opheilomen* is derived from חייב was confirmed by Delitzsch's translation.
[25]My translation of the text found in W. Staerk, *Altjüdische liturgische Gebete* (2d ed.; Berlin: de Gruyter, 1930) 21. A short description and dating of these synagogue benedictions is given here by Staerk.
[26]On the "sacrifices of thanksgiving," cf. Ps 50:14; 107:23; and 116:17. Hebrew expressions for "seemly, right and proper" in regard to praying to God while suffering are נאה, יפה, ראוי and הגון in Lam. Rab. 3:1§1 (Soncino English 7.188-189; Hebrew in *Midrash Rabbah*, Deuteronomy volume 50a [Jerusalem: Lewin-Epstein, 1960]). See also חז (Jastrow 443).

sacrifice/offering.²⁷ Thus there is evidence that כראוי was a liturgical phrase and was associated with חיב, as in 2 Thess 1:3.

W. Bousset's assertion that the ἄξιον καὶ δίκαιον of the early Christian liturgies in regard to giving thanks²⁸ stems from the opening words of the *Emet We-Yaṣṣib,* the morning benediction spoken following the Shema',²⁹ cannot be substantiated.

That the Greek term *axios* was especially suitable in contexts of suffering is shown by other *axios* passages in Revelation (3:4; 5:9, 12), another apocalyptic writing. This usage eminently fits the situation of suffering in 2 Thessalonians 1, which has two additional words from the same stem: καταξιωθῆναι (v 5) and ἀξιώσῃ (v 11).

The two phrases *eucharistein opheilomen ... kathōs axion estin* are thus shown to be derived from Jewish liturgical language. They also fit the situation of suffering envisaged in 2 Thessalonians very well. V 4 states that the Thessalonians show steadfastness and faith in their persecutions and in the afflictions they are enduring. V 5 relates that they are suffering for the kingdom of God; vv 6-7 repeat the motif of affliction. The judgment theophany of vv 7-10 is intended by the writer of the letter to comfort those who presently suffer by assuring them that their suffering indeed has a positive value to it,³⁰ even if it does not effect the (second) coming of the Messiah, the Day of the Lord (2:2). Although the Lord Jesus has not come yet, he definitely will come, says the author, and God's judgment concerning the persecuted and their persecutors will be just, even if it does not appear so now. The recipients' belief that the Day of the Lord was in the process of coming or had come (2:2) was derived from their interpreting the sufferings they endured as the Messianic Woes.³¹

---

²⁷The Tanna R. Jonathan b. Joseph (= Nathan b. Joseph), one of the speakers, was active ca. 140 C.E. Cf. Str-B 5/6. 191. Soncino English 468.
²⁸Cf. the communion preface of the Lutheran liturgy, for example: *Minister:* "Let us give thanks unto the Lord our God." *Response:* "It is meet and right so to do." *Minister:* "It is truly meet, right and salutary, that we should at all times, and in all places, give thanks unto thee, O Lord ..." (*Service Book and Hymnal of the Lutheran Church in America* [Minneapolis and Philadelphia: Augsburg and Board of Publication, Lutheran Church in America, 1958] 58-59).
²⁹Cf. *Eine jüdische Gebetssammlung,* 442. For a description of this benediction, see *The Jewish Encyclopedia* (New York and London: Funk and Wagnalls, 1925), 5. 152. The Hebrew/Aramaic is found in Staerk, *Altjüdische liturgische Gebete,* 6-7.
³⁰See "Excursus I: Suffering and Retribution in II 1" (*Comfort in Judgment,* 64-75), for an extensive discussion of this suffering, relating it to that of 1 Thessalonians and to the Jewish "theology of suffering."
³¹The author of 2 Thessalonians clearly addressed a persecuted congregation, not one composed of Gnostics. For a Gnostic view, see W. Marxsen

It is precisely in this situation of suffering that the author of 2 Thessalonians tells the addressees that he and his fellow Christians ought to give thanks to God, as is proper, because the Thessalonians' faith is growing abundantly and their love for one another is increasing; they are steadfast and are demonstrating their faith (vv 3-4). The texts examined above, especially Herm Sim IX 28:5; *Pesaḥim* 10:5; *Berakoth* 9:5; and Rev 3:4; 5:9, 12, show that the two liturgical phrases the author of 2 Thessalonians employs to express the necessity and propriety of thanking God are indeed appropriate to a context of suffering.

In addition, all the theories enumerated at the beginning of this article are shown to be ungrounded, for they do not recognize the liturgical background of *eucharistein opheilomen ...kathōs axion estin.* The author of 2 Thessalonians neither refutes the Thessalonians' assertion that they are unworthy of the praise given them in 1 Thessalonians, nor does he show in 2 Thessalonians that he is also interested in the recipients' physical health (as opposed to his alleged interest in 1 Thessalonians in only their faith and spiritual condition). Also, there is no reason to say that *opheilomen* points to the divine side of the obligation to give thanks and *kathōs axion estin* to the human. These two phrases rather express the necessity and propriety of thanking God precisely for the reasons given in vv 3-4, which are within a situation of suffering.

Finally, the use of *opheilō* in 1:3 does not cause the letter to begin with a "cool" tone, as maintained by many of the commentators. Indeed, *opheilō* is much more personal than the other similar terms listed on pp. 195-96. Supporters of the non-Pauline authorship of 2 Thessalonians thus should not use the so-called "coolness" of "we *ought* to give thanks" for their cause.

(*Introduction to the New Testament* [Philadelphia: Fortress, 1968] 39), who does not even consider the persecution.

Index of Modern Authors

Aalen, S., 115
Adam, A., 90
Albeck, Ch., 2, 10, 15, 20, 32, 53-55, 60, 66, 69, 74, 77, 99, 130, 133
Avery-Peck, A., 54
Baess, P., 133
Bammel, E., 29, 58, 61
Barker, M., 47
Barrett, C.K., 47, 113-114, 118
Barth, M., 164
Bartsch, H.-W., 167
Bauer, J., 3
Bauer, W., 42
Beare, F.W., 96
Becker, J., 29
Behm, J., 82
Ben-Chorin, S., 62
Bensly, R., 156
Bernard, J., 47
Bernstein, A., 3
Bertram, G., 130
Best, E., 143, 153
Betz, O., 62, 136, 144
Bicknell, E.J., 193
Bietenhard, H., 38, 67, 68, 72, 76, 79
Billerbeck, P., 3, 12, 14, 25, 47, 57, 90, 128, 130, 134, 167-168, 177, 183, 187-188

Binder, G., 109-110
Black, M., 30, 46, 143
Bonnard, E., 45
Bornemann, W., 143-144, 194
Bornkamm, G., 90, 161
Bousset, W., 196
Bowker, J., 138
Box, G.H., 177
Braude, W., x, 5, 7, 12-14, 21, 38, 56, 76-77, 86, 103-105, 115-118, 121-123, 132, 135, 144, 150, 152, 168, 178, 181, 183, 185, 189
Bridges, R., 66
Bright, J., 32, 97
Broer, I., 91
Brown, R., 30, 32, 34, 62, 95-96
Brownlee, W.H., 136
Buber, S., 7, 12-14, 20-22, 38, 52-55, 66-68, 74, 79, 105, 107, 133, 155, 178
Büchsel, F., 59
Bultmann, R., 1, 4, 30, 58, 88
Carlston, C.E., 91
Cary, E., 34, 110
Cassel, P., 3, 9, 11, 13, 17, 19, 22
Catchpole, D., 29
Charles, R.H., 114, 132, 161, 165, 175, 185

Charlesworth, J., 105-106
Chavel, C., 2
Clines, 4, 6, 9-10, 16, 18, 20
Coakley, J., 62
Cohn, H., 23, 27
Colson, F.H., 3, 120
Conzelmann, H., 91
Coppens, J., 144
Cullmann, O., 58, 143, 147, 160, 164
Dahl, N., ix, 23, 67, 165
Dalman, G., 44
Damrosch, D., 67, 77, 86
Danby, H., 2, 8, 37, 45, 54, 57, 60, 71-72, 74, 99, 116, 187, 197
Daube, D., 54-55, 81
de Lagarde, P., 12
Deichgräber, R., 198
Delitzsch, F., 113, 135, 150, 152, 198
Delling, G., 96
Denis, A.-M., 132, 175, 177
Derrett, J., 82, 89
Dibelius, M., 23, 160, 194
Dieterich, A., 110
Dodd, C.H., 58, 61
Donski, S., 104
Dupont-Sommer, A., 136
Edsman, C.M., 156
Eissfeldt, O., 114, 126, 173
Ellis, E., 92
Ernst, J., 23
Etheridge, J.W., 55-56, 120-121, 190

Fascher, E., 22
Fiebig, P., 65
Findlay, G.G., 194
Finegan, J., 30, 173-174
Flusser, D., 65-66, 77, 93
Fohrer, G., 98, 101, 147, 169-170
Frame, J.E., 148, 193
Freed, E., 61
Freedman, H., 32, 56, 66, 130-131, 163
Fridrichsen, A., 80
Friedlander, G., 8, 11, 14, 66-67, 69-71, 74-75, 78, 88, 104, 117, 183
Friedmann, M., 21, 103-104, 135
Georgi, D., 166, 171, 186, 191
Gerlemann, G., 5
Giblin, C.H., 144, 157
Ginzberg, L., 8, 10-11, 18-19, 22, 37-38, 56-57, 75, 107, 114, 116-117, 121-123
Gnilka, J., 58
Godley, A., 107
Goetz, K.G., 121
Goldin, J., x, 10, 66, 69-71, 74-75, 78, 86, 116, 132-133, 188
Goppelt, L., 93, 164
Gray, 175, 177
Greenburg, M., 11
Greenspan, F.E., 58
Greeven, H., 100
Gressmann, H., 65
Grimm, W., 62

Index of Modern Authors

Grossfeld, B., 8, 12, 15, 17, 19
Grundmann, W., 23, 61, 101
Gögler, R., 31
Haacker, K., 62
Haenchen, E., 29
Hahn, F., 30
Hammer, R., x
Harder, G., 195-196
Harnisch, W., 134
Harrington, D., 50
Harvey, A.E., 29
Harvey, D., 98
Hauck, F., 198
Hayward, C., 16, 43
Heinemann, I., 25, 67
Hengel, M., 11, 62, 168, 171
Hengstenberg, E., 40
Hentschel, G., 32
Herford, R., 60
Héring, J., 184
Hirsch, E., 5
Hofius, O., 81-83
Howard, W.F., 60, 95
Hunter, A.M., 66
Israelstam, J., 33, 131
Jastrow, M., 2, 10, 15, 18-21, 32, 36, 39, 44, 57, 59-60, 68-70, 72-75, 80-81, 113, 173, 198
Jellinek, 179, 186
Jeremias, J., 7, 41, 44, 65, 79-81, 91, 93, 101, 120, 177
Jung, L., 12
Käsemann, E., 119, 167, 182, 190

Kagan, Z., 67, 70, 72, 74, 79, 85-87, 89
Kapstein, I., x, 38, 56, 76, 86, 103-105, 117, 121
Katz, P., 140
Kee, H.C., 95
Klein, G., 113
Klinzing, G., 119
Klostermann, E., 23, 101
König, F., 17-18
Köster, H., 39
Kraus, H.-J., 126
Krauss, S., 18, 68-69, 73, 107
Krupp, M., 116, 178
Kümmel, W., 24, 89, 96, 110, 180
Kutsch, E., 152
Lachs, S., 3
Lagrange, M., 42
Lake, K., 124, 161, 168
Lauterbach, J., x, 77, 81, 104, 120-122, 134
Leenhardt, F., 167-168
Levey, S.H., 38, 122-123, 182, 190
Levine, E., 29
Levy, J., 72
Liebermann, S., 2, 53, 57
Lietzmann, H., 167
Lightfoot, J.B., 25, 194
Lindars, B., 61
Lohmeyer, E., 96, 101
Lohse, E., 30
Loisy, A., 92
Luz, U., 95-96, 109-110, 168

Mandelbaum, B., 104
Marcus, R., 8, 17, 51, 102, 120
Margulies, M., 33, 35-36, 69, 77
Marmorstein, A., 119
Marxsen, W., 199
Mastin, B.A., 46
McCasland, S.V., 96
McNamara, M., 132, 137-138, 141
McNeile, A.H., 47, 101
Meeks, W., ix
Merx, A., 32
Messina, G., 96, 109-110
Metzger, B., 159
Michel, O., 62, 164-165, 167-168
Milikowsky, C., 8, 35, 38
Mohr, T., 30, 61
Montefiore, C.G., 25, 27
Moore, C.F., 4-5, 9, 17-18, 119
Morris, L., 153, 193
Moule, C.F.D., 29, 47, 61
Muilenburg, J., 97, 126, 152, 173
Munck, J., 143, 147, 164, 166-167, 186-187
Murray, J., 167-168
Muszynski, H., 119
Neil, W., 193
Neusner, J., x, 2, 5, 7, 25, 32, 37, 45, 53-54, 57-58, 60, 67, 69-70, 72-73, 75, 78-79, 85, 89-90
Nickelsburg, G., 4, 38
Nickle, K., 166, 187, 191
Nolland, J., 106

Oldfather, C.H., 18
Oswald, N., 66, 115
Paton, L.B., 5
Perrin, B., 34
Plag, C., 164, 181
Pöhlmann, W., 78
Popkes, W., 59
Porton, G., 25
Prigent, P., 127
Reim, G., 61
Rengstorf, K.H., 81, 90, 92
Rigaux, B., 144, 163
Robinson, J., 62
Saldarini, A., x, 38, 50, 57, 66, 68-71, 74-75, 78, 84, 88-89
Salm, W., 65
Sanders, E.P., 119
Sanders, J.N., 46
Sanders, J.T., 91-92
Schalit, A., 110
Schechter, S., 38, 57, 66, 74-75, 78, 84, 88, 119, 121
Schlatter, A., 39, 42, 61
Schlier, H., 134
Schmithals, W., 91, 93
Schnackenburg, R., 46, 49
Schneemelcher, W., 90, 124
Schneider, J., 11
Schnider, F., 91
Schniewind, J., 80, 96
Schöttgen, C., 90
Schottroff, L., 78, 91
Schrenk, G., 120
Schulten, A., 173-174
Schürer, E., 3, 16, 30, 34, 37, 56

Schweizer, E., 168
Sellers, O.R., 11
Simon, M., 5, 16
Simonsen, D., 8
Singermann, F., 38
Smart, J., 152
Smith, M., 25
Sperber, D., 33
Sperber, S., 43, 50, 131-132
Spiegel, S., 10
Staerk, W., 198-199
Stemberger, G., 5-8, 12, 14-16, 20, 25, 33, 37, 39, 60, 66, 68-69, 76, 88, 98-99, 103-104, 115-118, 120, 122, 130-132, 134-135, 163, 176, 178-179, 183-185, 188-190
Stenning, J., 100, 126, 131, 138, 141, 153, 180, 186, 190
Stephenson, A., 137
Stern, M., 3
Strack, H.L., 5-8, 12, 14-16, 20, 25, 33, 37, 39, 60, 66, 68-69, 76, 88, 98-99, 103-104, 115-118, 120, 122, 130-132, 134-135, 163, 176, 178-179, 183-185, 188-190
Strathmann, H., 49
Strobel, A., 143-144, 146, 155, 157-158, 160
Stuhlmacher, P., 164, 181
Sukenik, E.L., 136
Sulzbach, A., 19
Thackeray, H., 5, 37, 102
Theodor, J., 10, 15, 20, 32, 53-55, 66, 74, 77, 130
Trilling, W., 144, 160

Trudinger, L.P., 128
Van Beek, G., 98
van der Woude, A.S., 137
van Unnik, W.C., 175
Vermes, G., 3, 30, 136
Via, D., 52, 66, 91, 99, 101, 171
Violet, B., 156
Volz, P., 134, 177-178, 187
von Dobschütz, E., 150, 153, 158, 194
Waldstein, W., 3, 37
Weiser, A., 183
Weissbach, F.H., 109-110
Westermann, C., 97, 99, 147, 170, 173, 180
Wettstein, J., 31-32
Wikenhauser, A., 31
Wilcken, U., 34
Wilckens, U., 113, 123
Windisch, H., 31
Winter, P., 1
Wohlenberg, G., 194
Wolff, C., 29
Wünsche, A., 33, 35, 52-56, 95, 178-179, 186, 189
Young, F., 95
Zahn, T., 57, 59, 102
Zeller, D., 164, 168
Ziegler, J., 97, 128
Zuckermandel, M.S., 2, 53, 57

About the Author

Roger David Aus, b. 1940, studied English and German at St. Olaf College, and theology at Harvard Divinity School, Luther Theological Seminary, and Yale University, from which he received the Ph.D. degree in New Testament Studies in 1971. He is an ordained clergyman of the Evangelical Lutheran Church in America, currently serving a German-speaking congregation in Berlin, Germany. The Protestant Church of West Berlin kindly granted him a short study leave in Jerusalem, Israel, in 1981. His study of New Testament topics always reflects his great interest in, and deep appreciation of, the Jewish roots of the Christian faith.

South Florida Studies in the History of Judaism

240001	Lectures on Judaism in the Academy and in the Humanities	Neusner
240002	Lectures on Judaism in the History of Religion	Neusner
240003	Self-Fulfilling Prophecy: Exile and Return in the History of Judaism	Neusner
240004	The Canonical History of Ideas: The Place of the So-called Tannaite Midrashim, Mekhilta Attributed to R. Ishmael, Sifra, Sifré to Numbers, and Sifré to Deuteronomy	Neusner
240005	Ancient Judaism: Debates and Disputes	Neusner
240006	The Hasmoneans and Their Supporters: From Mattathias to the Death of John Hyrcanus I	Sievers
240007	Approaches to Ancient Judaism: New Series Volume One	Neusner
240008	Judaism in the Matrix of Christianity	Neusner
240009	Tradition as Selectivity: Scripture, Mishnah, Tosefta, and Midrash in the Talmud of Babylonia	Neusner
240010	The Tosefta: Translated from the Hebrew: Sixth Division Tohorot	Neusner
240011	In the Margins of the Midrash: Sifre Ha'azinu Texts, Commentaries and Reflections	Basser
240012	Language as Taxonomy: The Rules for Using Hebrew and Aramaic in the Babylonia Talmud	Neusner
240013	The Rules of Composition of the Talmud of Babylonia: The Cogency of the Bavli's Composite	Neusner
240014	Understanding the Rabbinic Mind: Essays on the Hermeneutic of Max Kadushin	Ochs
240015	Essays in Jewish Historiography	Rapoport-Albert
240016	The Golden Calf and the Origins of the Jewish Controversy	Bori/Ward
240017	Approaches to Ancient Judaism: New Series Volume Two	Neusner
240018	The Bavli That Might Have Been: The Tosefta's Theory of Mishnah Commentary Compared With the Bavli's	Neusner
240019	The Formation of Judaism: In Retrospect and Prospect	Neusner
240020	Judaism in Society: The Evidence of the Yerushalmi, Toward the Natural History of a Religion	Neusner
240021	The Enchantments of Judaism: Rites of Transformation from Birth Through Death	Neusner
240023	The City of God in Judaism and Other Comparative and Methodological Studies	Neusner
240024	The Bavli's One Voice: Types and Forms of Analytical Discourse and their Fixed Order of Appearance	Neusner
240025	The Dura-Europos Synagogue: A Re-evaluation (1932-1992)	Gutmann
240026	Precedent and Judicial Discretion: The Case of Joseph ibn Lev	Morell
240028	Israel: Its Life and Culture Volume I	Pedersen
240029	Israel: Its Life and Culture Volume II	Pedersen
240030	The Bavli's One Statement: The Metapropositional Program of Babylonian Talmud Tractate Zebahim Chapters One and Five	Neusner
240031	The Oral Torah: The Sacred Books of Judaism: An Introduction: Second Printing	Neusner

240032	The Twentieth Century Construction of "Judaism:" Essays on the Religion of Torah in the History of Religion	Neusner
240033	How the Talmud Shaped Rabbinic Discourse	Neusner
240034	The Discourse of the Bavli: Language, Literature, and Symbolism: Five Recent Findings	Neusner
240035	The Law Behind the Laws: The Bavli's Essential Discourse	Neusner
240036	Sources and Traditions: Types of Compositions in the Talmud of Babylonia	Neusner
240037	How to Study the Bavli: The Languages, Literatures, and Lessons of the Talmud of Babylonia	Neusner
240038	The Bavli's Primary Discourse: Mishnah Commentary: Its Rhetorical Paradigms and their Theological Implications	
240040	Jewish Thought in the 20th Century: An Introduction in the Talmud of Babylonia Tractate Moed Qatan	Schweid Neusner
240041	Diaspora Jews and Judaism: Essays in Honor of, and in Dialogue with, A. Thomas Kraabel	Overman/MacLennan
240042	The Bavli: An Introduction	Neusner
240043	The Bavli's Massive Miscellanies: The Problem of Agglutinative Discourse in the Talmud of Babylonia	Neusner
240044	The Foundations of the Theology of Judaism: An Anthology Part II: Torah	Neusner
240045	Form-Analytical Comparison in Rabbinic Judaism: Structure and Form in *The Fathers* and *The Fathers According to Rabbi Nathan*	Neusner
240047	The Tosefta: An Introduction	Neusner
240048	The Foundations of the Theology of Judaism: An Anthology Part III: Israel	Neusner
240049	The Study of Ancient Judaism, Volume I: Mishnah, Midrash, Siddur	Neusner
240050	The Study of Ancient Judaism, Volume II: The Palestinian and Babylonian Talmuds	Neusner
240051	Take Judaism, for Example: Studies toward the Comparison of Religions	Neusner
240052	From Eden to Golgotha: Essays in Biblical Theology	Moberly
240053	The Principal Parts of the Bavli's Discourse: A Preliminary Taxonomy: Mishnah Commentary, Sources, Traditions and Agglutinative Miscellanies	Neusner
240054	Barabbas and Esther and Other Studies in the Judaic Illumination of Earliest Christianity	Aus
240055	Targum Studies: Volume One: Textual and Contextual Studies in the Pentateuchal Targums	Flesher
240059	Recovering the Role of Women: Power and Authority in Rabbinic Jewish Society	Haas
240061	The First Seven Days: A Philosophical Commentary on the Creation of Genesis	Samuelson